Contrasting Models of State and School

Contrasting Models of State and School

A Comparative Historical Study of Parental Choice and State Control

by Charles L. Glenn

continuum

2011

The Continuum International Publishing Group
80 Maiden Lane, New York, NY 10038
The Tower Building, 11 York Road, London SE1 7NX

www.continuumbooks.com

Library of Congress Cataloging-in-Publication Data
Glenn, Charles Leslie, 1938-
Contrasting models of state and school : a comparative historical study of parental choice and state control / by Charles Glenn.
   p. cm.
Includes bibliographical references and index.
ISBN-13: 978-1-4411-5801-7 (hardcover : alk. paper)
ISBN-10: 1-4411-5801-4 (hardcover : alk. paper)
ISBN-13: 978-1-4411-4562-8 (pbk. : alk. paper)
ISBN-10: 1-4411-4562-1 (pbk. : alk. paper)
   1. Education and state–Europe–History–Cross-cultural studies. 2. School choice–Europe–History–Cross-cultural studies. 3. Comparative education–Europe. I. Title.

LC93.A2G57 2011
379.4–dc22   2010044023

ISBN: HB: 978-1-4411-5801-7
         PB: 978-1-4411-4562-8

Typeset by Newgen Imaging Systems Pvt Ltd, Chennai, India
Printed in the United States of America

To my children: Joshua, Patrick, Peter, Matthew, Laurie, Elizabeth, and Lydia, and to Mary

Contents

Introduction

This book is about four countries that, although closely related in culture and in many respects sharing a common historical space, have come to illustrate very different ways of conceiving the relationship among Society, State, and schools.

Although I seek to offer an accurate historical account of the development of popular education in Germany, Austria, The Netherlands, and Belgium, my concern is not with school attendance or literacy rates, but with the ways in which schooling has been promoted and controlled in these countries over the past three or four centuries, and what this says about evolving concepts of the purposes of education and the role of families, Society, and the State.

I write as a specialist on comparative educational policy, concerned for many years with three interrelated questions: how the freedom of parents to choose how their children will be educated can be balanced with the opportunity for educators to create and work in schools with a distinctive character, and how both of these in turn should be limited by some form of public accountability to ensure that all children in a society receive a generally comparable and adequate education.

With a Belgian colleague, I published in 2004 a multivolume study of how this balance has been worked out in forty different national education systems.[1]

What our account of current laws and policies could not answer is how the particular arrangements in the various countries, all of them responding to basically similar needs, came to be so distinctive. The present study seeks to answer that question by looking at four of these systems in historical context. For heuristic purposes it has seemed useful to separate them into two pairs of countries, exaggerating somewhat the differences between them. The differences which concern me in this book are not variations in the structure of secondary schooling or the process by which individuals become qualified to teach, but what the arrangements for the provision of schooling tell us about how each country conceives of the roles of the State and of Society in educating the young and thus in shaping the future.

In Germany and Austria, I will argue, a long historical tradition sees education as a function of the State, while in The Netherlands and Belgium it has—as a result of political struggles in the nineteenth and again in the twentieth century—been entrusted primarily to civil society institutions.

In order to illustrate why this question is important it will be useful to introduce a concept unfamiliar to Americans but important in policy discussions in the European Union since it was incorporated into the founding Treaty of Maastricht, that of "subsidiarity." The classic statement of the principle of subsidiarity appeared in the papal encyclical *Centesimus Annus* (1991), concerned with social questions in the modern world. Pope John Paul II wrote:

> Malfunctions and defects in the Social Assistance State are the result of an inadequate understanding of the tasks proper to the State. Here again the principle of subsidiarity must be respected: a community of a higher order should not interfere in the internal life of a community of a lower order, depriving the latter of its functions, but rather should support it in case of need and help to coordinate its activity with the activities of the rest of society, always with a view to the common good. By intervening directly and depriving society of its responsibility, the Social Assistance State leads to a loss of human energies and an inordinate increase of public agencies, which are dominated more by bureaucratic ways of thinking than by concern for serving their clients, and which are accompanied by an enormous increase in [public] spending. In fact, it would appear that needs are best understood and satisfied by people who are closest to them and who act as neighbors to those in need. It should be added that certain kinds of demands often call for a response which is not simply material but which is capable of perceiving the deeper human need.[2]

The principle, which has passed into secular political and legal doctrine, has been taken to mean that central government (including that of the EU) should not make any decisions which can be made more adequately at a lower level, nearer those directly affected. This is often called vertical subsidiarity, and resembles administrative decentralization, though without the implication that the authority is simply "loaned" from the center to the periphery. Thus the extent to which individual schools enjoy autonomy within an educational system is a measure of vertical subsidiarity.

Horizontal subsidiarity is a further development of this principle, arguing that the freedom and dignity of citizens requires entrusting "the human care of human beings," so far as possible, to the "third sector" of voluntary associations and other civil society institutions.[3] Privatization of spheres of activity like education and social work and youth services which had been absorbed into the Welfare State is in some sense a precondition for enlisting the energies of civil society in solving problems which government has not been able to address successfully. New forms of competition are likely to result from such a devolution of responsibility from government to civil society associations and institutions, and this could produce efficiencies, though this is not the main purpose behind horizontal subsidiarity.

The conviction behind the strategy is, rather, that "mediating structures . . . are the principal expressions of the real values and the real needs of people in our society. They are, for the most part, the people-sized institutions. Public policy should recognize, respect, and, where possible, empower these institutions"[4] and, in so doing, will ensure that social services and education are provided more effectively. Market forces are incapable of generating the sense of moral obligation which is essential to good education and effective social services.[5] Thus subsidiarity in education is concerned not only with organizational forms and dynamics but also and more centrally with the spirit and the values which may animate schools. What they do and how they treat those entrusted to them is, for good or ill, the expression of deeply held beliefs about human life. As ethicist Helmut Thielicke pointed out, "the state—if it is not to be an ideological and totalitarian state—dare not have a specific view of man."[6] But arguably a school which does not have such a view, shared by all or most of its participants, cannot be fully effective or claim to educate.

It was his recognition of the dynamic and sustaining role of civil society associations that led Wilhelm von Humboldt, two centuries ago, to write that "the best efforts of the State should . . . aim at bringing men into such a condition by means of freedom that associations would arise with greater ease, and so take the place of political regulations in these and many kinds of similar instances."[7] This theme was reiterated by Tocqueville in his account of American society for a European audience which had grown—he argued—too dependent upon the State to solve every problem. In France, where Jacobin excesses had reinforced Ancien Régime absolutism, he warned, "it is the government alone which has inherited all the prerogatives snatched from families, corporations, and individuals; so the sometimes oppressive but often conservative strength of a small number of citizens has been succeeded by the weakness of all."[8] As a result, there was no sphere within which freedom and civic virtue could be practiced in the interest of that "social prosperity" which depends upon "the collective force of the citizens," not "the authority of the government."[9] "What political power," Tocqueville asked,

> could ever carry on the vast multitude of lesser undertakings which associations daily enable American citizens to control? . . . The more government takes the place

of associations, the more will individuals lose the idea of forming associations and need the government to come to their help. That is a vicious circle of cause and effect . . . The morals and intelligence of a democratic people would be in as much danger as its commerce and industry if ever a government wholly usurped the place of private associations. Feelings and ideas are renewed, the heart enlarged, and the understanding developed only by the reciprocal action of men one upon another . . . If men are to remain civilized or to become civilized, the art of association must develop and improve among them at the same speed as equality of conditions spreads.[10]

If decentralization and school autonomy are the expression, in education, of vertical subsidiarity, parental choice of schools that are civil society institutions rather than government agencies is the expression of horizontal subsidiarity. The right of parents to have access, for their children, to schooling other than that provided by the State was established in international law after the Second World War, and in part in response to the use of schooling by fascist regimes. The International Covenant on Economic, Social and Cultural Rights, adopted by the United Nations in 1966, was intended to set an international legal standard. Paragraphs (3) and (4) of Article 13 of the Covenant was specific about the rights of parents and also the rights of those who establish nongovernment schools.

(3) The States Parties to the present Covenant undertake to have respect for the liberty of parents and, when applicable, legal guardians to choose for their children schools—other than those established by the public authorities, which conform to such minimum educational standards as may be laid down or approved by the State and to ensure the religious and moral education of their children in conformity with their own convictions.
(4) No part of this article shall be construed so as to interfere with the liberty of individuals and bodies to establish and direct educational institutions, subject always to the observance of the principles set forth in Paragraph 1 of this article and to the requirement that the education given in such institutions shall conform to such minimum standards as may be laid down by the State.[11]

More succinctly, the International Covenant on Civil and Political Rights (also adopted in 1966) provided that "The States Parties to the present Covenant undertake to have respect for the liberty of parents and, when applicable, legal guardians to ensure the religious and moral education of their children in conformity with their own convictions."[12]

Unresolved in these provisions was the question whether this language about educational freedom was intended simply to restrain the State from infringing upon the rights of parents, or whether it imposed an obligation upon the State to take measures to make it possible for parents to choose schools providing "religious and moral" education consistent with their own convictions. If only the former, it is obvious that many parents would not be in a position, for financial and other practical reasons, to act upon their choices.

The Committee on Economic, Social and Cultural Rights of the United Nations addressed this issue in 1999 in a lengthy *General Comment* on the Right to Education as spelled out in the Covenant on Economic, Social and Cultural Rights. This includes a significant set of four characteristics that an educational system should possess, one of which was,

> Acceptability—the form and substance of education, including curricula and teaching methods, have to be acceptable (e.g., relevant, culturally appropriate and of good quality) to students and, in appropriate cases, parents.[13]

While the other three criteria are the sort of standards that educational experts might be called upon to measure, the criterion of acceptability gives a sort of Copernican twist to the process of determining whether a particular country is meeting its obligation to ensure that its citizens enjoy their right to education. Only the pupil and his or her parents can decide whether the schooling provided is acceptable.

As we will see, the educational systems of The Netherlands and Belgium are an especially striking example of horizontal subsidiarity; the large role played by civil society institutions in providing schooling contrasts with the central role of the State in education in Germany and Austria. How these contrasting models developed historically is the theme of this book.

WHY GERMANY AND AUSTRIA?

Germany and Austria, I will argue, have for the past several centuries and still today understood popular schooling as an instrument by which the State can extend its influence among the common people, creating political loyalty, and civic and economic virtues such as steady application to tasks and obedience to rules. During certain unhappy historical periods, this subordination of school to State has lent support to authoritarian and even totalitarian regimes.

It will not do to exaggerate; both Germany and Austria have been the cradle of some of the most original alternative schools and (unlike the United States) provide public funding to many nonpublic schools chosen by parents. There will be no suggestion in these pages that there is anything like a Germanic propensity toward totalitarian control of the minds of children.

Nor, in a formal sense, is the educational system in Germany and in Austria as centrally controlled as are those in France and Italy, to take two examples about which I have written elsewhere. The federal system of control of schools by the *Laender* in Germany, in fact, is currently only an aspiration in Italy, where the national Ministero dell'Istruzione, dell'Università e della Ricerca retains detailed control over schools despite recent constitutional changes that open the way to assumption of responsibility by regional governments.

What makes Germany and Austria especially appropriate, however, as examples of the dominant role of the State in popular schooling is that the evolution of this role can be traced over more than three hundred years in Prussia and in Austria. Unlike in France, where the aspiration for State control of schooling had been articulated for as long a period, but where constant political instability largely frustrated that aspiration until the 1880s, there is something inexorable about the enduring role of the State in German and Austrian schooling.

It is also significant for the development of the government role in education in other countries that the Prussian model was frequently cited admiringly by reformers in France, England, and the United States. North American educational reformers during the nineteenth century looked enviously at the dominant role in education of the various German-speaking governments, in contrast with the American and Canadian growth of schooling from the bottom up, through local initiatives only lightly guided and supported by government. Prussia, in particular, seemed a prime example of how a vigorous government could set about transforming society through schooling the young.

One of the earliest American visitors to express admiration for Prussian popular schooling was future president John Quincy Adams. While serving as diplomatic representative in Berlin, he traveled extensively and in an 1801 letter to his brother praised "the earnestness with which the King of Prussia laboured to spread the benefits of useful knowledge among his subjects."[14]

In subsequent decades an increasing number of bright and ambitious young Americans began to study at German universities. One of them, the son of Yale University President Timothy Dwight, published a comparative study of schooling in Protestant and Catholic areas of Europe after extensive visits to Prussian schools in 1825. "It may be said with truth of Prussia," wrote Henry Dwight, "that it is one of the most enlightened countries in the world; for among the younger of the population, it is rare to see an individual who cannot both read and write." While noting that the government was thoroughly authoritarian, Dwight wrote that the king "is still not afraid of the general diffusion of intelligence among his subjects. He is here laying a broad foundation for the future prosperity of Prussia, and it is to be hoped also, for the future liberty of the nation."[15]

It was above all the report on Prussian popular education by a French philosopher, Victor Cousin, published in Paris in 1833 and in English translation in London in 1834 and in New York in 1835, that galvanized attention on what had been occurring in what was still considered a backward part of Europe. Cousin placed special emphasis on the provisions in Prussia for teacher training in *Lehrerseminaren* since "the state has done nothing for popular education if it does not watch that those who devote themselves to teaching be well prepared."[16] Creation of a network of teacher-training *normal schools* would thus be a key element of the Elementary Education Law adopted by France under the leadership of Cousin's ally François Guizot.

Cousin's report was widely influential; the Massachusetts and New Jersey legislatures had it reprinted and distributed to schools. As an American visitor to Germany wrote,

[t]he attention of many intelligent and distinguished men in England and America, was now much excited, to investigate more fully, the statements of these reports. The very fact, that the head of a military despotism had set on foot a system of instruction, designed to benefit every subject in his dominions . . . in a word, that for forty years he had been engaged in promoting the moral and intellectual improvement of all his people, and that these efforts had been crowned with unexampled success.[17]

A Massachusetts clergyman, Charles Brooks, became an enthusiast for Prussian schooling and especially its teacher-training institutions in 1834. "I fell in love with the Prussian system; and it seemed to possess me like a missionary angel. I gave myself to it; and . . . I resolved to do something about State Normal Schools."[18] Brooks lectured and organized conferences on this theme with such success that a few years later his ally Horace Mann was able to establish the first state-operated normal schools to train teachers in the United States.

This was followed by a report to the Ohio state legislature by Calvin Stowe (husband of Harriet Beecher) in 1836, which was in turn reprinted and distributed widely by the legislatures of Massachusetts, Michigan, North Carolina, Virginia, and Pennsylvania. Stowe expressed special commendation for "the religious spirit which pervades the whole of the Prussian system," since "[w]ithout religion—and, indeed, without the religion of the bible—there can be no efficient school discipline."[19]

Admiring American visitors did not come only from New England, with its strong tradition of popular schooling, and from the frontier of New England settlement in Ohio; Benjamin Smith made an extensive study of German schools in 1836 and reported on them to the Virginia legislature, as usual with a particular emphasis on Prussian arrangements for teacher training. He noted of the Prussian normal schools that "[t]here could scarcely be devised a more efficient means of promoting the cause of common school education, with the same amount of money." Nor was the educational progress limited to Prussia:

> [I]n its practical operation, the system has advanced to a greater degree of perfection, perhaps, in the kingdom of Wurtemberg, and the duchy of Baden, than in Prussia itself. Bavaria is by no means behind it, and the kingdom of Saxony is in some features of her system superior. In the stronghold of legitimacy and despotism, Austria, we find an edict by the emperor, with characteristic arbitrariness, stating, that "no person shall henceforth be permitted to marry, who cannot read, write and cypher." He is, however, benevolently providing means, by which all his subjects may comply with these requirements.[20]

Horace Mann, already celebrated on both sides of the Atlantic for his work revitalizing the common schools of Massachusetts and his persuasive writing about the mission of those schools, made a honeymoon trip to visit European schools in 1843, and devoted one of his highly influential annual reports to his findings. In an editorial the next year in his *Common School Journal*, he wrote that "the most interesting portions of the world in regard to education are the Protestant states of Germany." Mann's ally in Connecticut (and from 1867 to 1870 the first national commissioner of education), Henry Barnard, was equally admiring.[21]

Canadian education official Egerton Ryerson went on an extended visit to Europe and, in his influential *Report on a System of Public Elementary Instruction for Upper Canada*, provided a detailed, though selective, description of the school systems of Ireland, Prussia, France, and Massachusetts.[22] This report, under his guidance, led to the enactment of a new school law for what would later become Ontario in 1846, but its results remained unsatisfactory to Ryerson and his allies: too much was still left up to local initiative and judgment. While, in 1826, as a Methodist minister, he had opposed the claims of the State to take over the direction of schooling from the churches, by 1846 he was commenting favorably on mandatory school attendance laws in Prussia and other European countries.[23]

English visitors to German schools were also impressed and envious. Joseph Kay, author of a comprehensive study in the 1840s of the weaknesses of schooling in England, noted of Bavaria that "perhaps there is no country in

Europe which possesses such an admirable and minutely considered series of enactments on the subject of national education."[24] Poet, essayist, and school inspector Matthew Arnold reported admiringly on German schools in 1858 and 1865.[25]

While the initial fascination with Prussian popular schooling declined as the American states and Canadian provinces developed their own systems of government oversight and teacher preparation, an official survey of European school systems commissioned by the American government in 1867 continued to express the perception that "Prussia is fully entitled to its present rank as first in the educational world." As late as 1891, an American school official from New York State, after an extensive study of education in France and Germany, concluded that a "careful observer of the work done in Prussian elementary schools . . . will return to this country with the feeling that Prussia is far in the lead of us." Similarly, a school superintendent from Massachusetts, in a book on comparative methods of instruction and school organization published in 1897, concluded that "our schools are poor in comparison with the schools of Germany."[26]

Foreign visitors thus came to admire the organization of popular schooling under government control in German states and the system of state-sponsored teacher training which seemed, to them, to guarantee uniform results. The impulse for American state and Canadian provincial governments to take the leading role in promoting and regulating education owed a great deal to the German example, so much in contrast with that of England, where local and voluntary efforts predominated.

In tracing the historical development of the distinctive German and Austrian understanding of the role of the State with respect to schooling, we should thus be aware of how significantly this influenced North American and British thinking about how government should use popular education as an instrument of control and reform.

WHY THE NETHERLANDS AND BELGIUM?

The Netherlands and Belgium (especially Flanders, the Dutch-speaking region) offer a different sort of model, one in which most schooling is entrusted to nonpublic schools sponsored by organizations and associations of the civil society. Among the world's nations with universal schooling, the Dutch can justly claim to provide the most freedom to parents to choose schools which correspond to their convictions about the most appropriate education for their children; Dutch laws and policies sustain the most pluralistic school system in the world, with dozens of models of education enjoying full public financing.

As a result, apart from the French-speaking area of Belgium, only about 30 percent of all pupils attend schools owned and operated by government. Freedom of education is guaranteed, under Dutch law, in three forms: nongovernmental groups have the right, within quality standards set by the government,

- to establish schools (*vrijheid van oprichting*);
- to give these schools a distinctive religious or philosophical character (*vrijheid van richting*); and
- to organize schools as they wish, included the choice of materials and teachers (*vrijheid van inrichting*).

These freedoms were won during the course of a seventy-year struggle of Protestant and Catholic "little people" against the dominance of an urban elite that sought to use popular schooling to impose its understanding of enlightenment and liberal religion.

The Belgian educational system is not as lavishly pluralistic as the Dutch, but it provides similar guarantees of parental choice and school autonomy, with nearly as high a proportion of pupils attending nongovernment schools. Educational freedom has been one of the pillars of the Belgian legal, political and social order since the country gained its independence from The Netherlands in 1830–31. The independence movement itself was inspired in part by Catholic and Liberal resistance to measures, first under French and then under Dutch occupation, to impose a state-controlled educational system in which religious instruction was turned into nonconfessional moral instruction.

Belgian patriots saw a close connection between political liberties—freedom of association and of the press—and freedom of conscience to provide confessional schooling. As a result, they anchored educational freedom in their new Constitution, and this guarantee is maintained in the present version. Intermittent political conflict over the independence and public funding of Catholic schooling during the late nineteenth and the twentieth century were finally laid to rest by the School Pact of 1958, an interparty agreement that continues to serve as the framework for law and policy. Secularists and Catholics put aside their struggles for hegemony and returned to the earlier emphasis upon freedom, establishing a *Schoolvrede* (school peace). The focus was no longer on protecting the rights of the Church or of the State but instead on protecting the rights of parents to determine on what philosophical basis their children would be educated. Belgians are guaranteed the right to establish and operate nonstate ('free') schools that meet quality standards set by public authorities, and to choose such schools for their children.

Perhaps even more remarkable than the strong legal and policy support for educational freedom in the two countries is the general lack of political controversy over the system of public subsidies for the costs of schools that are not operated by government. This has not always been the case, however; in fact, both Belgium and The Netherlands experienced bitter political struggles over the right to operate nongovernment schools and, once this right was won, over the right to receive public funding for these schools. In both cases, the issue was entwined with controversies over the role of religious instruction in public schools. The Belgian situation is complicated, in addition, by continuing tensions over language.

How did these two educational systems, models of educational freedom and school autonomy, emerge from many decades of conflict? It was, on the one hand, the "enlightenment" of the common people through schooling which inspired the successful Dutch efforts to create an effective system of near-universal schooling during the early nineteenth century, and it was, on the other, the growing resistance of these *kleine luyden* (little people) to the worldview promoted by the schooling offered in public schools that led eventually to the present system. In Belgium, as in The Netherlands, the controversies were about elementary schooling until at least the second half of the twentieth century.

Ironically, the Dutch educational system was celebrated, during the first half of the nineteenth century, for its apparent success in bringing together children from different religious confessions in a single common school. During the period when The Netherlands formed part of Napoleon's empire, Dutch schools were the object of a formal inspection in 1811 by a pair of French officials, one of them the distinguished scientist Georges Cuvier. Their enthusiastic report attracted great attention in France.[27]

This was only the first of many favorable reports by foreign visitors to Dutch schools over the next several decades. Just after the end of the Napoleonic wars, for example, a distinguished American scientist visited Dutch schools and praised their provisions for the education of poor children.[28]

The visitors noted especially the uplifting moral character of Dutch schools, their consistent emphasis, in all details of instruction and discipline, on morality and natural religion. These schools, they pointed out, were under the control of public authorities rather than of the churches, and thus avoided denominational instruction.[29] They were instruments of national purpose, as French philosopher Victor Cousin would write after his visit to Dutch schools in the 1830s: "Undoubtedly, government is made for society, but it is government alone which makes society function; if you want to organize a society, begin by organizing its government; if you are serious about the education of the people, be well aware that the essence of this education is in the government which you give it."[30]

Thus government itself should be educational in intention as well as effect, and naturally the schools were a primary focus of government activity. Whereas in France, even after the Guizot reforms of the 1830s, the control of schools was still very much in the hands of local "notables" with only limited oversight by government inspectors, in The Netherlands supervision by government officials was already well established, and foreign observers found in this the primary explanation for the generally high level of literacy as well as social morality. Characteristically, they missed the greater role played by social context: a popular piety which placed great emphasis on reading the Bible and devotional works.

Popular schooling in The Netherlands—like that in Prussia—was frequently praised by foreign visitors during the first decades of the nineteenth century, as other countries like the United States, France, and England sought to create effective educational systems. Benjamin Franklin's grandson, for example, admired the way the common people in The Netherlands were served by schools under the supervision of school inspectors, and the method used in nonsectarian religious instruction:

> While the necessity of religious instruction has been strongly felt, it has been made to stop short of the point at which, becoming doctrinal, the subjects taught could interfere with the views of any sect. Bible stories are made the means of moral and religious teaching in the school, and the doctrinal instruction is given by the pastors of the different churches on days appointed for the purpose, and usually not in the schoolroom.[31]

Henry Barnard, then secretary of the Connecticut Board of Education, wrote to his Massachusetts counterpart, Horace Mann, to ask whether he had read this report. "Our school systems on this side of the water," Barnard noted, "look very disjointed and imperfect" when compared with those Bache had visited in Europe.[32]

A description of Dutch and German schools by an English Quaker was also read with interest and excerpted in Mann's *Common School Journal* in March 1841. Hickson concurred with other visitors in attributing great virtues to the system of school inspection in The Netherlands, and noted the importance of neutral religious instruction as a key to the popular support which the Dutch schools enjoyed.[33]

Other visitors who were loud in their praise of Dutch schools included Horace Mann himself, Matthew Arnold of England, and Ramon de la Sagra of

Cuba. Dutch elementary education seemed to have accomplished what other nations were seeking with more limited success to achieve for themselves. Arnold wrote in 1851, "I have seen no primary schools worthy to be matched, even now, with those of Holland."[34]

While Prussian schools were also visited and admired, it was regarded as a fault in their case that separate schools served children of the different Christian confessions. Unitarian minister Charles Brooks, addressing "the schools and citizens of the town of Quincy" on July 4, 1837, quoted Dutch education leader Adriaan van den Ende's insistence that "the primary schools should be Christian, but neither Protestant nor Catholic. They should not lean to any particular form of worship nor teach any positive dogmas; but should be of that kind that Jews might attend them without inconvenience to their faith."[35]

It is one of the ironies of educational history that Mann and the other reformers of the 1830s looked to The Netherlands as the leading example of how a common school could serve a religiously diverse population. It was only a few years later that bitter conflict would break out over the demand of both Protestant and Catholic parents to have confessional schools, conflict that (as we will see) led to the present Dutch system, the world's leading example of subsidized diversity and educational freedom.

Belgium, through a different but often parallel process of conflict and compromise, arrived at arrangements for the organization of schooling which, in practice, have substantially similar effects in guaranteeing parental choice among schools and protecting to a considerable extent the distinctiveness of those schools.

Again, we must not exaggerate. The Dutch national government and the governments of the language-based regions in Belgium are very active in guiding and regulating schooling, and they fully fund almost all nonpublic schools. American private-school leaders might be appalled at the extent to which their counterparts in Holland or Flanders are regulated. Nevertheless, there is a basic principle in Dutch and Belgian educational policy, that each nonstate school has a right to its own distinctive character based on religion or philosophy or pedagogical theory, which government may not violate.

OVERVIEW

As we will see, the different direction taken by Belgium and The Netherlands, in contrast with Germany and Austria, can be traced to specific developments and decisions at various points in the nineteenth century. There was no obvious reason, before mid-nineteenth century, to expect that they would have followed a different course; reformers in both countries had called for an expanded State role in providing and managing popular schooling. Nor is there an obvious explanation in their religious make-up. The Netherlands, like the much larger Germany (and like Prussia), was a Protestant-dominated society with a large Catholic minority which became politically mobilized in the late nineteenth century. Belgium, like Austria, was a strongly Catholic society and all the more so because in the sixteenth century their Protestant movements had been suppressed by the Catholic Counter-Reformation.

This account begins with a brief overview of popular schooling before and after the sixteenth-century Reformation, and a somewhat more extensive account of schooling under the influence of Pietism and during the period of enlightened absolutism followed by the Romantic nationalism of the early nineteenth century. In each of the countries the State took the lead in promoting systems of popular schooling, and controversies ensued.

Two chapters are then devoted to the completion of State control of popular schooling in Germany and Austria, and the contrasting reduction of the role of the State in Belgium and The Netherlands as political conflict led to new arrangements protecting the role of civil society institutions in providing popular schooling. These are followed by a chapter describing how totalitarian regimes—first National Socialist, then Communist—in Germany used schooling as a means of ideological control. The final two chapters describe developments between World War II and the end of the twentieth century.

What lessons can we draw from this long and complex experience? One is clearly that state control of schooling can bring it to a high degree of efficiency and uniformity, the qualities which foreign visitors admired so much in Prussia during the nineteenth century. Another is that giving the State a powerful instrument to shape the minds of children and youth poses dangers to families, to individual freedom, and to societal diversity.

As we will see, the post-war educational policies in each of these countries (extended to the former East Germany after reunification) have sought to find the appropriate balance between the Social Welfare State (including now the super-State of the European Union) and the free associations of individuals. Vertical and especially horizontal subsidiarity continue to be central to the policy debate in education.

Chapter One

Background

The minor and occasional role that the state played in education in antiquity—apart from Plato's imaginary realms—vanished entirely in the Middle Ages. Apart from some gestures on the part of Charlemagne around 800, any education available was either under religious auspices or by local initiative. Wealthy families, naturally, employed tutors for their children. Most schooling, though, was under Church sponsorship. Religious orders provided for the schooling of their postulants and novices to ensure that they could join in the daily and yearly cycle of worship, and it was not uncommon for well-born children whose parents did not intend to devote them to such a vocation to receive some basic schooling in a convent or monastery. Periodically, Church leaders called for basic schooling at the parish level for boys who might become priests or serve in other capacities, and by the twelfth century many cathedrals provided schools which offered more advanced instruction, sometimes free to poor children.

As city life re-emerged, first in Italy and then in northern Europe, municipal governments began to take an interest in the adequacy of the schooling available, though schools continued to be what we would consider "private," generally owned by a local parish or a guild, a charitable foundation or an individual. Already in the fourteenth century, in the commercial cities of Germany and the Low Countries, a new type of school had developed, often private enterprises by individual teachers which over time might receive guild or city subsidies. These "writing and reading schools" taught the skills necessary for business without any pretense of offering higher culture.

The distinction continued to exist between schools that instructed through the vernacular, preparing boys, or in some cases girls (but seldom both together), for employment or domesticity that did not require a mastery of the classical languages, and Latin schools. The former were "slowly progressing from the stage where the chief purpose was to give catechetical instruction," and toward the end of the sixteenth century there were an increasing number of schools whose "purpose . . . was to give special preparation to such boys as expected to enter the service of the state or [local] community in the capacity of clerks, secretaries, and the like."[1] Latin continued to be taught even to boys who were not destined for the priesthood or for learned careers because it was the language of law and international communication.

The goals of municipal schools were usually quite different from those of Latin grammar schools intended to prepare for university. In the latter,

> that part of mathematics now found in arithmetic books . . . was regarded as a practical art, useful chiefly to tradesmen. Reading meant the ability to read Latin words. The (grammar) school had no use for the former, and it very frequently expected the pupil to bring the latter ability with him, just as he brought the ability to talk.

The growth of commerce, however, made a very different sort of schooling necessary.

> The origin of the elementary school as such is to be found in the demand made by commerce and industry for junior clerks and for workmen who could read and write the vernacular and, in fewer instances, make out or at least understand a bill. Such schools, quite distinct from grammar or song schools, grew up in the great commercial and industrial centres during the fourteenth century in Italy and in Germany.[2]

As long-distance commerce developed in the later Middle Ages, merchants required new skills, or wished their sons to acquire them, to deal with administrative and business documents and with increasingly complex accounting. There was a growing demand for schools which would prepare for worldly occupations. The ground had been prepared in northwestern Europe— especially in the Low Countries and along the Rhine in Germany—by the Brothers of the Common Life, founded in the fourteenth century in The Netherlands to encourage an intense spiritual life on the part of both clergy and laity, inspired by the enormously popular devotional work *Imitation of Christ*, attributed to Thomas à Kempis (c. 1378–1471). Soon the movement began to provide schools that emphasized a warm devotion to Christ and the formation of habits and dispositions that would sustain a godly life in the world, rather than in the shelter of a monastery.

In The Netherlands and Flanders what we would call primary schooling— reading and writing Dutch and a little arithmetic—was provided by privately owned and usually very small schools, while preparation for commercial careers was then continued in "French schools," where that language and sometimes German or English were learned as well, or in schools operated by the guilds, with a strong practical emphasis.[3]

THE REFORMATION

The Reformation of the sixteenth century gave an impetus to fundamental changes in the provision of schooling. One effect was to give these essentially vocational schools an additional, confessional mission which had not seemed so urgent when confessional differences did not exist.[4]

> The churches had to undertake massive pedagogic campaigns, which they conducted via preaching, education, printed propaganda, church discipline, and revamped rituals. In all these areas Protestant reformers broke new ground. They made the sermon the centerpiece of Protestant worship. They required that children receive elementary religious instruction, either at school or through special catechism classes. They released torrents of printed propaganda and encouraged ordinary Christians to read scripture. They established new institutions and procedures to supervise parish life.[5]

Another effect of the Reformation, in those areas which became Protestant, was to transfer responsibility for the schools operated by religious orders or supported by church endowments to town authorities, since the orders had been dissolved and the endowments confiscated. While schools for the children of the urban elite had already developed, the emphasis of the Reformation upon literacy as a precondition for reading the Bible, catechisms, and hymns led also to the spread of popular schooling.

Problems arose in those territories where princes and municipal authorities confiscated the religious endowments which had supported schools, and many parents, impressed by Luther's condemnation of the existing monastery and cathedral schools as "devil's training centers," decided to withdraw their children. To make matters worse, the Reformation slogan of "the priesthood of all believers" convinced some that no training was required for the ministry. Luther wrote to an ally, in 1524, warning that "the neglect of education will bring the greatest ruin on the gospel." He felt obliged to respond to misinterpretations of his intentions, in an open letter to municipal officials lamenting that

> we are today experiencing in all the German lands how schools are everywhere being left to go to wrack and ruin . . . it is becoming known through God's word

how un-Christian these institutions are, and how they are devoted only to men's bellies. The carnal-minded masses are beginning to realize that they no longer have either the obligation or the opportunity to thrust their sons, daughters, and relatives into cloisters and foundations . . . "Why," they say, "should we bother to have them go to school if they are not to become priests, monks, or nuns?"

'Twere better they should learn
a livelihood to earn.[6]

Such views, Luther argued, were a trick of the devil to persuade parents to neglect their children. In fact, a true understanding of the Gospel should lead to a renewed commitment to education, from municipal officials as well as from parents:

We are on the alert against Turks, wars, and floods, because in such matters we can see what is harmful and what is beneficial . . . Even though only a single boy could thereby be trained to become a real Christian, we ought properly to give a hundred gulden to this cause for every gulden we would give to fight the Turk, even if he were breathing down our necks . . . My dear sirs, if we have to spend such large sums every year on guns, roads, bridges, dams, and countless similar items to insure the temporal peace and prosperity of a city, why should not much more be devoted to the poor neglected youth—at least enough to engage one or two competent men to teach school?[7]

This could easily be done, Luther argued, by using the money that individuals were saving by no longer paying for "masses, vigils, endowments, bequests, anniversaries, mendicant friars, brotherhoods, pilgrimages, and similar non-sense." They should instead "contribute a part of that amount toward schools for the training of the poor children."[8] Fatefully, Luther was calling for assumption by secular government of what had been until then the self-assumed responsibility of either religious organizations or private initiatives. In effect, this was secularization of the organization, though not in any respect of the content, of schooling.

Luther argued that parents were generally not competent and could not be expected to educate their children themselves, and that, if the younger generation was sinking ever further into ignorance and uselessness, it was the fault of the municipal authorities, "who have left the young people to grow up like saplings in the forest, and have given no thought to their instruction and training."[9] He advocated and took steps to establish schools for girls as well as boys, since women were under the same obligation to study the Bible for themselves. In his sermon "Keeping Children in School" (1530), Luther used especially strong language, even for him:

> I maintain that the civil authorities are under obligation to compel the people to send their children to school, especially such as are promising . . . If the government can compel such citizens as are fit for military service to bear spear and rifle, to mount ramparts, and perform other martial duties in times of war, how much more has it a right to compel the people to send their children to school, because in this case we are warring with the devil . . . The Turk does differently and takes every third child in his empire to educate for whatever he pleases [here Luther refers to the tribute of Christian boys to be trained as Janissaries]. How much more should our rulers require children to be sent to school, who, however, are not taken from their parents, but are educated for their own and the general good.[10]

Luther's more tactful colleague Philip Melanchthon urged in 1528 that "preachers should exhort the people of their charge to send their children to school, so that they may be raised up to teach sound doctrine in the church, and to serve the state in a wise and able manner." He conceded, however, that "in our day there are many abuses in children's schools,"[11] and personally engaged in school inspections before proposing, with Luther, a plan for establishing and maintaining schools.[12] The rulers of the newly Protestant states of Germany frequently called upon the reformers for help in writing regulations for the schools under their jurisdiction. Melanchthon did so in at least nine cases, including Nuremberg (1526) and Saxony (1528), as did Luther in other towns and regions.[13]

The summons by these and other Reformers did not pass unheeded; more than a hundred school ordinances were adopted in Protestant cities and territories in Germany during the sixteenth century.[14] In 1559, for example, the Duchy of Wuerttemberg in South Germany adopted an ordinance providing for "German" schools in villages, to provide instruction for children of the common people.[15] In many territories the laws establishing and regulating churches included provisions for schools, including detailed provisions for controlling curriculum and instruction.[16]

Luther's great contribution to popular education in Germany was less through such exhortations than through his hymns and his Bible translation, which greatly increased the interest in being able to read, though this would not reach full force until the Second Reformation of Pietism. The results of his innovation in educational policy—calling upon public authorities to take responsibility for schools, while insisting that the religious instruction provided continue to be a concern of the clergy[17]—lay in the future.

> Luther made necessary what Gutenberg made possible: by putting the scriptures at the center of Christian eschatology, the Reformation made a technical invention into a spiritual obligation . . . If the Reformation is not the sole origin of this change [in literacy], it was certainly the most spectacular sign of it, a revolution in society even more than in the Church. The proof is the rapidity with which the Catholic Church adapted itself to the new socio-cultural conditions: to respond to the Protestant challenge, it had to accept the battlefield of its adversary, fight the Reformation with the Reformation's weapons.[18]

Indeed, it was often in areas where Catholics and Protestants were in juxtaposition that Catholic efforts at popular education were most vigorous, with Catholic authorities unapologetically adopting many of the reforms pioneered by their Protestant rivals.[19]

Although many ordinances providing for popular schooling were adopted during the sixteenth century, there were, unfortunately,

> a great many forces that operated against the fullest fruition of these good laws . . . Life in the country was crude and stagnant; economic resources were extremely deficient, an effective teaching personnel was lacking, and the arm of the central authorities was weak. The law was put into effect in some localities, while in others it was neglected, but even where schools were established, they remained, with the outstanding exception of a few states, in a state of miserable inefficiency until well into the eighteenth century or even beyond.[20]

In the flourishing commercial towns of the Low Countries, where there was already a good provision of schooling, the Reformation led to a greater emphasis upon religious instruction. This was inevitably the case in communities where (unusually for the sixteenth and seventeenth centuries) schools operated by different religious groups were tolerated. A study of Rotterdam, for example, describes how Catholic schools and several varieties of Protestant schools were permitted alongside the schools affiliated with the majority (Calvinist) Reformed Church.[21]

In 1618 the Synod of Dordt, a sort of constitutional convention of the Dutch Reformed Church, stressed that the responsibility for religious instruction of youth was shared among the family, the school, and the church. Dutch municipalities were already reasonably well supplied with schools, but the synod called for the extension of schooling into rural areas as well. "Schools, in which the young shall be properly instructed in the principles of Christian doctrine, shall be instituted, not only in cities but also in towns and country places where heretofore none have existed." Magistrates were urged to ensure that "the children of the poor may be gratuitously instructed, and not be excluded from the benefits of the schools." Local ministers were responsible to oversee the schools and

> if necessary, with a magistrate, to visit all the schools, private as well as public, frequently, in order to excite the teachers to earnest diligence, to encourage and counsel them in the duty of catechizing, and to furnish an example by questioning them [the pupils?], addressing them in a friendly and affectionate manner, and exciting them to early piety and diligence.[22]

The tone makes it clear that—in what would become characteristic of Protestant areas—the church was in no position to require these educational provisions: "the magistracy [that is, the local government] shall be requested . . ." to take these actions. In response to this plea, provincial and municipal authorities began to make funds available—in some cases from the confiscated property of monasteries and other religious establishments—to subsidize the schooling of poor children.[23]

As might be expected, the Dutch War of Independence (1572–1609) and the subsequent Thirty Years War (1618–48) had a devastating effect on schooling in many parts of the Low Countries and Germany, but as the crisis passed it had a stimulating effect as well. Its effect upon society, both heightening the significance of confessional identity and loosening the ties of authority, created an enhanced appreciation among elites of the contribution of popular schooling to the disciplining of the common people. Catechetical instruction was an essential element of making youth aware that they were Catholic or Protestant, and the new territorial arrangements which resulted from the wars made a simple form of political education seem essential.[24]

> In Germany . . . the trend toward segregation was marked. There, many schools that had been attended by both Protestants and Catholics in the sixteenth century were subsequently split into separate ones, and confessional schools that originally attracted cross-over students ceased to do so . . . In the wake of the Peace of Westphalia [1648] . . . secondary education in Augsburg was strictly segregated, with Catholic and Protestant institutions receiving equal funds, regardless of student numbers. Biberach also ended up with separate, parallel school systems for Catholics and Lutherans, as did Erfurt, Hildesheim, Regensburg, Maastricht (the one Dutch parity city), and the biconfessional Swiss town of Glarus. In Transylvania, with its multiple establishment of faiths, all four received religions had their own schools by the late sixteenth century.[25]

Although the network of popular schooling—the *Volksschule*—did not really begin to develop in Germany until after the crisis of the wars over religion, when it did the most rapid development was in Protestant areas. Perhaps the most influential development was in Gotha, whose Duke Ernst the Pious—under the influence of Wolfgang Ratke (1571–1635)—felt responsible for the piety and virtue of his subjects, and in 1642 provided detailed instructions for schools, including specification of organization, textbooks, inspection, tests, and discipline.[26] It was the first German school legislation that stressed practical subjects such as natural history, geography, and botany in primary education, explaining about plants, and animals, and the planets.[27] In his advice to rulers, Ratke argued that schooling should be a primary concern of government, "since on and out of the schools the whole regime issues and depends."[28]

Here, as elsewhere in the period before development of effective central governmental administration—in a Germany highly fragmented in any case—implementation depended heavily upon local initiatives, and progress could be fragile; in Gotha, for example, the quality of schooling declined in the eighteenth century.[29] Wuerttemberg, Prussia, and Saxony all mandated school attendance at one point or another, but as Wehler points out, "these were proclamations, certainly symptomatic, but difficult to put into practice, as the disillusioned inspection reports made clear"—a reminder of the vast distance between political planning and school realities and results.[30]

It was Pietism which gave new energy to the effort, spearheaded by local pastors and by devout members of the landed nobility, to provide popular schooling. In Scandinavia and to some extent in Prussia, indeed, it was the Second Reformation inspired by Pietism rather than the earlier Reformation of the sixteenth century which did more to promote popular literacy.[31]

Pietism grew out of the work of Jacob Spener in the late seventeenth century, seeking to renew the fervor of the Lutheran churches with an emphasis upon personal devotion and sanctified living. Schools inspired by this new emphasis upon religious experience and a virtuous life were established by August Hermann Francke (1664–1727) in Halle. Francke has been described as "the first real educator";[32] certainly he deserves special recognition for combining innovative ideas with the ability to build lasting institutional expressions of those ideas. The goal of schooling, wrote Francke in his instructions for the schools for orphans established by the Pietist movement, was that children come to a living knowledge of God and to a solidly established Christian character. He founded the first such school in 1695, and over the following decades was able to expand his efforts considerably—including a teacher training *Seminar*—through charitable contributions. Pupils in these schools should learn to read and write and to do arithmetic, while those who went on to the secondary level should study Latin, Greek and Hebrew.[33] By 1727, there were more than 2,000 pupils and 175 teachers in the complex of Halle schools.[34]

Among the lasting contributions of Pietism to education was the development of formal training for future teachers as well as literature aimed specifically at children and "many pedagogical techniques that survive today, such as hand raising (to ask a question) or the collective instruction of pupils in primary school classrooms."[35] Whole-class instruction (as contrasted with the practice, common as late as the nineteenth century, of the teacher working with one or two pupils at a time) had been introduced a little earlier by the Brothers of the Christian Schools in France. In Francke's schools, pupils were assessed four times a year and put in classes based on achievement rather than age. As in the Gotha schools, pupils studied nature, including through direct observation outdoors.[36]

There was a growing—though still very limited—demand for secondary schooling in Prussia and other German states in the eighteenth century, derived in part from the growing number of opportunities for employment in the bureaucratic systems which were being elaborated by the hundreds of autonomous or semi-autonomous German-speaking princedoms, bishoprics, and other states large and (mostly) small, as well as some three hundred "free cities." Some of the more enterprising states sought to consolidate territories into larger units and to create centralized administrative structures. This created new employment opportunities as public officials and civil servants in the various competing states, and this in turn gave an impetus to the development of secondary and tertiary education.

Francke's efforts were supported by King Frederick William I of Prussia, who is reported to have said, "Wenn ich baue und bessere, und mache keine Christen, so hilft es mir nit [sic]" (what do I gain if I build and improve, but produce no Christians?). He enacted school laws in 1713 and 1717 requiring that all children be sent to school, and several hundred new schools were created.[37] Local communities were ordered to pay the tuition for poor children, and over the course of the eighteenth century several laws were enacted requiring school attendance and regulating the calendar and hours of schooling. Implementation was, in all cases, rather haphazard, since neither enforcement nor adequate funding was a priority for successive governments; the Prussian law of 1717 has been called "little more than an exercise in wishful thinking, since it contained no workable provisions for financing school construction or hiring schoolmasters . . . As long as parishes alone shouldered the financial responsibility for school masters and school construction, further expansion was impossible."[38]

Few elementary school teachers had more than an elementary education themselves and—apart from orphans who had been trained in one of the schools inspired by Francke—very few had any specific training to teach.[39] A report from a Prussian community in 1729 of the selection of a new teacher provides a vivid insight into what was actually expected from popular schooling. There were five candidates, all men aged thirty to sixty; one was a former soldier with a missing leg. The account devotes much attention to what was sung and how well. Each of the candidates first sang several hymns so that the gathered congregation could judge how well he would lead congregational singing. Each was then required to read a passage from the Bible— the eventual winner read seven verses, making ten errors in the process. Each was also asked to read samples of handwriting—though several could not— and to write several lines from dictation, with errors noted. Three (including the one eventually selected) were reported completely unable to do arithmetic; a fourth knew some addition; and the fifth a little subtraction as well. "What was the use of a requirement to attend school," it has been asked, "if these were the teachers?"[40] Along the same lines in 1779 an arrangement was put in place to give preference for teaching positions to disabled or retired soldiers to save the state the cost of their pensions.[41]

As might be expected, the actual effect of the various government initiatives on popular literacy was quite limited. In East Prussia, in the middle of the eighteenth century, there were around 1,500 parish schools, but only ten percent of the adult peasants could sign their names. In fact, even within the Prussian territories—and despite the frequently cited legislation—there were vast differences in the provision of schooling. As late as 1805, all of the villages in Halberstadt/Hohenstein and 96.5 percent of those in Magdeburg had schools, but this was true of only 17.5 percent of those in South Prussia and 8.3 percent of those in New East Prussia.[42] The situation was better in towns and cities, less because of government than in response to the economic benefits of literacy; unofficial *Winkelschulen* provided focused instruction on useful skills.

On the other hand, in local communities under strong Pietist influence there were much higher rates of schooling and of literacy, and to a considerable extent the Halle model spread throughout Protestant Germany, Scandinavia, The Netherlands, and the German settlements in the American colonies. Gradually, the situation improved in Prussia. In 1736 Frederick William I established regulations for Prussian schools, including the salaries to be paid by parishes to teachers and the tuition to be paid by parents, while permitting schoolteachers to supplement their income by practicing a craft or working on a farm. State subsidies were for the first time provided for villages without schools, and a fund was set up to support teachers in the poorest communities. The results were significant; in the Koenigsberg region, for example, the number of rural schools increased from 384 in 1736 to 572 in 1742.

The Reformation, in shifting the responsibility for popular schooling to secular authorities, did not make the purpose of schools any less religious, and indeed its emphasis upon the responsibility of every Christian for his or her own soul unquestionably increased the demand for instruction and for reading material, both the Bible itself and also countless devotional manuals and works of popular edification. In the face of Protestant competition, religious and secular authorities in Catholic areas also increased their efforts to provide popular schooling; it is notable that the parts of Europe where schooling lagged most seriously were those, like Spain and Italy, where the Counter-Reformation triumphed completely and eliminated religious competition.

While most schools in Rotterdam—apart from the Latin school—were concerned largely to teach the skills useful for business and the professions, the "poor schools" had a strong emphasis on "teaching children from needy families not only reading and writing but also generally accepted ways of behaving." The function of these schools was strongly educational in the sense of being focused on shaping the person, and not primarily on imparting skills. Toward the end of the eighteenth century, as the Dutch economy stagnated, the number of families who could not raise their children in what was considered an appropriate manner increased greatly, and "the school had to take over the abandoned task of the parents." Teachers placed a strong emphasis upon personal and civic virtues. In order to ensure that poor children received this instruction, the financial assistance provided by the churches to their parents was contingent upon the children attending school consistently.[43]

While the Bible continued to play a central role in the instructional program of Dutch schools during the late seventeenth and the eighteenth century, Dodde suggests that eventually it was treated not as a sacred text so much as a set of guidelines for virtuous living. "The religious texts had the goal of imprinting upon the pupils 'good morals and civic politeness.'"[44] There was a new emphasis upon recent history, with a schoolbook giving an account of the wars to obtain independence from Spain and to preserve independence from France going through at least twenty printings between 1620 and 1670. History was by no means taught as a "value-free enterprise"; it was intended to promote, in children, "resistance in adversity, dislike of religious persecution, hatred of the Spaniards and French, trust in God and admiration of the Orange house"—that is, the hereditary political leadership.[45] Use of popular schooling to promote political loyalty would continue as a primary focus for several centuries.

In the Austrian Netherlands (now Belgium), efforts by the government to reform secondary education, which until 1773 was entirely in the hands of the Jesuits, failed completely. Emperor Joseph II visited Belgium in 1781 in an attempt to promote his reforms of the Catholic Church; it is reported that this model enlightened despot "suffered because he could not make men happy." His efforts succeeded only in arousing bitter opposition in the name of traditional "Burgundian liberties" and a rebellion which his successor had to put down with Austrian troops in 1794.[46]

We should not confuse activity at the government level, adopting laws and regulations, with actual progress in the provision of education; there may indeed be an inverse relationship between the two phenomena. More, in fact, was achieved in the northern European countries where government's role was modest than in those to the south where the authority of government was invoked in support of schooling. Nor should we assume too quickly that it was economic factors alone which made literacy a valued possession, as some neomarxist historians have argued; the vigor of civil society may have had more to contribute. In fact, in literate Scandinavia, education (whether in schools or in the home) was seen as essentially a religious matter, and as an expanded function of the local church.[47]

The emphasis of Pietism on individual religious experience and moral responsibility helped undermine traditional authority. During the same decades of the late seventeenth and early eighteenth centuries there was also a ferment of expectation that somehow social and individual conditions would improve.[48] The form taken by the Enlightenment in Germany drew upon these developments. It would differ from the French Enlightenment in being basically friendly toward while in profound ways transforming religion—Schleiermacher would be the great example—and also in putting into practice, at least in experimental form, ideas which in France remained matters for passionate discussion without results. These characteristics were in no sphere more evident than in education.

Chapter Two

The Enlightenment and Romantic Nationalism

As the influence of Pietism ebbed during the late eighteenth century, Enlightenment-inspired rulers of Prussia and Austria continued to assert the authority of the State in education, tempered by a policy of working through and in alliance with the Protestant and Catholic churches. This strategy was only one aspect of what it has become traditional to call "enlightened absolutism," at the time often referred to as Cameralism, "state intervention in virtually every realm of social and economic life."[1] The Cameralists were convinced of the importance of increasing the economic strength of the state by making peasants and manufacturers more efficient, and schooling was one of the instruments which they sought to use to this end.

This was a period of many proposals for change of social and economic and political institutions, and the new institutions that were imagined would require changes in the individuals who populated them, as we will see in the case of Pestalozzi's fictional village.

Many eighteenth-century monarchs ruled over territories without long traditions of unity and often without even a common language, territories put together almost haphazardly through dynastic marriages, wars, and the chances of history. The Hapsburg Empire centered on Austria was the prime example, with subjects speaking a dozen languages and looking to very distinct historical traditions; the same fragile unity characterized the growing Prussian dominions as well as Russia and even France. Under these circumstances, creating a sense of loyalty to the ruling house (it would be anachronistic to speak of a sense of "nationality") was a primary consideration.

> The administrative autocracies of Prussia and Russia . . . were the most efficient possible instruments of collective power for territories whose historic divisions, artificial connections, and economically localized communities offered few points of social cohesion . . . In Prussia, therefore, government had to supply, through the artifice of reason, all the connections that nature, history, or social intercourse had helped to provide elsewhere.[2]

AUSTRIAN TERRITORIES

Although the Catholic states of Germany had lagged educationally behind their Protestant counterparts during the sixteenth and seventeenth centuries, at the end of the eighteenth century it was, for a time, Austria which had the most notable developments, and these were copied in smaller Catholic states.[3]

The complacency of Catholic rulers, which had been nourished by the defeat of Protestant forces at the Battle of the White Mountain (1620) and the subsequent suppression of Protestantism in Bohemia, as well as the Revocation of the Edict of Nantes and the suppression of Protestantism in France, had been shaken by the middle of the eighteenth century. The victories of Prussia and other Protestant powers between 1741 and 1763 led to a sense of crisis among Catholic religious and political leaders. "Catholic rulers, prelates, and scholars began to suspect that the Catholic territories of the empire were lagging far behind their Protestant counterparts. Catholic uneasiness, fueled by complaints about widespread irreligion, immorality, and crypto-Protestantism, bred doubts about the efficacy of traditional pastoral practice." Making parish schooling more effective seemed an urgent necessity, not only in the Habsburg dominions but also in Bavaria, Mainz, and other Catholic states.[4]

Habsburg Empress Maria Theresa, in 1752, established state supervision of secondary schools, and in 1759 the Court Commission for Studies. Her government began in 1760 to create the administrative structure to oversee education; she declared that "school affairs are and remain always a 'politi-cum,'" under the oversight of the state. In 1769 she ordered the administrators of the Austrian provinces of her empire to suggest how schooling could be improved in response to a warning from the Catholic hierarchy that heresy (i.e., Protestantism) and unbelief were widespread. Proposals were developed to improve the training of teachers and to issue instructions for the organization of primary schooling. The most ambitious of these, modeled upon the plan developed by Breton parliamentarian La Chalotais and published in Paris in 1763, urged that schooling be made uniform and put under control of the state rather than of the Catholic Church.[5]

La Chalotais was instrumental in France's expulsion of the Jesuits who had operated most of the schools attended by sons of the nobility and bourgeoisie; his proposals were concerned with how to staff and manage schools without dependence upon a Catholic order. When Pope Clement XIV, under pressure from several Catholic sovereigns, abolished the Society of Jesus altogether in 1773 "as having occasioned perpetual strife, contradiction, and trouble," he surrendered to Maria Theresa all the Jesuit property in her domains; "the subsequent reform and expansion of Austrian parish schooling would never have been possible without the wealth left by the Jesuits. It explains above all why school reform proved more successful in Austria than in [Protestant] Prussia, where the Hohenzollern monarchy benefitted little from the demise of the Society."[6]

The most important figure in the development of popular schooling in the Habsburg territories was Johann Ignaz von Felbiger (1724–88), abbot of an Augustinian monastery in Silesia, in which capacity he was responsible also for six local parishes. He was shocked to find that Catholic parents were sending their children to Protestant schools because these schools were more effective. In 1762 he made a visit to Berlin to learn more about instruction in Pietist schools, and adapted what he learned to Catholic schools; "it was highly irregular for a Catholic abbot to visit a Protestant school in Protestant Berlin," and even more unusual that he subsequently sent two young men to spend a year studying the Pietist methods of instructing poor children.[7]

As Felbiger's reputation grew, Maria Theresa summoned him to Vienna in 1774 and made him general commissioner of education for all her German-speaking dominions. The same year he drafted for her the *Allgemeine Unterrichtsordnung*, defining primary schooling as a "national institution," with the goal of implementing uniform norms for schooling through a gradual rationalization of the diverse system of church-sponsored and private schools that had developed over the previous centuries; this would serve until 1869 as the basis for Austrian elementary education. Attendance was made compulsory between the ages of six and twelve, and a hierarchy was established of *Trivialschulen*, providing elementary instruction, and urban *Hauptschulen* in each administrative district for middle-class pupils, covering both elementary and more advanced instruction. A normal school was to be established in each province for the preparation of teachers, and no one was authorized to teach without the approval of the normal school director. "Uniformity (*Gleichfoermigkeit*) was a central theme of the reforms."[8]

The impact was especially marked in Bohemia (now part of the Czech Republic), where vigorous measures were taken after 1778. In 1775, there had been about a thousand elementary schools (*Trivialschulen*) in Bohemia, with some 30,000 pupils; by 1789, there were 2,294, with 162,000 pupils in the summer; 170,000 in the winter.[9]

Although the *Allgemeine Schulordnung* established the obligation of school attendance, actual compliance varied greatly in different areas and on average represented only about a third of those required to attend school.[10] In Hungary, pressure was put upon Catholic parishes to establish schools (Protestant and Jewish communities had already done so), and the *Ratio Educationis* (1777) offended all religious groups by seeking to bring all schools under government oversight. Despite the effort to use government-controlled schooling as an instrument of unity, the effect was to further differentiate the country religiously.[11]

Much the same situation prevailed in the Habsburgs' Czech territories, where official persecution had not prevented the Protestants from establishing at least fifty schools, and the Jews, twenty-eight. Habsburg efforts to centralize and control education was related to the imposition of German as language of instruction, which in turn helped to stimulate the Czech nationalism—much promoted by schoolteachers—which became so significant in the nineteenth century.[12]

In 1781, Maria Theresa's son and successor, Joseph II, while withdrawing support from Felbiger, reinforced the requirement that all children whose parents did not provide private tutors attend school from ages six to twelve, and that their teachers use a standard method of instruction; they were forbidden to use nonauthorized textbooks.[13] He provided funds directly to parish schools through further confiscation of properties and endowments of the Catholic Church.

These measures had an uneven effect on popular schooling, which existed only as a function of some Catholic parishes and (where these existed) other religious institutions. Even in the area in and around Vienna in the late eighteenth century most children of the age for mandatory schooling were not in school. A Jesuit missionary reported from a village in Austria that only four of the 650 inhabitants could read.[14]

The efforts at education reform under Maria Theresa and Joseph II did not continue beyond the latter's death in 1790. The government of absolutist states had real control only over their taxation and military affairs; their ability to intervene in society was very limited. Only in the wake of the Napoleonic wars would the bureaucratic capacity be developed to do so.[15]

PRUSSIAN TERRITORIES

The situation of popular schooling in Prussia continued to improve somewhat after 1763 as a result of measures taken to promote general recovery from the Third Silesian or Seven Years' War. The *General-Landschul-Reglement*, the first education ordinance to apply to all of the (repeatedly enlarging) Prussian territories, sought, in the spirit of the Enlightenment, to promote "a reasonable as well as a Christian instruction of youth in true piety and other useful things."[16] Compulsory attendance between ages five and thirteen was pre-scribed, though pupils could be excused from the requirement earlier based upon demonstrated mastery of the skills taught in elementary school, and the requirement did not apply to Catholic children, for whom a separate law was enacted in 1765. Schools were to be supported by parental contributions (*Schulgeld*), while the charitable funds of the church or community paid for children of poor families. The local pastor was expected to meet each month with the schoolmaster, and assign the religious songs and catechism responses which should be learned;[17] higher church officials were to inspect schools annually. Anyone wishing to teach was required to obtain both government and church approval.

While these governmental measures were progressive compared with most other countries at the time, and German historians have often pointed to such decrees with pride, compliance was very uneven in the territories attached directly to the crown; in those under territorial magnates some of the latter were very active in promoting schooling, while others ignored it altogether. After all, it was up to local communities to build the schools and pay the teachers; in fact, "until the end of the 18th century, the schooling of the people remained dependent upon local initiatives of the lords of manors or ecclesiastical officials."[18] By 1816 only 60 percent of children of school age were in school, and many rural schools were in session for only a few winter months.[19] There was, however, growing interest among the educated classes in the provision of popular schooling, and more practical measures were taken in Germany than in contemporary France where talking and writing about enlightenment of the common people was equally fashionable. This Enlightenment program, with its emphasis upon making the peasantry more economically productive rather than creating possibilities for social mobility, was summed up by Heinrich Zerrenner, editor of *Der Deutsche Schulfreund* (*The German Friend of Schools*), in 1786, as "making [the people] rational and good to the degree necessary for them to become useful to the state as well as in every circumstance and relationship with other men, to be happier with their own lives, and to be more satisfied with their estate."[20]

In the same spirit, philosopher Immanuel Kant—who did not think it beneath him to write a little book about education—would observe, as an obvious truth requiring no justification, that "Man can only become man by education. He is merely what education makes of him."[21] The necessary fundamental recreation of mankind (*Umschaffung des Menschen*), Kant warned, was a risky and above all a political project.[22] On the other hand, as dean of the University of Koenigsberg, Kant issued a warning that poor youths should enter practical employment;[23] there were apparently limits on what education could be expected to accomplish. Kant began offering lectures on pedagogy in 1776–77, for the benefit of students of theology who would be constrained to teach while waiting for an opening in a parish.[24]

One of the enlightened Prussian noblemen, Friedrich Eberhard von Rochow (1734–1805), established schools on his estates in the early 1770s in response to problems he observed among his peasants in the wake of crop failures; he was convinced that they needed to be helped to develop the capacity for independent thinking and action in place of fatalism.[25] In 1779 Rochow urged that the "character and disposition of an entire people might be given direction" through education and could produce for Prussia a "common spirit" or "national character,"[26] a theme that would be revived by Fichte a quarter-century later. Rochow composed textbooks, including a widely used primer called *The Friend of Children* (*Der Kinderfreund*) that offered moral and biblical lessons through fables drawn from rural life, and wrote pamphlets to urge his fellow Junkers to support schooling on their estates.[27] He would earn the admiring title, among his contemporaries, of "the Pestalozzi of the borderlands."[28]

Rochow's example was followed by a few of his peers; by 1790 there were sixty-four estate schools in Germany.[29] While these schools served only a very small part of the peasant population, they had an influence beyond Germany's borders and provide support for Schmale's claim that the revival of German schools was not simply a reaction to developments in revolutionary France. [30]

The Friends of Mankind (Philanthropen), deeply influenced by Rousseau's writing, sought to provide an impetus to society-wide efforts through their own writing and through establishing schools. Unlike Rousseau, however, they sought to provide practical training that would increase prosperity: Campe contended that the inventor of the spinning wheel had done more for mankind than the authors of odes and epics. Their concern was to expand human happiness through making men and women more useful to society and to themselves.

Johann Basedow (1724–90) was, like many of his contemporaries, an enthusiast for the educational ideas of Rousseau; indeed, he named his daughter Emilie in tribute (as Pestalozzi named his son Hans Jakob—thus Jean Jacques). Basedow prepared a complete plan for the reform of schooling, with a central state supervising authority and a unitary, sequential structure of schooling. In an anticipation of Fichte forty years later, Basedow asked in 1768, "Where else can that patriotism which has died out be restored to life other than in schools and academies?" This would require, he insisted, "a complete remaking of schools and of schooling" under the direction of the state.[31] He placed special emphasis on teacher training *Seminare*, schoolbooks, and how-to-do-it handbooks on teaching for parents and teachers.

Basedow's proposals, with their emphasis upon "public virtue," aroused widespread enthusiasm, and he received many contributions to establish a model boarding school in Dessau in 1771; Kant wrote that this was the start of a true revolution in education, not a slow process of reform but a rapid revolution through the power of an experiment.[32] Basedow's pupils combined physical exercise, hikes, and handicrafts with their studies, and lived with the teachers and their families in an intimate relationship intended to build character. Like many educational experiments, Basedow's school flourished for only a decade, then gradually declined into extinction.[33] His influence, however, went far beyond the school, and it was said at the time that he had made education a popular fad, even among the most sophisticated circles. Perhaps more significantly, a number of the most influential teachers of the age had worked at his school.[34]

A more successful effort was that of Christian Gotthilf Salzmann (1744–1811), whose school in Schnepfental combined gymnastics, physical labor, and elements of self-governance with academic studies, and survived for two centuries. Salzmann was able to establish and maintain his school with support from Freemasons, and he insisted on its nonconfessional character. Before his death it had drawn pupils from Amsterdam, London, Copenhagen, Lisbon, Geneva, Bordeaux, Moscow, Boston, and Baltimore.[35] Salzmann's novel *Konrad Kiefer* (1794), often considered the German *Émile*, avoids the radical themes of the latter, and presents a picture of natural education within the family, with a strong emphasis upon moral instruction and illustration; religious instruction, he insists, should begin with moral stories rather than with the Bible or catechism.[36] His special concern—an anticipation of a central theme of twentieth-century pedagogy—was to draw pupils out of their passivity and engage them with their own learning.[37]

Joachim Heinrich Campe (1746–1818) was the most active writer among the Philanthropen, producing many successful books for children as well as guides to education for adults. Sixteen volumes of a comprehensive reference work "by a society of practical educators" appeared between 1785 and 1792, including the German translation of Rousseau's *Émile*. This required three volumes because of the extensive annotations by his enthusiastic German disciples; on some pages there was only a single line of Rousseau and all the rest was commentary.[38] Rousseau's suggestion that Defoe's novel *Robinson Crusoe* should serve as the basis for encouraging youth to imagine how they would survive in isolation from society was adapted by Campe in his *Robinson Junior*, which went through many editions and was widely imitated.[39] Like Pestalozzi and Schiller, Campe would be made an honorary citizen of revolutionary France.[40]

Campe's judgment upon contemporary schools—"schools of laziness, of stupidity, and of uselessness for life"—was especially harsh, and he insisted that efforts to remake the German nation must begin with children, since adults were already hopelessly ruined. "In the schools, or nowhere, can a nation be developed to industriousness and to every other moral and political virtue." Thus, in an anticipation of Pestalozzi, he called for keeping pupils busy with productive labor when they were not actually being instructed.[41]

In 1787 Friedrich Wilhelm II of Prussia established a government office for education, the Oberschulkollegium. The responsible state official, Karl Abraham von Zedlitz, proposed a comprehensive plan that sought to create a uniform (though internally differentiated) system of schooling under state oversight, and this was quickly approved by the king. Zedlitz had published his proposals in the Berlin Monthly, indicating that he was appealing for support to the newly emerging force of educated public opinion.[42]

The heart of his reforms, and of the government's efforts, was to improve the quality of teachers and of school inspection.[43] One of his concrete measures was to appoint in 1779 one of the Philanthropen, Ernst Christian Trapp (1745–1818), as the first professor of pedagogy at the University of Halle in an effort to build up pedagogy as an academic field independent from theology to which it had previously been attached; in fact, however, Trapp and his successor (like many education professors in subsequent centuries) chose to turn it into a scholarly field, which had little to do with classroom practice.[44]

Zedlitz also provided subsidies to Rochow that enabled him to raise the annual salaries of the teachers on his estates to such an extent that families no longer had to make tuition payments, with the result that attendance rose dramatically.[45]

Zedlitz was succeeded in office in 1788 by Johann Christoph von Woellner who imposed government censorship on Prussian teachers, including those at the university level. This provoked a strong reaction against the idea of state control of education, most famously expressed by Wilhelm von Humboldt whose objections will be discussed subsequently. Another opponent was Trapp who argued that the state should support but not control public schools and should have no authority over curriculum or teacher training.[46]

A fundamental distinction in Zedlitz's program, and, in fact, throughout most of the nineteenth century, was between rural and urban schooling. Rural schools were exclusively elementary—until well into the nineteenth century most had only one teacher—while most urban schools were what we could call secondary schools with preparatory classes at the elementary level. Zedlitz had written in 1777 that what was needed was an education of useful subordinates; each pupil, according to his destination in life, should learn no more and no less than he would need in his future position in life.[47] "The metaphysical education of peasants," he insisted, "should not be driven too far," as suggested by cosmopolitan enthusiasts who sought to "convert peasants into philosophers."[48]

In cities, there were two sorts of private schools, those which served the elite and charged a lot, and those which were inexpensive and often served many poor children whose tuition was paid by the charity funds. Secondary schools—*Gymnasien*—included preparatory classes taken by many who did not go on to the upper classes, which prepared for "learned" occupations requiring further study in university.[49]

"Schools and universities are state institutions [*Veranstaltungen des Staates*]" proclaimed the *Allgemeine Landrecht* of 1794, and, even if privately sponsored and funded, could be established only with state approval. Educational institutions "must at all times submit themselves to examinations and inspections" by government, and could not appoint teachers or change their program "without the previous knowledge and consent of the provincial school authorities." The Prussian state thus made it clear that its relationship with popular schooling would no longer be mediated through the churches. The new code of civil laws made school attendance compulsory, at least in theory.[50] More significantly, it gave the state control over the accreditation of teachers and approval of their appointment to schools. But all this could only begin to be effective after 1807 when the public administration was reorganized; gradually, in the following decades, Prussia extended its authority over all aspects of schooling.[51]

These measures have often been identified as the nationalization of Prussian education, but, in fact, "substantial collaboration between the state and the church characterized the school administration in Prussia until the end of the monarchy in 1918."[52] Indeed, the Protestant and Catholic clergy, like those in Baden, Brandenburg, or other German states, had a wide range of government responsibilities, such as keeping the list of military recruits and making government announcements in church.[53] The state lacked the administrative structures to bring schools under its direct control; "although the civil code defined schools as 'state establishments,' it stipulated that the Church and clergy were to continue to perform the major function of school supervision, although now in theory as agents of the state."[54] Of course, the fact that the Protestant and Catholic clergy were salaried by the state and were thought of as responsible for public morality made the role a natural one. It came to be deeply resented by teachers, however, and the abolishment of clergy oversight would be a periodic demand of their organizations—in 1848 and again in the last decades of the nineteenth century.[55]

During the period of ferment and disruption arising from the French Revolution of 1789, the ideas promoted by the Philanthropen came under general suspicion on the part of the authorities, and there was a turn among influential thinkers toward what came to be called *Neuhumanismus*, the emphasis placed by Herder and Wieland upon the inward cultivation of the individual, the development of a "beautiful soul."[56]

On the other hand, the crisis of Napoleon's invasion and conquest of the various German states made it urgent to find some means of building upon the ruins of the Old Regime. Popular schooling came to seem, to many, the key to building a new humanity worthy of the new society under construction. Rousseau had already suggested as much in his *Social Contract*, and it was a Swiss-German admirer of Rousseau, Johann Heinrich Pestalozzi (1746–1827), who captured the attention of many in Europe and, eventually, North America with his account of how that schooling should take place.

At the low point of Germany's fortunes, when victorious Napoleon was consolidating states and humiliating their rulers, a philosopher in occupied Berlin gave what were perhaps the most publicly influential series of lectures ever delivered. As we will see, Fichte called for a new birth of a German nation through education; in his *Addresses to the German Nation*, he invoked Pestalozzi's theories and methods as the nucleus of his scheme for national transformation.

Late in the nineteenth century, when many attributed the astonishing rise of a unified Germany as an industrial and military power to its educational systems, a French author would write that the "present greatness" of the country was "in a large measure" owed to Pestalozzi.[57] An English author wrote, a few years later, that "the nineteenth century humanitarian motive in impulse takes its definite beginning from Pestalozzi, not from the antisocial doctrines of Rousseau, nor the abstract theoretical legislation of the French revolutionaries, nor the benevolent intentions of the Philanthropinists."[58]

Indeed, Pestalozzi became "the symbol of pedagogy itself . . . the center and object of a 'pedagogical cult,' a myth which the reality of his actual [largely unsuccessful] pedagogical practice did not disturb."[59] This was especially the case because, through what the cynical might see as relentless self-promotion in such works as *How Getrude Teaches Her Children* (1801), Pestalozzi identified himself as the educator of poor children par excellence. "Friend," he writes, "there is no presumptuousness in my heart; I have wanted nothing else for my whole life, and will want nothing else, than the Good of the People, whom I love and whose misery I feel, in that I bear their suffering with them, as few have borne it with them."[60]

> Since poor children would ordinarily be taught by poorly trained men or women, Pestalozzi sought "to simplify and determine methods to such a degree that they might be employed by the most ordinary teacher, and by the most ignorant father and mother. In a word, he hoped to organize a pedagogical machine so well set up that it could in a manner run alone."[61]

Pestalozzi had been profoundly influenced by Rousseau's *Émile*, published when Pestalozzi was sixteen; Rousseau's picture of an education unfolding 'naturally' in a country retreat had a profound influence on Pestalozzi's determination to create a rural educational utopia. In an autobiographical reflection, Pestalozzi reported that

> [t]he moment Rousseau's *Émile* appeared, my visionary and highly speculative mind was enthusiastically seized by this visionary and highly speculative book. I compared the education which I enjoyed in the corner of my mother's parlour, and also in the school which I frequented, with what Rousseau demanded for the education of his Emilius. The home as well as the public education of the whole world, and of all ranks of society, appeared to me altogether as a crippled thing, which was to find a universal remedy for its present pitiful condition in Rousseau's lofty ideas. The ideal system of liberty, also, to which Rousseau imparted fresh animation, increased in me the visionary desire for a more extended sphere of activity, in which I might promote the welfare and happiness of the people.[62]

It should be noted, however, that he "eventually came to characterize *Émile* as an 'unpractical dream book.' For one thing, his efforts to educate [his son] according to Rousseau's precepts had failed miserably."[63]

After a personal bankruptcy, Pestalozzi became a teacher of poor children, and decided to create a household workshop to combine work with their studies: "I needed, for the poor children whom I took into my home to seek work and education [note, *Bildung*, not *training*]. But I didn't want only this, and wanted during and through their work to warm their hearts and develop [literally, unfold: *entfalten*] their minds. I didn't want simply to teach them; my intention was that their lives and actions themselves would teach them, and that by self-education the feeling of the inner worth of their nature would be aroused."[64]

Unfortunately, this effort failed, and Pestalozzi was forced to support his family by his writing. In 1781 he published the first version of his novel about education, *Leonard and Gertrud*, which was widely read and gave him—as *Émile* had given Rousseau—a reputation as an educator despite his lack of practical success. In 1792, the revolutionary French National Assembly made Pestalozzi an honorary citizen of France, and, with the French occupation of Switzerland in 1798, he was asked to take on the education of a group of orphans in an abandoned convent at Stans. This effort was also unsuccessful, in part because of the hostility of the local population, which saw him as a heretic and the tool of a foreign government, but it resulted in a *Letter from Stans* which would be profoundly influential as a brief statement of his educational theories.[65]

The Bern government then gave him the opportunity to try out his pedagogical methods with primary-level children in Burgdorf; after some months with little success, he was fortunate to gain a young disciple who did the actual teaching; in 1800 the government provided him with a chateau and the opportunity to create a small teacher-training institute. An admiring official report in 1802 captures the essence of what would be Pestalozzi's influential adaptation of the education which Rousseau had imagined:

> There is no trace of memory drill. Everything which the child learns is the result of his own observation, of his own experience. He learns nothing which he does not understand; he understands everything which he learns . . . The children are then led to notice the objects in greater detail, their situation, and the relations of their parts, their permanent and changing qualities, the qualities that are general and those that are peculiar to them, their influence, their functions, and their destiny. Thus they pass from simple to complex ideas, from mental images and names to judgments, descriptions, conclusions—in one word, to the definite and intelligent use of language.[66]

After further crises, Pestalozzi was able to move to Yverdon in 1804 and create the institute and laboratory school which would draw visitors from all over Europe and North America. A Pestalozzian school was opened in Berlin, and Yverdon became a mandatory stop on the tour of Europe by reformers, including the British industrialist/reformer Robert Owens. Pestalozzi (perhaps fortunately) did little teaching there; he "wrote letters and essays, received guests and gave talks."[67] Dissension among his disciples, and his own incapacity as a manager, led to the decline of the institution; a young American visitor in 1819 wrote that "[a] painful visit it was for me, to see this good old man and real philanthropist going broken-hearted to his grave, for broken-hearted he must be, in contemplating the ruined state of the institution which he has been laboring his whole life to establish."[68] It is one of the more intriguing paradoxes of educational history that among its most influential figures in their own time and subsequently are three—Rousseau, Pestalozzi, and John Dewey—who by all accounts were complete failures as teachers.

Leonard and Gertrude is a fictional account of the home schooling which a mother provided to her own and a neighbor's children, and of how this was then generalized to serve as the basis for a village school. For Pestalozzi, the education received in the family was not simply a preliminary to that received in school, but was, in fact, the model for the latter; "the more family-like all of life is formed, the more true and virtuous it is."[69]

Pestalozzi's primary objection to education as it was commonly practiced was that it put too much emphasis upon abstraction, and especially upon reading; one is reminded of Rousseau's outburst, in the middle of a very long book, "I hate books. They only teach one to talk about what one does not know."[70] Pestalozzi became convinced that real education must be self-directed and begin from sense impressions, with an emphasis upon real-life experiences. He wrote:

> We leave children, up to their fifth year, in the full enjoyment of nature; we let every impression of nature work upon them; they feel their power; they already know full well the joy of unrestrained liberty and all its charms . . . And after they have enjoyed this happiness of sensuous life for five whole years, we make all nature around them vanish from before their eyes; tyrannically stop the delightful course of their unrestrained freedom; pen them up like sheep, whole flocks huddled together, in stinking rooms; pitilessly chain them for hours, days, weeks, months, years, to the contemplation of unattractive and monotonous letters and (contrasted with their former condition) to a maddening course of life.[71]

In his own program for the children in the poorhouse at Stans, Pestalozzi used neither books nor other conventional school materials:

> While instructing the children in drawing, writing, and physical exercises, Pestalozzi encouraged them to cooperate with each other and to share their work . . . As he was convinced of the value of the natural environment for this purpose [of using sense impressions as the basis of instruction], the children were frequently taken on excursions to study natural history and the surrounding countryside.

Though external circumstances soon forced the institution to close, it has been called "the cradle of the modern elementary school";[72] more accurate, perhaps, would be to call it the source of recurrent progressive education theory.

One can find anticipations of current fashions in pedagogy in the fact that, for example, "Pestalozzi's major principle in teaching geography was to move from the near to the far. Not until they had become thoroughly familiar with their own locality were children introduced to broader areas." Similarly, science was taught "entirely without plan," through observation and examination of "such objects and phenomena as were within reach." The problem with this approach was already noticed by an early biographer, writing in 1831, who pointed out that, as a result, "the students did not acquire a comprehensive view of the sciences" and their knowledge "had a tendency afterwards to remain fragmentary." Similarly, in teaching music, Pestalozzi's concern was not that children acquire the discipline necessary to proficiency but that they experience "the marked and most beneficial influence which it has on the feelings."[73] His method required all knowledge should "have its origin in the child himself'"; the teacher should not give the child ready-made answers but should stimulate him to arrive at his own solutions. This required that "his own powers of perceiving, judging, and reasoning should be cultivated, his self-activity encouraged."[74] Child-centered education then, as now, tended to give students an incomplete command of the knowledge and skills which serve as the basis for effective participation in society—or, at least, in a society which already, in Pestalozzi's time, was undergoing rapid changes.

Pestalozzi himself made no apologies for his emphasis. "The aim of education," he wrote, "is not to turn out tailors, boot makers, tradesmen, or soldiers, but to turn out tailors, boot makers, tradesmen, and soldiers who are in the highest meaning of the word, men. Consequently, the aim of all education and instruction is and can be no other than the harmonious development of the powers and faculties of human nature."[75] In this respect, again, we find him following Rousseau faithfully. In his novel *Leonard and Gertrude*, the children of a widowed neighbor come to Gertrude's humble house

> almost every day, and constantly learned from her to take more heed to themselves and all about them. While they were spinning and sewing, she taught them to count and cipher, for she regarded arithmetic as the foundation of all intellectual order. Her method was to let the children count their threads or stitches both forwards and backwards, and add and subtract, multiply and divide the result by different numbers. The children vied with each other in this game, trying to see who could be quickest and surest in the exercise.[76]

The novel tells us that the good effects of this home-based education came to the attention of the local benevolent nobleman, who had expressed to the pastor "an earnest desire to labor for the improvement of the village, and asked the clergyman if he could recommend an upright, able man from among the people who could help him in furthering his designs." The pastor took him, and his assistant, Lieutenant Gluelphi, to see a cotton spinner named Meyer, who advised that "we can do very little with the people, unless the next genera-tion is to have a very different training from that [which] our schools furnish. The school ought really to stand in the closest connection with the life of the home, instead of, as now, in strong contradiction to it." Gluelphi agreed, arguing "that a true school should develop to the fullest extent all the faculties of the child's nature," and resolved that he would himself undertake to estab-lish and teach such a school, if someone would show him how. Meyer at once suggested Gertrude, and accordingly the pastor, the nobleman, and Gluelphi visited and were charmed by the little home school which they observed in action. Pestalozzi comments that Gertrude's "whole scheme of education"

> embraced a true comprehension of life itself. Yet she never adopted the tone of instructor toward her children; she did not say to them: "Child, this is your head, your nose, your hand, your finger" . . . but instead she would say, "Come here, child, I will wash your little hands" . . . Her verbal instruction seemed to vanish in the spirit of her real activity, in which it always had its source. The result of her system was that each child was skillful, intelligent and active to the full extent that its age and development allowed. The instruction she gave them in the rudiments of arithmetic was intimately connected with the realities of life . . . Above all, in every occupation of life she taught them an accurate and intelligent observation of common objects and the forces of nature. All that Gertrude's children knew, they knew so thoroughly that they were able to teach it to the younger ones; and this they often begged permission to do.[77]

Gluelphi "asked her whether she thought it would be possible to introduce into a regular school the same method she pursued at home with her children," and she replied that she thought it possible if a schoolmaster could be found "who would tolerate such an arrangement in his school." Gluelphi told her that he was determined to do so, and he and the pastor and nobleman "explained to her that they regarded the proper education of the youthful population as the only means of elevating the condition of the corrupt village."[78] In the new village school organized by Gluelphi, Gertrude pointed out that "the reading, writing and arithmetic are not, after all, what they most need; it is all well and good for them to learn something, but the really important thing is for them to be something—for them to become what they are meant to be, and in becoming which they so often have no guidance or help at home."[79]

The ultimate vindication of Gertrude's approach to education came when an official from the court of the Duke visited the village to observe the school, where he

> paid especial attention to the union of study and manual labor. Then he expressed to the somewhat anxious lieutenant the warmest approbation of his methods. "I find your plans in harmony both with the inner nature of man and his actual social condition," he said. "Man is only happy and secure in this world, when he is so developed as to be able to fill well that place in society to which he can legitimately lay claim. This demand is met by your methods in a more perfect degree than I have ever seen before."[80]

Returning to brief the Duke, the official advised him that there was only one way to improve the condition of his realm, and that was "for the government to exert an influence on the development of the people." This could be accomplished by "the establishment of a new professorship, for the purpose of acquainting the noblemen of the realm with better principles of popular government, and also the appointment of a commission whose duty shall be to counsel and assist everyone who shows a disposition to carry out these principles."[81]

In short, community and family life would be transformed by the intervention of the authorities, and there could thus be no conflict of interest between the people and their overlords.[82]

This fictional official endorsement was, in fact, echoed in real life. A number of able young men were sent by their governments to learn Pestalozzi's methods, and a constant stream of visitors arrived on their own initiative. It is reported that in residence at Yverdon were not only Swiss, German, and French enthusiasts but also Italians, Spaniards, and Russians, even Americans.

Pestalozzi had become known very extensively through the publication of an enthusiastic report on his earlier institute at Burgdorf by the Bern authorities and by his books. His educational "discovery" was discussed in widely read German periodicals by such distinguished writers as Wieland, Herbart, and Friedrich Schlegel, who "considered it to be among the most important innovations of the new century."[83]

In an "atmosphere of general enthusiasm for Pestalozzi," Prussian education authorities sent teachers to Switzerland to study Pestalozzi's methods; Minister of Education Suevern told a group of a dozen young men about to depart that they were being sent, not so much to learn Pestalozzi's methods, which they could learn elsewhere and at less expense, but that they might warm themselves at the sacred fire glowing in his bosom, full of power and love, so that they could walk with a similar spirit in the path of truth and in the observation of the laws of nature.[84] They returned after several years full of enthusiasm; the king himself helped to fund the publication of an edition of Pestalozzi's writing. Educators were not the only ones, Tenorth observes, who were filled with almost limitless hopes by this new method, which promised—as one official told the king—to "teach the child nothing that he does not understand, and to understand everything that he learns."[85]

By 1825 Pestalozzian ideas "had substantially taken possession of the whole common school system" in Prussia;[86] they served the same function for popular schooling that Humboldt's "Neo-Humanism" served for the highly selective secondary schools.

What explains this enthusiasm, in conservative as well as progressive circles, for the pedagogical theories of an unsuccessful Swiss teacher? No doubt an important factor was his reputation as the primary continuer of Rousseau's 'child-centered' approach to the education of an (imaginary) boy from infancy to adulthood, and the prophet of the application of this idea to a policy of reform of the common people through schooling. The fact that the schooling which he described was explicitly intended to prepare the children of the poor to remain in their parents' humble condition was probably an important element of the enthusiasm; this was a central concern in Enlightenment discussion of popular schooling. Elementary education of the poor, Pestalozzi insisted, ought "by no means to encourage 'fantastic dreams' of abolishing class distinctions"; its purpose was "to educate the poor child in such a way that he will, though remaining poor, be able to lead a life both useful and satisfying, of dignity and human worth."[87] He wrote that "the poor must be educated for poverty, and this is the key test by which it can be discovered whether such an institution [school] is really a good one. Education of the poor demands a deep and accurate knowledge of the real needs, limitations, and environment of poverty, and detailed knowledge of the probable situation in which they will spend their lives."[88]

The implication of this focus upon the immediately useful was that Pestalozzi opposed the teaching of algebra and geometry, except to the brightest students, and that "history is mentioned by him only occasionally in discussing education, and literature is scarcely mentioned at all."[89]

Spinning cotton or wool while reciting passages from the Bible, taking rambles in the countryside, learning arithmetic through work-related tasks, could all be educationally valuable activities, but nothing in these activities encouraged the children of peasants to lift their heads above their parents' condition or exposed them to a wider world of possibilities, of the sort that books could have revealed to them. What is more, as the young American visitor to Yverdon pointed out, Pestalozzi's method, well intentioned as it was, "would exclude memory altogether as a medium of instruction, and make use of reason alone, which is absurd. Reason must be furnished with ideas for the materials of its ratiocinations, and many of these must be laid up in and recalled by the memory . . . This is the misery of all systems, that the makers of them are never satisfied with putting them in practice as far as they are true, merely, but have a foolish vanity of giving them universal applicability."[90]

It may, in fact, have been this limit of the Pestalozzian model which made it so attractive to Fichte and to the Prussian authorities whose concern was to train the hearts of the common people, not to lift their heads above their inherited social and economic position.

The Prussian disciples of Pestalozzi were given responsibility for training other teachers through special institutions, teacher *Seminare*, established for the purpose. For example, in 1809 the Prussian authorities appointed one of them, Karl August Zeller, to be the supervisor of elementary education in East Prussia, where he established several *Seminare* to train teachers, as did several other young men who had been sent by their government to learn Pestalozzi's methods. These teacher-training *Seminare* were to be one of the most notable aspects of Prussian education, with a strong emphasis on moral and religious formation to form reliable teachers. Between 1826 and 1840, forty-five *Seminare* were founded in Prussia alone, and there were others elsewhere in Germany.

The actual tendency of this Pestalozzian emphasis was expressed in a Prussian cabinet order in 1809, in which the first three of four principles for the organization of primary instruction could be derived directly from *Leonard and Getrude* and other works of Pestalozzi. "First, education was henceforth to be considered the state's responsibility; second, teachers must prepare themselves for their profession; third, the aim of primary schools was not to impart knowledge but to help form judgment, common sense, morality, and religious spirit." The fourth concerned the practical arrangements necessary.[91]

The self-understanding of teachers was also deeply influenced by both the idealized image of Pestalozzi and by his accounts of child-centered schooling. For elementary school teachers, underpaid and poorly educated as most of them were, "the proud feeling of being an instructor of the People" created a self-understanding which gave them the courage to take a pedagogical standpoint and to claim to be an advocate for the interests of the child. Teachers came to see themselves as mediators of humanity and of the progressive spirit.

They possessed this high mission, not because of their social origins or the respect which they enjoyed, but because of their mastery of the pedagogical method of Pestalozzi, which gave them a privileged insight into both the nature and the goals of human development, and thus of the future of humankind.[92] It was a natural step to seeing themselves as the advance scouts of a movement for universal emancipation;[93] "the reform called on [the teacher's] self-understanding, gave him a perspective upon the wide framework of the schooling of Mankind and opened the opportunity to understand himself, in his [lowly] office, as an active agent."[94] Despite all subsequent efforts to limit their goals and to constrain their methods, teachers of popular education became a continuing source of agitation for social change and especially for recognition of what they considered their own crucial role in social progress—often going far beyond anything that Pestalozzi would have imagined.

Although elements of Pestalozzi's approach to popular schooling—often in a form that would have been unrecognizable to him—remained influential throughout the nineteenth century and into the twentieth, in actual practice it served more often as a reason to limit the scope of the schooling provided than as a means to make it more liberating. He seemed to nineteenth-century education reformers, especially in Germany, to have shown how to "educate men without at the same time unfit them for actual life," since he proposed an education "directly adapted to the duties the child will probably have to fulfil in the future"[95] in the humble station that would be his lot. It is clear that the peasant child in Gertrude's schoolroom, spinning while reciting lessons, was a world away from the professor's child in John Dewey's Laboratory School, playing at weaving like Penelope in order to "experience" Homer's Odyssey.

THE NETHERLANDS

The eighteenth century had been a period of long decline for The Netherlands from its "Golden Age" in the previous century. While farmers continued to do moderately well, and Dutch merchants continued to engage in oversees trade, there was growing poverty in the cities and a general sense of social and economic stagnation. Historian Guillaume Groen van Prinsterer would write as late as 1847 of "an unmistakable and sometimes vivid sense of humiliation and decline" which extended not only to commerce and industry and to the increase of pauperism, but also to political disarray.[96]

How that situation was understood by contemporary opinion would have particular importance for the development of popular schooling in the following century. The stagnation was blamed by some on the lack of national unity and thus of central executive authority. The provinces that made up the United

Netherlands had retained a large measure of autonomy, surrendered only reluctantly and in part when military emergencies required leadership by the hereditary *stadholders*.[97] In each of the provinces, political as well as economic power was in the hands of the oligarchic regents and of the guilds. The conviction had been growing that social and economic progress required fundamental reforms and national unity. Thus "the Enlighteners sought to concentrate all power in the central authorities."[98]

Influential voices were calling for a more unified educational system under the supervision of central authorities, as the basis for national revival from the long economic slump of the eighteenth century. The Patriot movement, which would welcome the support of revolutionary France in the 1790s had for several decades already been blaming the troubles of The Netherlands on the autonomy of the provinces with respect to education, among other matters.[99]

A second diagnosis of the stagnation of The Netherlands placed the blame on falling away from the virtues which had characterized the great generations that fought for independence from Spain and then built a worldwide commercial empire. The form which the Enlightenment took in The Netherlands, in contrast with France, did not posit a fundamental opposition between faith and reason, and placed a strong emphasis upon the restoration of moral norms among the Dutch people.[100]

"With what heavy darkness the majority of the Nation is still covered," wrote Y. van Hamelsveld in 1791 in an influential book entitled *The Moral Condition of the Dutch Nation at the End of the Eighteenth Century*. Van Hamelsveld deplored not only what he believed was a serious decline in morality but also the "unbelief and superstition" (*Ongeloof en Bijgeloof*) which he held equally responsible. The decline threatened to end in disaster, he warned. "Netherlands, Netherlands, you stand on the very brink of your own destruction. Your ruin is inevitable unless reforms . . . can avert the final blow." Virtue and duty could be restored to social life by reforms to increase the moral influence of schools, prisons, and almshouses.[101]

The first diagnosis led to three decades of political upheaval and also— once a more unitary state had been established—to efforts to create a system of national schooling that would help to "knit the nation together" through popular education using prescribed texts of a patriotic character. The second diagnosis of the crisis ensured that this schooling and these texts would be strongly committed to moral education on the basis of what came to be called a "Christianity above [confessional] differences."

It was very much in the Dutch tradition that voluntary associations played a major role in defining and then developing this approach to popular schooling, along with reading rooms, discussion groups, and publications aimed at "enlightenment" of the common people. Advocates of popular schooling were primarily rising merchants, small manufacturers, notaries, lawyers, dissenting clergymen, and schoolteachers, a new class living on their brains rather than their inherited capital and owing little to the Golden Age of the seventeenth century or its theological certainties.

> Their Christianity was very watered down, what would later be called "modernism," and their faith was essentially a faith in the improvement of the world and the educability of mankind through rational interventions . . . They wanted to centralize and modernize the state and at the same time dismantle the power of the old oligarchy . . . The "democrats" wanted a centralized state in which citizens would form a homogeneous "nation"; separation of church and state was a necessary precondition, given the religious diversity of the population.[102]

This emerging class had everything to gain from a restoration of the energy and sense of common purpose which (in their imagination, at least) had once characterized the Dutch Republic.[103] The gradual growth of the literate middle class during the course of the eighteenth century supported a new periodical literature on the model of Steele and Addison's *Spectator* in England. These publications, the first of which appeared in 1731, addressed themselves to men, and women as well, who possessed a lively curiosity about new developments in science and social life. The Dutch periodicals "stressed . . . the conviction that mankind could lay a basis for knowledge, virtue, and happiness through voluntary associations in circles of friends, organizations, and societies."[104] They sought to inspire and advise, with a focus on the reasonable, virtuous life based upon a correct understanding of human nature and of duty. While upholding Christianity as the basis of virtue, they called for tolerance and criticized prejudices based on doctrinal differences.[105]

The most significant—though not the first—of the voluntary associations concerned with popular enlightenment was the Maatschappij tot Nut van 't Algemeen (Society for the General Welfare, known as the 'Nut'), founded in 1784 by a dissenting Protestant pastor who had read a publication of the Holland Association of Haarlem, "On the Moral and Physical Education of Children" and reflected that

> it's too bad . . . that as a result of its high price this [publication] cannot be bought and read by the common man; after all, without a good education, children cannot become upstanding people, true patriots, virtuous Christians, nor can they come to know, to value, and to exercise wisdom with all her noble virtues. To achieve a

goal so beneficial for the Fatherland, I thought that nothing would be more useful than to establish a society of such honest and true friends of humanity.[106]

Such efforts were in the air. The Zeeland Society for Sciences, echoing the French societies which played such a significant role in the Enlightenment, had offered a prize in 1778 for the best essay on the subject, "What improvements are necessary in the common or public, especially the Dutch, schools to improve the culture of our Nation? How can these, in the most beneficial manner, be implemented, and maintained on a durable basis?"[107] The first prize went to an essay by H. J. Krom that called for creating institutions in each province to train teachers.[108] Another essay submitted was by Kornelis van der Palm, a teacher in Rotterdam, whose son would be a central figure in establishing the role of the national government in education. Van der Palm senior urged that religious instruction should be adapted to the understanding of children, and thus rejected the traditional use of catechisms.[109] A more radical note was struck in 1790, as the French Revolution was gathering momentum; the Utrecht Society for Arts and Sciences held a similar competition, and one of the essays insisted upon the right of the state to form the young. It was not enough to improve the existing schools, the author argued, but rather they should be replaced with an entirely new system, under the control of the state.[110]

J. H. Swildens published in 1781 a *Fatherlandish A. B. Book for Dutch Youth*, intended to "spread necessary fatherlandish accomplishments and thus to promote the enlightenment of the people." Swildens called for removing schooling from the responsibilities of the national Church and placing it under the state as its most important task.[111] This by no means meant that schools should abandon their traditional role of shaping a religious consciousness, but Swildens argued that this should be so formulated that it would be acceptable to all Christians.[112]

The ambitions of the Nut were more modest, however: the action plan adopted in 1784 called for publication of simple books intended for those with little schooling, along with local efforts to improve the quality of schools. A "school library" of inexpensive texts for classroom use was widely distributed.[113] By 1787 the Nut had eleven branches, and its publications— religious essays, schoolbooks, uplifting biographies, works of popular morality, folksongs—were appearing in large editions of five or six thousand copies. These publications were influenced by Enlightenment themes, but as mediated through an essentially conservative liberal Protestantism. Contemporary German educational reformers like Campe and Basedow were more directly influential than were Rousseau or Diderot. The ground for this movement, indeed, had been prepared by Pietism with its emphasis upon making Christian teaching directly relevant to young minds as much as it had by the Enlightenment.[114] This had gradually evolved into an emphasis on (in Kant's terms) God, virtue, and immortality. Jesus was presented as a teacher and a moral example, not as a redeemer from sin; he was described as fighting against the prejudices of his day, with the implication that he would have been appalled at the differences between Calvinists and Catholics. The Nut's publications avoided mentioning the various churches in their presentation of a confessionless Christianity.[115]

Soon the Nut turned to establishing its own schools, seeing this as the most essential "foundation for the formation, improvement, and cultivation of citizens." By 1800 several dozen Nut primary schools were in operation, and teacher training institutions had been established in Amsterdam, Haarlem, and Groningen; there were fifty-two local branches of the organization with 3,678 members. A study of the members of the Nut in Utrecht in 1786–87 found that about a third were from small-scale business and industry, with the next largest group coming from their free professions: doctors, lawyers, notaries. Forty-three percent belonged to the liberal dissenting churches, compared with their 0.4 percent representation in the population as a whole; the four clergymen were all dissenters. Sharply underrepresented were Catholics, then almost exclusively of low status in Utrecht, and members of the established church, which included both the social and economic elite and many workers, were somewhat underrepresented.[116]

Members of the Nut were instrumental in the implementation as well as the planning of the public system which, within a few years, had attracted international admiration. It was the hopes and anxieties of this emerging middle class about the future of their nation, and not a concern about—for example—labor-force needs that provided the energy to push and cajole local authorities into making adequate provision for schools. In 1796, for example, a commission appointed by the municipal council of Leiden recommended that the "poor-children schools" be given the "nobler" name of "public schools" (*openbare scholen*) and serve children of all religious groups, while avoiding doctrinal instruction "which is in addition inappropriate for young children." There should, of course, be religious education, but it should be such "that no one can take offense at it."[117]

The French invasion of 1795 in support of the Patriot Party which had sought fundamental changes in the oligarchic Dutch society brought an end to the Republic of the Seven United Netherlands. "The Netherlands Republic no longer exists . . . as a confederate state of independent territories, but as one single sovereign People," the Patriots proclaimed.[118] The new Batavian

Republic was a unitary state with a central government which made education a priority as the surest means to create a sense of nationality. In the face of a "crisis . . . of national self-esteem," the program of national unification came to seem of overriding importance. Thus the "Representatives of the People of Rotterdam" proclaimed in the year of the French invasion that "without Unity our Republic can never succeed in being either important and valuable for her allies [i.e., republican France] or redoubtable to her foes. Common interest dictates that the whole Batavian nation unite to form a single indivisible Republic."[119]

> The word *national* was a key concept. In 1796 the National Assembly came together, the top leadership of the country, chosen under the principle of universal [male] suffrage. It considered one of its most important tasks the central organization of education. It quickly appointed a "Commission for the development of a proposal for National education." In the *Staatsregeling* of 1798, the first constitution of the country, reference was made to the establishment of schools "through which the National character can be improved" and, in addition, to the appointment of an agent for national education. The document that played a large role in the actual reform, written in 1796, was published two years later under the title *General Thoughts about National Education.*[120]

This report was by the Nut, calling for a system of national education and endorsing Swildens's position that education was the business of the state and not of the churches.[121] In these *General Thoughts*, the Nut called upon the new Batavian National Assembly to undertake a comprehensive program of popular education: "Every well-ordered society constitutes the unity of its citizens for the ordering of the general happiness . . . Society has the right to demand from each of its citizens full and unstinting collaboration in the achievement of this goal. Society is especially obliged to its young citizens to provide them with the necessary knowledge for their future participation in the national commonwealth."[122]

To these ends, the report discussed the training of teachers, the subjects that should be in the curriculum, the maximum number of pupils in each class, the education of girls and boys together, the way pupils should (and should not) be punished and encouraged, and the best means of arousing the interest of parents in the schooling of their children.[123] The Nut "was concerned to train a generation of teachers who were not only versed in the new techniques but prepared to treat their charges as something other than small animals, kept in order only by regular doses of brutal punishment and the most mechanical forms of learning by rote."[124] Through publications and conferences, the Nut promoted whole-class instruction in contrast with the inefficient individualized practices then prevalent, and new methods of teaching reading. The fundamental assumption behind these efforts was that effective instruction, widely diffused, would lead inevitably to virtue throughout the society; this placed much higher expectations on the skill as well as the character of the teacher.[125]

The educational program of the Batavian Republic and its successor governments was to a large extent based upon the initiatives and publications of the Nut, and those appointed to implement the program were members of or in sympathy with the organization. Members of the organization played leading roles as school inspectors as the system developed. The Nut, in turn, drew upon a Dutch tradition of civic engagement which had developed through hundreds of years of civic life under a weak central government. The presence of branches of the Nut in all parts of the country (as well as in the Dutch colonies), linked together through frequent correspondence, goes far to explain why popular education developed more rapidly in The Netherlands than it did in France, as a civil society, rather than a government, initiative.

In Utrecht, for example, the influence of the Nut led to establishment in 1795 of a Committee of Public Education, and the adoption of the first of a series of school regulations in 1796. This called for a confessionally neutral system, a policy applied immediately to the two publicly funded schools, though the church-sponsored schools, providing free education to poor children, did not comply. For the first time in The Netherlands, the potential emerged for conflict over education between church and government.[126]

There is another aspect of the Nut's influence which made its program widely acceptable: it was not a semisecret organization like the Masonic order, which over the next century played a significant role in the agitation for state control of schooling in Belgium, France and Italy. Nor was it anticlerical, much less anti-Christian. Many of the Nut's early publications, indeed, were intended to present a nondoctrinal form of Christianity to a popular audience, including schoolchildren; the organization has been described as "a kind of social church."[127]

The liberal leadership of the predominant Protestant Church, the Hervormde church (which, even after it was officially "disestablished" in 1796, continued to play a semiofficial role in Dutch life) supported these reforms as contributing to the promotion among the common people of their own religious views. Liberal theologians like Professor Muntinghe of Groningen were popular among Nut members for their unchallenging teaching that Jesus's death should be seen, not as an act of redemption from sin, but as a moral example, encouraging us to live better lives.[128] Later in the nineteenth century, in fact, and until the 1860s, Petrus Hofstede de Groot and other liberal Protestant theologians at the University of Groningen would be among the most ardent supporters of the state school and among the strongest opponents of denominational schooling.[129]

Initially the Catholic leadership supported these educational reforms as an improvement upon the previously preponderant influence of the Protestant church establishment on schools. Thus The Netherlands—during the first decades of building a system of schooling—avoided the conflict between school policies and the wishes of parents which did so much damage in France at the same period. By the time such conflict broke out, the system was well established.

BELGIUM

Efforts by the Counter-Reformation Catholic Church and religious orders to provide popular schooling as a means of countering Protestantism faded as the southern Netherlands became reliably Catholic under Spanish and then Austrian rule in the late seventeenth and the eighteenth centuries. Scattered efforts were made later in the eighteenth century by individual clergy or benevolent laymen to establish schools for poor children, but there was a general educational stagnation except for children from wealthier families.[130]

Under the treaties of Utrecht (1713) and La Barrière (1715) the frontier between France and what is now Belgium had been defined and control of that portion of the Low Countries passed from the Spanish to the Austrian branch of the Habsburg dynasty. Efforts by the government in the Austrian Netherlands to reform secondary education, until 1773 almost entirely in the hands of the Jesuits, failed completely. In the Austrian Netherlands as in Austria itself Maria Theresa "profited from the suppression of the Jesuits [by the pope] in 1773 to laicise and modernise secondary education by creating her own colleges in place of those formerly run by the Jesuits, and in 1777 set about the formidable task of killing analphabetism among the teeming thousands of her subjects by elaborating an all-embracing plan for a state system of primary education. It came to nothing."[131]

Maria Teresa's son and successor, Joseph II, visited Belgium in 1781 to attempt to promote his reforms of—and reduce the power of—the Catholic Church, but his efforts succeeded only in arousing bitter opposition in the name of traditional "Burgundian liberties." Proposals for teacher training institutions were blocked by questions about their funding, and by the resistance of the clergy to government intervention in this area.[132] Significant popular unrest broke out in 1787 in reaction against these efforts at reform, and for a brief time rebels were able to seize Brussels and announce—on the American model—the establishment of a Sovereign Congress of the United States of Belgium. This rebellion was put down with Austrian troops, just before the French invasion brought a permanent end to Habsburg rule in The Netherlands.[133]

Chapter Three

The State Takes Charge

As we have seen, the governments of Austria and Prussia took various measures, during the eighteenth century, to promote and impose a measure of uniformity upon popular schooling, but it was not until after the convulsions of the French Revolution and the subsequent wars that such efforts began to have a significant effect. The popular school of the nineteenth century was above all an instrument of emerging nationalism, reflecting the Romantic concern with national unity based upon cultural uniformity and requiring the engagement of peasants and workers as loyal participants in that project. It was also during this period that linguistic unity, and thus the suppression of the countless local dialects, became an urgent project for the theorists of nationalism and thus a mission of the school.

The foremost theorist of the educational project of nation-building was that great admirer of Pestalozzi, philosopher Johann Gottlieb Fichte (1762–1814). Prussia had been profoundly affected by the French Revolution and its aftermath, especially when defeated and over-run by the French army in 1806–7. "In Prussia the idea of retrieving through the schools the fortunes lost in battle had taken definite shape after the battle of Jena [1806]."[1] In the process of national revival, the "new humanists" demanded a dramatically changed role for the school. As the reforming prime minister, Baron vom und zum Stein, wrote in his Nassau Program of 1807, it was necessary to awaken the sleeping and misdirected strengths of the people and arouse in them a strong feeling for the Fatherland, independence, and national honor, thus uniting State and Nation (*Volk*).[2]

To the post-1806 reformers the "national community" promised political as well as cultural salvation. Their goal was to transform the rigid hierarchy of subjects into a community of citizens who shared a common national identity and participated actively in public life . . . The imperatives of national renewal required a revitalized, dynamic state administration, distinguished from the officialdom of the old regime not only by its organic union with the nation but also by its more centralized, efficient structure. The "development [*Bildung*] of a nation," Hardenberg wrote in his Riga Memorandum of 1807, must go hand in hand with a "doubling of the powers of the state."[3]

In his *Addresses to the German Nation*, delivered during the French occupation in Berlin that same year, Fichte abandoned his earlier criticism of the state and identified it as "the means for achieving the higher purpose of educating and developing the element of pure humanity in the nation." Fichte called for a truly "national education" to fashion a "new self," a "new life," to "mold the Germans into a corporate body, which shall be stimulated and animated in all its individual members by the same interest." Only in this way, he argued, could the nation rise again from the destruction which it had suffered at the hands of Napoleon: "in the education of the nation, whose former life has died away and become nothing but a supplement to that of another [nation], to an entirely new life . . . In a word, I propose a total change of the former system of education as the only means to preserve the existence of the German nation."[4] Fichte "assumed that the state would be guided by ethical right, and would know the morale suitable for the community;" thus he "deplored family instruction."[5]

The weakness of the existing schooling was that it had been unable to present to its pupils the image of a moral world order so vividly that they were filled with a burning love and desire for it, with such glowing emotion that they would seek to realize it in their lives. The old education had been unable to penetrate with sufficient power to the very roots of impulse and action; the new national education must possess that power. "By this new education we want to build Germans into a single body [*Gesamtheit*], that in all its members will be stimulated and animated by a single interest." Thus it must be applied to every German, so it would not be the education of a single class but that of the Nation itself, not just popular education but national education.[6]

The phrase *national education* would come to be loaded with meaning over the course of the nineteenth century, and not just in Germany; it signified education seeking to shape, even to create, a national consciousness. This was certainly the meaning that Fichte attached to the phrase, and it was significant, for example, when Mussolini renamed the Italian Ministry of Public Instruction the Ministry of National Education—and significant, also, when the post-war Italian government changed the name back again. Similarly, the French Ministry of Public Instruction became (and has remained) the Ministry of National Education in 1932, reviving a title employed during the 1790s by supporters of state control of education, as a way of signaling an expanded mission of schools to transform society.

This national education, Fichte argued, would possess sufficient power only if it abandoned the error of the old education, which stressed the free will of its pupils, and instead undertook to suppress freedom of the will completely and substitute for it the absolute necessity of obeying the moral imperative of duty. All true education, Fichte asserted, seeks to produce steadfastness of character; he who must be continually exhorted to do the right thing, or must exhort himself to do so, lacks such a character. "If you want to have influence over him, you must do more than talk to him; you must fashion him in such a way that he cannot will anything contrary to what you want him to will . . . The new [national] education must develop this stable and unhesitating will."[7]

One is reminded of Rousseau's 1773 essay on how to restore the collapsed Polish nation, and it seems likely that Fichte had this in mind. Rousseau had written that

> [i]t is the national institutions that form the genius, the character, the tastes, and the morale of a people, and make it different from every other people . . . This is the all-important article. It is education that must give the souls of the people a national form, and so shape their opinions and their tastes that they become patriots as much by inclination and passion as by necessity. A child ought to look upon his fatherland as soon as his eyes open to the light, and should continue to do so until the day of his death. Every true patriot sucks in the love of country with his mother's milk. This love is his whole existence. He thinks of nothing but his country. He lives only for his country. Take him by himself, and he counts for nothing.[8]

Thus Fichte contended that "it is essential . . . that the pupil be entirely and without interruption under the influence of this education, and entirely separated from the community and all contact with it," as Rousseau had insisted in the case of his imaginary pupil Émile, and as Robespierre and his allies recommended during the radical phase of the French Revolution. The result, Fichte promised, would be that the pupil would complete his education as a fixed and unchangeable piece of machinery that cannot go otherwise than in the manner for which it had been designed, and is self-regulating without external compulsion.[9] Though he may have read Rousseau's essay, it is unlikely that Fichte had also read the American "Founding Father" Benjamin Rush's essay asserting that it was "possible to convert men into republican machines.

This must be done if we expect them to perform their parts properly in the great machine of the government of the state."[10] The image, and confidence in the power of popular education, was in the air on both sides of the Atlantic.

As an instrument of the state, the school should become the primary institution for remaking the scattered elements of the kingdom into a Prussian—indeed, a German—people. Distinctions of the traditional social orders should be abolished, with only talent determining one's position in society.[11] Germans were suffering from excessive individualism, Fichte argued, and he called instead for devotion to a fatherland defined by the use of the German language, over-reaching the boundaries of the many states, large and small, that shared that language.

This "national education" would be something entirely unprecedented, something that no people had ever experienced; it would create a new identity and a common will. Citizens of this larger German nation—which did not exist as an organized state—must be educated to have a sense of a common fatherland; only in this way could Germany be raised from the ruins of the now-abolished but for centuries ineffective Holy Roman Empire and given its independence.[12]

How could this be accomplished? "We give to this question the answer: by adopting the form of education discovered, proposed, and already put into practice under the supervision of Johann Heinrich Pestalozzi." The Swiss educator only wanted to help the common people, but in fact his method had the effect of removing the distinction between them and the educated class, and provided, "in place of the intended popular education, national education, and indeed has the potential to help the nations, and all of humanity, out of the depths of their misery."[13]

Pestalozzi, Fichte wrote elsewhere, would

remain in the history of our age one of the most extraordinary and beautiful phenomena. This his contemporaries feel; posterity will appreciate it still more deeply. To the course of instruction which has been invented and brought forward by Heinrich Pestalozzi, and which is now being successfully carried out under his direction—must we look for our regeneration . . . With this system of popular education for the entire rising generation must the nation address itself—at once and persistently.[14]

In recent decades, Fichte lamented, "enlightened" governments had come to believe that they could rely upon coercion to achieve their goals, and had thus neglected the religious and moral education of their subjects. With the proposed system of national education, however, it would no longer be necessary to employ coercion, since in every heart would burn a love of the community, of the State, and of the Nation, a love which would destroy every selfish impulse.[15]

Fichte was not distressed by Pestalozzi's low estimation of the importance of literacy; in national education, he argued, that could indeed be harmful if given too much emphasis or introduced too soon. "Only at the absolute end of education, and as the last gift to take on the way," should the pupil be made acquainted with the letters by which—having fully mastered spoken language through Pestalozzi's method of oral instruction—he could learn to write and to read that language. That would be the practice in the ordinary, common national education; of course, Fichte added, it would be different in the education of children of the educated classes.[16]

Such national education, Fichte told his Berlin audience, was the only means of rescuing Germany from all the evils and weaknesses which were oppressing the divided and prostrate nation. The State, as the highest manager of human affairs, responsible to God and to its own conscience for all those dependent upon it as its wards, had a complete right to compel its subjects for their own good. This compulsion, after all, was designed to restore complete freedom at the conclusion of education; surely intelligent parents would gladly hand over their children to the State's system of national education.[17]

Another convert to state action in education was Fichte's fellow-philosopher Wilhelm von Humboldt (1767–1835). Like Fichte, Humboldt experienced a partial change of heart under the impact of the crisis brought on by the French invasion and Prussia's defeat by France. Humboldt became de facto minister of culture in 1809 and drafted laws for elementary and secondary schooling, as well as for the new university in Berlin that since 1945 bears his name.

Humboldt had written in 1791–92 a powerful critique of the culture-shaping role of the state, a book which would later profoundly affect John Stuart Mill and other opponents of paternalistic government. Humboldt wrote that "national education—or that which is organized or enforced by the State—is at least in many respects very questionable." Rather, "the freest development of human nature, directed as little as possible to citizenship, should always be regarded as of paramount importance . . . all systems of national education, governed as they are by the spirit of regulation, impose on nature a special civic form."[18] While he became an agent of state authority, he continued to stress the role of the civil society in education; his 1810 report on how Prussia's schools should be funded recommended a separate national school fund apart from the state treasury and administered by local officials.[19]

Humboldt also sought to minimize the ways in which schooling reinforced and expressed social divisions. He proposed in 1809 a system of schooling for Prussian territories in the East with only three levels—elementary, *Gymnasium*, and university—that would provide a general education on a humanistic basis rather than around occupational expectations.[20]

Humboldt understood education (*Bildung*) in the broadest sense as the life-long process by which an individual became truly himself, though along the lines furnished by the ideal of ancient Greece, when the individual— he contended—was first invented. "'Humanity' thus took the position that Rousseau had attributed to 'Nature' . . . Modern man could, according to Humboldt, experience through the study of the Greeks what it really meant to be a human being [*Menschsein*], 'really' in the sense of beyond national, confessional, or social class and occupational boundaries"[21] and distinctions. It has been said that the nineteenth century in Germany saw the formulation of a religion of *Bildung*, asserting that the "highest happiness of mortals" was the result of a well-rounded education and a fully developed personality, and that the *Bildungsroman* was Germany's special contribution to world literature,[22] anticipated by Goethe's *Wilhelm Meister's Apprenticeship* (1795).

Vocationally oriented schooling, Humboldt argued, should be left up to private initiatives, while the State should seek to ensure that every one of its subjects, even the poorest, had the opportunity for a comprehensive education as a human being (*eine vollstaendige Menschenbildung*). In his enthusiasm for the *paideia* of classical Greece, he argued that "to have learned Greek would be no more useless for the carpenter than to have learned how to make a table would be for the scholar."[23]

Humboldt and other "Neo-Humanists" distinguished their recommendations from those of the Philanthropen of the previous generation, whom they accused of being overly concerned to prepare youth for the careers which they could be expected to follow rather than to provide a general education to fit them to be human beings. Pupils should not so much be taught specific knowledge and skills as encouraged to use their minds; once they were launched into the world, they would be too busy learning a trade or profession to continue to develop their minds for the "higher world of the Spirit [*hoehere Welt des Geistes*]," as Friedrich Niethammer wrote in 1808.[24]

Humboldt and others "planned the elementary school, or *Volksschule*, as the foundation of a new system, in 'organic' unity with academic institutions" such as the academic secondary *Gymnasium* and the university. "Their formula was a 'general education' [*allgemeine Bildung*] to develop the innate human potential for intellectual life and transmit the cultural traditions shared by all Prussians (and Germans). Only by transcending (but not, of course, eliminating) occupational and social distinctions would the school system equip all children to participate in public life," however humble their station.[25] This required that schooling be structured on a "horizontal" basis, with the primary school for all children leading on to the academic secondary school for the most talented and determined, in place of the "vertical" structure in which the *Gymnasium* was accessed only through special preparatory schools to which only children of middle-class families had access, while the *Volksschule* led nowhere. This was necessary so that "the most common daily laborer and the most carefully educated man" would receive the same early formation; thus the former would not fall below the level of human dignity and become crude and the latter would not fall under that of human strength and become sentimental and effete.[26] No doubt the classically trained Humboldt was thinking of Plato's insistence, in *The Republic*, that education in the arts and gymnastics be kept in balance.

All schools that serve the entire nation, Humboldt wrote in 1809, "must have as their purpose only general human development [*allgemeine Menschenbildung*]."[27] Again and again we find the echo of Pestalozzi that education is about forming human beings in the fullest sense, not useful members of this or that occupational group. In the new Prussia or Germany that was being created, Rousseau's warning that "one must choose between making a man or a citizen, for one cannot make both at the same time"[28] would no longer apply.

Friedrich Schleiermacher (1768–1834), one of the most important Protestant theologians of the nineteenth century (arguably the fountainhead of Liberal Protestantism), was also an education official—appointed by Humboldt and continuing in office after the latter's resignation—and delivered influential series of lectures on pedagogy which "are still among the most mature, rich in thought, and consummate works of pedagogy."[29] He was by no means the only education official in the Protestant states of Germany trained as a theologian, which reflects and also explains the fact that the development of popular schooling never had the strongly secularizing emphasis that, more than once, it had in France during the nineteenth century.[30]

In his 1814 lecture *The Task* [Beruf] *of the State in Education*, Schleiermacher wrote that

> we find times in the history of our modern world when peoples seem able to awake from a long dullness and roughness only if their government takes the reins of this important business [of education] in its hands and through other means seeks to stir up in the younger generation the wished-for higher strengths, which the elder [generation] is not able to awaken through the usual means of home

instruction because they are not present in them or have died out. . . . We ourselves, and most other German peoples and the many Slavic [peoples] who are ruled by members of German noble families [*Fuerstenhaeuser*] have found ourselves for several successive generations in the fortunate situation of a highly elevating influence of government on the education of the people.[31]

Next to politics and in close alliance with politics, Schleiermacher insisted, education was the means by which society could improve itself; indeed, it could make revolutions unnecessary.[32]

Like Humboldt, Schleiermacher insisted that the positive results produced in some cases by state oversight of education did not mean that it could be justified in all cases; after all, "one can say that the strongest bulwark of personal freedom and of individual development" argues for the other side, that the home, as the setting of the family, is holy ground in which public authority may under no circumstances intervene uninvited." After all, "one of the dearest and most pleasurable expressions of freedom is the way in which parents build up their children and seek to reproduce in them their own most inner natures." It would be paradoxical for government to leave its subjects free to dispose of their material property as they wish, but deny them that freedom with respect to their children.[33] Unfortunately, however, families and society as a whole were sometimes incapable of responding to new conditions and thus preparing the future.

The situation in which the State was justified in taking education into its own hands was when it needed to overcome the divisive effect of ethnic diversity [*eine Menge von einzelnen Staemmen*] through developing in a diverse population a feeling of common loyalty, so that love for a common fatherland and people (*Volk*) would replace that for the ethnic group. Under these circumstances, the State must not leave education up to the churches, much less to private initiatives, but must itself undertake the effort to raise its people to a higher spiritual unity. Once this has been achieved, education should be given back into the hands of the people—though even in this case it would remain "public" and common, so that it could fulfill its mission of making individuals into citizens capable of acting as living organic members of the whole.[34] The primary concern for Schleiermacher, as for Fichte, was not freedom but "order, organization, and the progressive elimination of chaos."[35]

Schleiermacher mistrusted the doctrinaire radicalism of Rousseau and Pestalozzi and their imitators who derived pedagogical strategies from abstract theories of human nature, or who placed a heavy emphasis on what each child must learn for himself. It is true, he wrote in his 1826 lectures on education, that each individual must begin from the beginning, but everything depends on how soon he is brought to be able to participate in humanity's tasks on earth. The older generation can hasten this process by passing on what it has acquired, and the more intelligence has been developed in the elders, the less the younger will be dependent on the working of chance for its own development.[36]

He was less optimistic than was Humboldt about the possibility of providing a humanistic education to the entire population. For Schleiermacher, extending and improving the education system was an aspect of the "defensive modernization" of Prussia during the period of reform up to 1819, when it was brought to a close by the reactionary alliance of Prussia and Austria to prevent further regime-threatening changes.[37] Public policy, he wrote, could never attain its goals without education as an integrating element, and this was particularly the case in times of transition when the older generation could not provide an adequate orientation to the younger. When the State had reason to believe that all families were in harmony with the spirit of the commonwealth (*Geist des Gemeinwesens*), it should leave education up to them, as was the case in England and in North America. When this was not the case, the State could not afford to leave education up to families and must take it as one of its own responsibilities.[38]

Writing from the perspective of 1826, when the reform movement had come to an end, Schleiermacher had appreciative words for Pestalozzi's intentions but suggested that either his premises had been wrong or the implementation of his method in popular schooling in Germany had been ineffective. Compared with other pedagogical formulae, such as that of Basedow, the Pestalozzian method had much to commend it, but it would need to be worked out with much more care.[39]

Fichte, Humboldt, and Schleiermacher, together with Kant, Froebel, Herbart, and other contemporaries, illustrate the extraordinary interest in education and in the details of pedagogy on the part of leading intellectuals of the early years of the nineteenth century in Germany. Not since Plato and Aristotle, it is fair to say, had education enjoyed such high-level attention, nor has such concentrated attention been given to fundamental thought about the purposes of education in the two centuries which have followed.

All of the elements for the creation of systems of popular education were present in the late eighteenth century, but it was only the crisis of the Napoleonic period that gave governments the capacity and the need to become "school states."[40] The need emerged in part from extensive territorial changes. As a result of Napoleon's dissolution of the Holy Roman Empire, its 294 member-states were consolidated into the 41 members of the new German Bund. Bavaria incorporated in 1806 about eighty previously distinct states;

the size of Baden quadrupled, and that of Wuerttemberg doubled. After Napoleon's eventual defeat, Prussia gained back its lost territories in the east and, in the west, added the Rhineland, Westphalia, and other territories, with a doubling of its population. Under these circumstances, popular schooling was seen as a means of consolidating previously separate territories and creating new identities and loyalties among the common people.[41]

Napoleon had been defeated, but the ideas which he represented, and those promoted vigorously by the French Revolution, were a grave concern to authorities in the various German states. A report prepared for a meeting of monarchs and their chief ministers in Aachen in 1818 identified three causes of the continued unrest: (1) the general insanity of individuals and social classes, (2) the dissolution of religious ideas, and (3) the growing misdeeds of public education.[42] Aware that they could not simply turn the clock back to the Old Regime, the leaders of Prussia and other states engaged in what Wehler has called "defensive modernization," building much stronger bureaucratic apparatuses to extend their control deeper into society.[43]

The opportunity to organize many aspects of society and government, including education, on a different basis coincided, as we have seen, with intense discussion about the purposes of education and even about specific forms of pedagogy. In contrast with the sporadic and generally superficial efforts of the preceding period of enlightened absolutism, the early decades of the nineteenth century saw, in several German states, a coherent effort to penetrate to the village level with a new and purposeful form of schooling. It was the results of these efforts, as well as the efforts themselves that aroused such interest and admiration in France, England, and the United States in the 1830s as those countries began the process of building their own state systems of educational oversight.

The period of reform which began around 1807 lasted for about a dozen years before political developments—the Holy Alliance which sought to re-establish the status quo upset by the French Revolution and the subsequent quarter-century of tumult and change—brought them to a halt. During this period the reforming governments of Germany made gestures in the direction of creating systems of universal schooling, though the actual effects were very uneven at first.

PRUSSIA

In these efforts, it was Prussia which took the lead, and the smaller German states of central and western Germany tended to imitate its efforts. Leadership for Prussian education reform during this period was provided by Johann

Wilhelm Suevern, continuing the agenda initiated by Humboldt. Like Humboldt, Suevern wanted neither to maintain the system of schooling partitioned by the social class of its pupils, nor to restructure schooling along vocational lines to support individual social promotion.[44] The reform program was summed up in Suevern's proposal for a comprehensive education law, in 1819.[45] There would be a general elementary school which all children would attend, with the opportunity for those with the most ability and effort, without regard to their backgrounds, to go on to intermediate, secondary and higher education. Suevern proposed to recognize as "public" and "common" only those schools which sought the general education (*allgemeine Bildung*) of pupils and not simply their preparation for work, and he insisted that these schools should form an integrated system.[46]

This fundamental reform of the educational system gained little support; it was opposed by most of the aristocracy who saw it as a threat to the existing social hierarchy; nor did it gain the support of the emerging business leadership, whose goals for popular schooling were strictly vocational and utilitarian.[47] The counterattack began with the Congress of the Holy Alliance (Prussia, Austria, and Russia) where, concerned about revolts in Spain, Naples, Portugal, and Piedmont, the rulers resolved to suppress any sources of dangerous ideas. King Frederick William III of Prussia would write in his *Self-Confessions* that "we do not confer upon the individual or upon society any benefit when we educate him beyond the bounds of his social class and vocation, give him a cultivation which he cannot make use of, and awaken in him pretensions and needs which his lot in life does not allow him to satisfy."[48] In early 1821 he was given a memorandum which blamed Fichte and Schleiermacher for having planted such ideas with the result that civic order and virtue had been greatly endangered.[49]

One of those behind this analysis, Ludolf von Beckedorff, would go on to argue that Suevern's proposal flew in the face of the natural inequality of human beings and would create unsatisfied ambitions and resentment on the part of those unable to go on to reach the highest positions. They should be taught to be satisfied with their humble position in life, rather than encouraged to try and fail to rise higher; rural children should not be stuffed with all sorts of abstract principles and useless knowledge. "This plan of 'general human development;'" he charged, "leads inevitably to a so-called common 'national education,' and this would, if carried out, infallibly destroy the only sort of equality that we should wish for all citizens, namely the equality in contentment, in satisfaction with their various lots in life and in mutual respect, love, and helpfulness, in short an equality in state of mind [*Gesinnung*]."[50] Suevern's proposal to provide a humanistic education to all children in common would create the illusion of social equality and thus nurture resentment and frustrated ambition dangerous to society.

The semblance of equality promoted by a common school, Beckedorff warned, would transform social relationships into "a true civil war," since all existing social relationships would be overwhelmed with expectations that could not be met. What Prussia required was not a *Volks-Bildung* but rather a *Standes-Bildung*, not the education of a people but the education of the different orders of society.[51]

Beckedorff was critical of the directors of teacher-training institutions (*Lehrerseminare*) who offered unnecessary subjects like algebra and physics and introduced the ideas of Pestalozzi. An education like that, he wrote, "was unwilling to accept authority and, instead, elevated the individual judgment as the touchstone of the correctness of each doctrine. [It] . . . will educate only sophists and doubters and, while it maintains that it fosters independence, will create undisciplined views and arbitrariness of character."[52]

In the climate of reaction that characterized the 1820s, this viewpoint prevailed. When Suevern's proposals failed, Wehler notes, it seemed as though all the efforts of previous decades had been in vain, but in fact the founding of *Lehrerseminare*, the improvement of schools in concrete ways, and the growing proportion of pupils attending school regularly kept having their effect. By 1848, about 82 percent of Prussian children were in school, a proportion equaled only by Scotland and New England.[53]

State policy, in Prussia and elsewhere in Germany (and, indeed, elsewhere in Europe), however, continued to be to promote improvements in urban schooling while essentially freezing that in rural areas in a primitive condition. In place of Humboldt's idea of a common elementary school for children from all social classes, it became the policy of the Prussian government to provide a popular formation (*volkstuemliche Bildung*) for the lower social classes, while continuing to develop the *Gymnasium* and its preparatory programs for children of the middle classes.[54]

While rural elementary schools (*Volksschulen*) were not developed into instruments of upward mobility, they were seen as playing an essential role. Where but in schools could children be taught to shun "artificial equality" and the "seductive expectation of revolution"? A circular from the Prussian government in 1822 warned against forming "half-educated," discontented peasants who would threaten the established order.[55]

Not that there was extensive demand for schooling in rural areas, especially in the more exclusively agricultural areas taken by Prussia in the partition of Poland. Although the German states financed their universities and— increasingly—elite secondary schools, the burden of popular elementary schooling, though state-mandated, fell on local communities and on parents who had to pay tuition.[56] Efforts to expand schooling often encountered resistance from local authorities and from parents unwilling to give up the labor of their children for an education which was of little utility under rural conditions.[57] As late as 1864, the average country school had 1.2 classes and the average rural teacher had eighty-three pupils in his class. Two decades after that, only 20 percent of rural pupils were in schools with three or more classes.[58] In fact, "the schools which developed in the cities, differentiated by grade levels, did not become role models for rural educational reform until the 20th century."[59]

It has been noted that

it is of very great significance for the subsequent social and political history of Germany . . . that the thoroughgoing organization of a national system of education in Prussia occurred at a time when Prussia had barely emerged from strictly feudal institutions and attitudes. In a country without any system of popular representation, even as modified by conditions of wealth or birth, the installation of a strong bureau of education represented simply an extension of the King's arm and constituted an additional force at his command for controlling the thought and actions of his people. The various councils and the different grades of executives did not reflect in any sense the will or feeling of a majority, but were rather appointees of an irresponsible central government and a part of a hand-picked bureaucracy.[60]

Schools in the countryside where the great majority of the population lived continued to be controlled—for good or more often for ill—by the local sponsors since the central government was not able to provide funding through which it could also exercise control. Despite these limitations, there was a growing sense that education could be thought of as a system which could be improved as a whole through the adoption of wise policies.[61]

The Prussian school system expanded rapidly during the first half of the nineteenth century, in part as a result of a great population increase and in part also through central direction in a "revolution from above" that, at least outside the growing cities, was not in response to popular demand. The central problem was somehow to reconcile the process of making the economy and social institutions more efficient while at the same time preserving the existing social and political order.[62] Among the measures employed to this end were an increased centralization of policy-making for popular schooling (including the beginnings of an education bureaucracy in 1809, further developed into a separate ministry of education in 1817), a specification of the contents of schooling in 1812, and—perhaps most significant for the long run—the specification of particular educational credentials for positions in government and society.[63]

In the cities, to a growing extent, the provision of schooling was highly differentiated:

> there were free schools for the poor and other public *Volksschulen* in which the scale of fees automatically segregated the pupils by social class. The *Buergerschulen* to which bourgeois families sent their children set higher educational goals and offered in the curriculum, besides the three Rs, a foreign language, history, geography, geometry, and natural science. The *Vorschulen*, or elementary classes, attached to the elitist secondary schools following a classical curriculum catered to the educated bourgeoisie.[64]

Children from ambitious middle-class families did not attend the ordinary primary schools, but rather the *Vorschulen*, followed by some form of selective secondary school. In addition to the traditional *Gymnasium*, with its strongly classical curriculum, middle-class youth could attend *Realschulen*, secondary-level schools for pupils whose career objectives were in business or in the middle levels of government employment for which university studies were not required.

Compared with rival France, Prussia had considerable success in promoting school attendance. By 1846, 78 percent of children of mandatory school age were attending, in contrast with 47.5 percent in France in 1850, and the Prussian proportion rose to 85 percent in 1864, contrasted with 70.4 percent in France in 1867.[65] When Prussia defeated Austria at Koeniggraetz in 1866, some of the credit was given to Prussian schoolmasters, just as earlier they had been blamed for the revolutions of 1848;[66] many in France attributed defeat by Prussia in 1870 to the same superior educational efficiency.

The systematic organization of schooling in Prussia was greatly admired in the 1830s and 1840s by foreign visitors like Horace Mann and France's Victor Cousin, but "school conditions never matched the high reputation that the Prussian *Volksschule* (elementary school) enjoyed abroad." Schools were supported largely by local taxes from which, especially in the eastern provinces, the large landowners were exempted, and "the state's investment in elementary education was paltry up to 1870 and thereafter quite modest."[67] Even the engaging pedagogy which foreign visitors noted in the (no doubt carefully selected) schools which they visited was less faithful to the Pestalozzian model than they assumed.

> Subserviency to the teacher had taken the place of subserviency to the textbook, and the pupils were attached by very short strings to the lead of their teachers.

The system was adapted to the wholesale indoctrination of pupils into desired social and political attitudes, and, moreover, it was so employed. While it substituted an animated and efficient system of drill for the spiritless learning of facts, yet it was essentially a system of drill in which the teacher was responsible for the pattern as well as the detail of the pupil's experience. The very exercises that were designed to foster thoughtful attitudes in the experience of the pupils represented more a thinking after the teacher on the part of the pupil than any development in him of experimental and problem-solving attitudes.[68]

Nevertheless, "it was in such a country, undemocratic by any standards that we recognize, that there was organized for the first time in Western history a comprehensive and efficient system of education for the common people."[69]

The system was presided over from 1817 to his death in 1840 by the Baron Karl von Altenstein under whom steady progress was achieved. The description of the system that became most influential in other countries was that by French philosopher Victor Cousin, based on a visit in the 1830s. Cousin admired the requirement that all children be educated—in school if not adequately otherwise—and that every community support a school. His comment reflects the admiration of many reformers at that time for the military as well as the educational focus of Prussia.

The duty is so national, so rooted in all the legal and moral habits of the country, that it is expressed by a single word, *Schulpflichtigkeit* (school duty, or school obligation). It corresponds to another word, similarly formed and similarly sanctioned by public opinion, *Dienstpflichtigheit* (service obligation, i.e., military service). These two words are completely characteristic of Prussia: they contain the secret of its originality as a nation, of its power as a state, and the germ of its future condition. They express, in my opinion, the two bases of true civilization—knowledge and strength. Military conscription, instead of voluntary enlistment, at first found many adversaries among us [in France]; it is now considered as a condition and a means of civilization and public order. I am convinced the time will come when popular instruction will be equally recognized as a social duty imperative on all for the sake of all.[70]

The school law that had been adopted in 1819 required that universal education be ensured by providing poor parents "with the means of sending their children to school, by providing them with the things necessary for their instruction, or with such clothes as they stand in need of." Parents who failed to send their children to school were subject to various sanctions, including fines and imprisonment, as well as deprivation of poor relief.[71]

Primary schools were either Protestant or Catholic, although the 1819 law provided that "Jewish residents in towns may establish schools at their own expense, on condition that they be organized, superintended, and administered by them conformably with the present law. They may equally send their children to other schools, but they are not permitted to have any share in the management of those schools." In rural communities with a religiously mixed population, children of the smaller group should have their convictions respected in the religious instruction which permeated the entire program. In exceptional cases when Protestants and Catholics were not in large enough numbers to justify a denominational school, an interdenominational or *Simultanschule* could be formed, with the provision "that each of these sects have within reach all that may be necessary for the religious education of the scholars belonging to it."[72]

The "first vocation" of primary schools, according to the law, was "to train up the young in such a manner as to implant in their minds a knowledge of the relation of man to God, and at the same time to foster both the will and the strength to govern their lives after the spirit and precepts of Christianity." Schools were also "to inculcate in youth the duty of obedience to the laws, fidelity and attachment to the sovereign and state, in order that these virtues may combine to produce in them the sacred love of country." It is interesting that the law provides that gymnastics "shall be considered as a necessary part of a complete system of education," and that provision is made for teaching the mother tongue of pupils in areas where that was not German—notably, the Polish provinces of Prussia. Both were unusual by the standards of the time. The law also made it clear that "instruction in religion, reading, writing, arithmetic and singing are strictly indispensable in every school."[73]

Primary schools were to be supported by a combination of local taxation, church funds (in turn based upon taxation), pious donations, tuition paid by parents, and grants from regional government. Secondary *Gymnasia* were to be supported by the national and provincial governments as well as by tuition.[74]

Altenstein introduced reforms in teacher training and certification, following the provision of the law that primary normal schools—*Lehrer-Seminare*—be maintained at public expense in each region of Prussia. These were to be denominational when numbers justified that, but when circumstances required, an interdenominational normal school could be established, provided that "each pupil can receive the religious instruction appropriate to his faith." The goal of these institutions, by law, was "to form men, sound both in body and mind, and to imbue [them] with the sentiment of religion, and with that zeal and love for the duties of a schoolmaster which is so closely allied to religion." In an interesting evidence of Pestalozzi's influence on teacher training, the law also specified that the emphasis of teacher training should not be "so much to inculcate theories on the pupils, as to lead them by enlightened observation and their own experience to simple and lucid principles."[75]

Cousin noted in the 1830s that local initiatives had already created a number of such institutions and that the 1819 law "does little more than methodize what already existed, not only in Prussia, but throughout Germany." As a result, the provisions of Prussian law were not simply "a metaphysical, arbitrary and artificial abstraction" like the laws so frequently adopted in France, but were "founded on reality and experience" and had been implemented effectively.[76]

Formal examinations for teacher certification were introduced in 1826— though Altenstein's successor, Friedrich von Eichhorn, would decide that "the professionalization of elementary teaching [was] a potential threat to the social status quo."[77] Historians disagree about the extent to which elementary teachers played a significant role in the revolutionary events of 1848, though in the period of reaction which followed they were blamed for unsettling the common people and new measures were put in place to seek to ensure their docility and to limit their ambitions for their own education and that of their pupils.

The teacher seminaries—by 1845, they enrolled 2,000 future teachers in Prussia—were boarding establishments where an intensive experience was intended to develop a strong sense of duty and of loyalty to Church and State; after graduation, the government continued to influence teachers through conferences, meetings, and special publications.[78] They were not connected in any manner with the universities, and "the years spent in such an institution could not be used as a stepping stone to a higher level of education or to a higher teaching career."[79] In effect, as in the normal schools which developed a little later in France and in the United States, they were designed to turn primary school graduates into primary schoolteachers by furthering their knowledge to only a moderate extent but more importantly by shaping their character and habits.

There was a similar concern in Bavaria, where King Ludwig mistrusted schoolteachers who were "overeducated" and likely to be subversive of the established order. He issued regulations reducing the academic content of teacher education and placed top priority on character building and the "stimulation and awakening of a truly religious spirit" in prospective teachers.

After 1837, under Ludwig's archconservative cultural minister, Karl von Abel, schoolteachers were the targets of harsh discriminatory policies which prohibited communities from granting them tenure or pensions, restricted their community residence and marriage rights, and placed them under increased surveillance by their clerical school inspectors. In addition, through a series of much-resented ordinances which forbade teachers from visiting taverns, attending dance halls, growing beards, or going hunting, the state authorities sought to dictate the image and way of life which it considered appropriate for teachers.[80]

By contrast, a leading figure in teacher education and in agitation for progressive reform during this period was Adolf Diesterweg (1790–1866) whose copious writings urged that teachers should form a self-regulating profession, freed from supervision by local clergy, with the mission of popular enlightenment.[81] Educators, Diesterweg insisted, should be free from the oversight of the churches as they undertook to reshape and improve humanity; he called for secular (*weltliche*) elementary schools. During his years as head of a teacher-training *Seminar* in the Rhineland (1820–32) and in Berlin (1832–47), he inspired his students with a vision of the great cultural mission to which they were called as schoolteachers.[82]

Activist educators chafed at church supervision of local schools, and called for interconfessional schooling (*Simultanschulen*), along the lines pioneered by the ruler of Nassau in 1817; "in an effort to consolidate territories acquired during the French Revolutionary Era, he ruled that Catholics and Protestants should attend the same schools. After an attempt to introduce common religious instruction, which proved impracticable, he permitted separate Protestant and Catholic religion classes to be established in the same school."[83] In Prussia, however, a decree which Altenstein issued in 1822 rejected that model in favor of continuing the system of public denominational schooling.

> Experience has taught us that in the interconfessional schools the principal element of education, religion, is not properly fostered, and it lies in the nature of these schools that this cannot happen. The aim of promoting greater tolerance among diverse religious believers through such schools is seldom or never achieved; rather, any tension which breaks out among the teachers and the parents of the schoolchildren degenerates too easily into religious dissension, which often tears an entire community apart.[84]

"Disillusionment with pure rationalism" continued to gain ground, and "in 1826 Altenstein issued a decree that had lasting influence. He pointed out that the Prussian state wanted to bring up true Christians in schools and that religious instruction must have real content, permeated with belief in Jesus Christ and the doctrine of Christian salvation."[85] Interconfessional schooling would weaken this effect, and

> would raise havoc with traditional school prayers, school communion services, group attendance at church services, and instruction in singing, which consisted in

large part of hymns. Instead of diminishing denominational differences *Simultan-schulen* would increase them, notably through separating pupils into special religion classes . . . [and] above all disrupted the common spirit which ought to pervade all instruction. Religion was not something to be separated out, but was an integral part of the whole school. Without unified Catholic or Protestant instruction the complete education of a child would suffer . . . The establishment of *Simultanschulen*, instead of solving the problem of the relationship of church, state, and school only increased its complexity.[86]

The governor of Posen, a primarily Polish territory seized by Prussia in the late eighteenth century, urged Altenstein to repeal this decree since, under the conditions of his area, denominational schools aggravated the differences between Catholic Poles and Protestant Germans. The education minister continued to insist, however, that pupils and teachers should be of the same faith, and in 1834 issued further instructions which made it difficult to establish interconfessional schools.[87]

Matthew Arnold, on an official visit to Continental schools in the 1860s, when political differences over the denominational—including variations of Protestantism—character of schooling were raging in England and in The Netherlands, noted that

the wide acceptation which the denomination evangelical takes in the official language of Prussia prevents a host of difficulties which occur with us in England . . . The State . . . not only declares itself Christian . . . but it expressly disclaims the neutral, colourless, formless Christianity of the Dutch schools and of our British schools . . . So the Protestant schools as well as the Catholic employ a dogmatic religious teaching.[88]

Prussia was divided into provinces, each of which had a school board nominated by the national government and responsible for secondary education, including the institutions for training elementary school teachers. These provinces were divided in turn into *Regierungsbezirke*, each of which had a school official, also nationally appointed, who included among his responsibilities the elementary schools in the area.

For purposes of school inspection, the *Regierungsbezirke* were subdivided into *Kreise*, or circles, each of which had its *Kreisschulinspector*, or circle school inspector. His authority extended to all the primary schools in his circle, and he was in close communication with the local inspectors and school officials. He was practically always a clergyman.[89]

The *Kreise* were in turn divided into *Gemeinden* (communities), each of which was required to maintain an elementary school, under the supervision of a committee which included local clergy who had responsibility for super-intending the work of the teacher, while the lay members were responsible for managing the funding and facilities. In rural areas, communities tended to be exclusively Catholic or exclusively Protestant, making this clergy super-vision a relatively straightforward matter, though resented by the more pro-gressive elements among teachers.

Even liberals who had reservations about the churches were anxious to preserve their influence on the moral character of the people and thus sup-ported their official role in the education system. In historical retrospect, in fact, one can suggest that the religious instruction which was so central to popular schooling in the growing cities as well as in the countryside had the positive effect of integrating to some extent the children of the poor into the common symbolic and conceptual world of German society at a time when no other institutions filled that role.[90]

Private elementary schools, though rare, were permitted, but the teacher's competence was subject to examination by the *Kreis* inspector and to con-tinuing supervision by public authorities.[91] Although early in the nineteenth century they played an important role in the cities, their expansion did not keep pace with enrolment in public schools and dropped to 8.5 percent of the total by 1864.[92]

THE NETHERLANDS

A system of nationally supervised common schools was implemented in The Netherlands in the first years of the nineteenth century, decades before state oversight began to be effective in Massachusetts and other American states, in France, or in England. The decisive steps were taken during the period of indirect rule by France—"of all the reforms that were undertaken between 1805 and the incorporation into France in 1810, the school law of 1806 was the most important because it was actually implemented and was the basis for the development of the public elementary school."[93]— but they built upon characteristically Dutch arrangements which pre-dated the Revolution and which led to greater success than contemporary efforts in France.

These arrangements included compromises over religious issues while maintaining the generally religious character of public schools. That this character was vaguely Protestant resulted in resistance in Catholic areas, and in consequence, a progressive emptying of all elements that could cause offence to any person, including Jews. In 1795, for example, a provincial ordinance was adopted in Brabant, a heavily Catholic area, requiring that the Heidelberg catechism—a summary of Calvinist teaching—be dropped from the instructional program of all schools.[94]

Among the administrative reforms adopted by the Batavian Republic in 1798, in its effort to become—in the spirit of the French Revolution—"one and indivisible," was the creation of eight national agencies answerable to the governing Directory. One of these was charged with national education. Schama notes that, though the general organization was based upon the model which had been adopted in France, the creation of an education agency was "the peculiar innovation of the Batavian Republic," and "reflected the Dutch preoccupation with governmental burdens hitherto shouldered by provincial and local bodies whose resources were now unequal to the task of sustaining their responsibilities."[95]

Another of these burdens, particularly acute at this time, was the administration of relief for the indigent, and the approach taken adumbrates what would eventually be the characteristic Dutch way of providing education as well. Most of the relief had traditionally been provided through denominational institutions, often funded by endowments and legacies and managed by boards made up of leading citizens. As the financial crisis brought on by the Napoleonic wars and the severe curtailment of international trade increased the number of poor families needing help, it was proposed that "the state—the collectivity of citizens—should have a monopoly over assistance to the poor . . . Quite apart from the principle of nondenominationally distributed relief, it was an axiom of the unitarist approach that what was corporate, local, and private was obnoxious to the dictates of reason and equality." Merging of all the local funds into a national system was successfully resisted, however, based in part upon "the French experience—where the liquidation, after 1790, of the church establishments for the poor had led to the rapid contraction in the funds available for their support." Those managing local and denominational funds for the poor insisted that they "would continue to . . . look after their own, and would never surrender them as 'children of the state.' "[96]

What did the reforms of education under the republican government amount to? They did not create a state school system: schools remained locally controlled. Some were public schools funded in part by local government and in part by parent tuition; the provincial and national governments made a contribution to these schools only under unusual circumstances. Other schools were operated by religious and other organizations, often with the help of endowments. The law adopted in 1801 applied only to the local government schools, but the reformers were determined to bring the endowed schools under the oversight of the state as well, and this was achieved by the 1806 primary education law, which remained in force for a half-century. Yet others were strictly private enterprises, often owned by individual teachers, and remained independent of the state; schools of this type depended entirely upon tuition income. There was, in fact, a bewildering variety of types of schools, but the concern of public policy was with those provided by public or charitable funds for the poor.[97]

A professor of oriental languages, J. H. van der Palm (the son of Kornelis), was appointed Agent for National Instruction. For Van der Palm as for his Patriot allies, the primary source of national weakness was political and religious factionalism, "old prejudices supported by new violence . . . to create a new lordship of ignorant priestcraft and oppression." National regulation of schools was essential to ensure that local authorities would not appoint or retain "opinionated and fanatical idiots in the position of teacher, lest rural youth in particular remain submerged in the wallow of prejudices whose destructive results have become all too apparent in these days of civic dissension."[98]

With the assistance of Adriaan van den Ende, who would then serve as his successor until 1833, Van der Palm set out to begin to influence the locally controlled schools. He warned that "in school instruction it's not a matter of putting things right here and there, but everything—each more leprous than the other—must be re-established and recreated."[99] In order to achieve such reforms in the face of local authorities controlled by "fanatical, ignorant, and ungenerous creatures" with no desire "that their children learn any more than they had," Van der Palm concluded that the central government would have to control curriculum and pedagogy, approve books, examinations, and school inspection, while leaving to regional authorities the financial support of teachers. "Decentralization was the great enemy of school reform."[100]

The law enacted in 1801—the first education law in Dutch history with national authority—provided that educational commissions, independent of local authorities, were to be established at the parish, district, and regional levels. Their assignment was to maintain and improve teaching standards, through examining potential teachers, making regular inspections of schools and reporting on their condition to the central authority progress, ensuring a supply of modern teaching materials, and making financial recommendations to local government, which was responsible for paying the bills. A clear distinction was made between "public" schools, those established by public authorities to serve the poor, and "private" schools, which were outside government jurisdiction.

The 1801 law stated as the purpose of schooling to teach

> reading, writing, and the first principles of arithmetic; this instruction shall be so organized that, through the development of the rational potentialities of the children . . . it shall form them into rational human beings, and further, will imprint in their hearts the knowledge and feeling or everything which they owe to the supreme being, to society, to their parents, to themselves, and to their fellowmen.

This definition of the purposes of schooling aroused the opposition of orthodox Protestants because of its deistic formulation and neglect of fundamental Christian beliefs, necessitated by the requirement that "any dogma which is differently understood by any church . . . must be omitted."[101] It is worth noting that a similar restriction was adopted by the Massachusetts legislature about twenty years later, under Unitarian influence.

The law proved too radical for Dutch sensibilities, and school inspectors—mostly "enlightened" Protestant ministers—complained that local authorities were working against their efforts. Sufficient resistance developed that a new school law, adopted in 1803 to conform to a new constitution, weakened considerably the emphasis on religious neutrality. Local authorities and parents reacted against the attempt to eliminate doctrinal teaching and demanded the return of denominational catechisms. As provincial authorities wrote from heavily Catholic Brabant, "fanaticism against the particulars of the various religions is also fanaticism."[102]

The 1803 law also expanded the definition of "public" schools—and thus the number of schools under state supervision—to include all church-sponsored schools. The distinction between "public" and "private" schools, then, was not the one with which we are familiar, between schools operated by government and those not; rather, a private school was one supported entirely by tuition, and a public school was one supported by some mix of local government and church or charitable funds. The distinction, therefore, was social rather than confessional.[103]

In effect, while the 1801 law defined "public" in terms of public financing, that of 1803 defined it in terms of serving the public, in contrast with private (household) schooling. The financial definition would again prevail in the 1806 law, and it would not be until 1857 that "public" would come to mean schooling provided by public authorities.[104]

Despite these bold provisions, and parallel to contemporary frustrations in Prussia, France, and the United States, "the sheer obstructionism of the local administrations made it impossible for the law to be implemented" as intended. Van der Palm and Van den Ende were convinced by this frustration of their efforts that a fundamental political reform was needed to ensure national sovereignty. One wrote, optimistically, that "the Commonwealth . . . is no longer composed of different nations; no department or town will henceforth have conflicting interests and the whole people, made up of individuals of each and every department, will all have the same interests, will be endowed with the same rights and have laid on them the same obligations." Van den Ende himself had written a handbook for teachers in 1803 in which he argued that society had a responsibility to provide instruction to youth, that the existing provision of schooling required fundamental reform, and that to that end the authority of the State was essential.[105]

In 1805 the central authorities gained increased power and were able to implement their policies more effectively. The elementary school law adopted in 1806 and in effect for half a century softened the requirements for schools and left the possibility open for establishment of new private schools, though only with the approval of local communities and under specific conditions, and in fact few were approved for many years.[106]

This idea of social as well as political unity, with its clear echoes of Rousseau's *Social Contract*, was in the air; we find it in Fichte's *Addresses to the German Nation*, and in the rhetoric as well as the policies of the succession of French governments of the period. More realistically, however, "the 'nation' in 1805 was still such a variegated, complicated entity that even the elementary facts of language and geography remained to be straightened out. There was little chance that Holland's Dutch would penetrate the remoter recesses of Friesland or coarsen the softer fricatives of Brabander dialects."[107] Administrative mechanisms in The Netherlands were still too limited to impose any sort of unity upon even publicly funded schooling, but the 1806 law created the framework within which a government-directed system would develop over the following decades.

Progress was made during this difficult period toward overcoming the extreme provincialism and localism which had characterized The Netherlands. "As a result, the government bequeathed to William I in 1813—after a three-year interval as departments of the French Empire—was the organ of a paternalist monarchy, radically different to the regime from which his father had made his exit in 1795. That change was one of the decisive transitions in the collective life of the Dutch people."[108]

The new king, William I, confirmed in 1814 that the education law of 1806 would remain in effect, and a constitution was adopted for the new regime in which, in language whose interpretation and application would later cause great difficulty, public education was declared to be a matter "of continuing concern to the government" (*aanhoudende zorg der regering*). Later in his reign, the king stated that "an appropriate public education . . . is the basis for all social happiness." Like his brother-in-law, the king of Prussia, the Dutch king wanted to promote the unity of Christians in his domain, and saw the public schools as the primary means of accomplishing this end.[109] Making subjects into virtuous citizens, rather than promoting social mobility for individuals or social groups, was the goal of these efforts.[110]

Van den Ende sent a bulletin to all schoolmasters in 1813, urging that

> only through unity can our State become what it once was . . . through the uprooting of old enmities . . . and an unlimited trust and the most hearty support for the present government. Develop therefore among all of your students a mutual love, unity, and unselfishness so that, when they are fully grown, they may carry the same principles over into society and into all their relationships. To this end, inflame your hearts with love for the Fatherland, for the prince who rules it, and for Christian virtue.[111]

Broader and broader circles of the population were entering into public life, whether peaceably or through mob violence, and it seemed essential to develop common loyalties and to inculcate norms of civic participation. As a German theorist of public policy wrote at about the same time, "the needy people pays little attention to improving the hearts of its children, to instilling in them a love of fatherland, or leading them into virtue and righteousness."[112] Schools, it was hoped, would make all the difference.

What had been the program of an enlightened minority before the French invasion came to seem an urgent necessity to liberals and conservatives alike in the early nineteenth century. Education could no longer be left to local initiative or allowed to take as many different forms as there were sponsoring organizations; too much was at stake, especially for political Liberals with their commitment to broadening the franchise. The Batavian Republic "transferred the enthusiasms of philanthropists, educationalists and amateur entrepreneurs from the voluntary into the public domain," and in no sphere more than that of popular education.[113]

> Through education and propagation of (Liberal) "culture" among all classes the circle of citizens could be broadened and the basis of the state as well. On this course a homogeneous Dutch nation would come into being, and would naturally take on a liberal coloration. This is the political core of the liberal school policies. The school as nation-forming institution must not be divided among competing "sectarian schools" or left in the hands of an exclusive political or church party. The Liberals considered themselves *algemeen* [i.e., common, nonpartisan, nonsectarian].[114]

We have seen that the mission of public schools, as defined in the 1806 law, was explicitly Christian, but in a general form intended to be inoffensive to all. Already in 1798 the National Assembly of the Batavian Republic had insisted that "the reverential knowledge of an all-governing Supreme Being strengthens the bonds of Society, and thus in all possible ways must be impressed upon the hearts of the Fatherland's Young People."[115] As the wording suggests, the understanding of religion that was advocated did not correspond with the beliefs of ordinary Protestants and Catholics. Indeed, those beliefs were perceived by the guiding elite as a danger and a restraint upon progress. The primary source of national weakness, van den Ende and his colleagues believed, was political and religious factionalism, "old prejudices supported by new violence . . . to create a new lordship of ignorant priestcraft and oppression."[116] In place of such prejudices, youth should be taught a "Christianity above doctrinal differences [*Christendom boven geloofsverdeeldheid*]." This formulation, which came to have a central place in the common school agenda in The Netherlands, seems to have made its first appearance in connection with efforts to unite the various religious communities as part of the Patriot program of national unification. Thus, for example, a society of young men was formed in Delft in 1797 with this objective and employing that slogan.[117]

To this end, teachers were strictly forbidden to provide doctrinal education. They were required to teach in a "Christian spirit" while avoiding anything which could give offense to anyone's beliefs or moral convictions.[118] Van den Ende wrote to the leadership of the various denominations in 1806 requesting that they take on the task of doctrinal instruction outside school hours while the historical and moral aspects of the Christian religion would be taken care of in school.[119] Regulations adopted for the implementation of the 1806 law provided that "All primary education shall be so instituted that while the children are learning applied and useful skills, their rational faculties will be developed and they themselves reared to all social and Christian virtues." As Protestant theologian Herman Bavinck pointed out toward the end of the century, the religion that informed the Dutch common school "made God a Supreme Being, Christ a teacher, man a rational being, sin weakness, conversion improvement, and sanctification virtue." It was inspired by the teaching of liberal theological professor P. W. van Heusde, according to which "Christ was not the Redeemer of sinners but merely the perfect teacher of the human race. It was not conversion and regeneration that people needed but education and development."[120]

Among the strategies inspired by the Nut and then mandated by law for promoting national unity through the schools was the creation of a list of books for public elementary schools, on which there should be no books which could cause controversies or divisions;[121] thus the Bible was not included among the approved texts, though selected stories taken from the Bible were represented, and there might be invented tales about "Jesus, the best little boy who ever lived," and books featuring Virtuous Hendrik and Virtuous Maria. The sentimentality and moralism of such books reflect the Romantic rediscovery of religion, purged of its more demanding characteristics and its more offensive doctrines, a "religion without crisis" or conversion, tamed to serve social and cultural goals. Unlike in revolutionary France, this imposition of "politically correct" books did not cause massive resistance, no doubt because the Dutch books were infused with religious language and themes, and were morally uplifting in ways consistent with the views of parents.[122]

The Agent for National Instruction was responsible for setting standards for the qualifications of teachers, and established a system of four levels of competence, requiring each prospective teacher to be examined by one of the government's school inspectors. Since authorization to be appointed as schoolmaster of urban schools—which paid better salaries—depended upon reaching one of the higher levels, there was a continual incentive for teachers to study so that they could improve their qualifications.[123]

The responsibility of part-time school inspectors, often clergymen, appointed by the central government for each region of the country, was

> to maintain and improve teaching standards; examine potential teachers; make regular visits to schools within their jurisdiction and report on progress; ensure a regular supply of modern teaching materials; and make financial recommendations where appropriate. From the government's point of view, the great strength of these commissions was their independence from local authorities.[124]

We should not form an exaggerated image of the schools, most of them already in existence but gradually improved through the persuasion and chiding of school inspectors and the mutual support of teachers. The 1806 law presupposed a one-room school with a single teacher for all ages, though it required that an assistant be appointed if there were more than seventy pupils. Most children were taught only reading; for instruction in writing, parents had to pay extra.[125] As late as 1858, indeed, 10 percent of children between six and twelve did not attend school at all during the winter, and this rose to 25 percent in the summer, when they were needed for farm work.[126]

In a growing number of schools, on the other hand, "the use of wall charts, arithmetical models and slides, nature projects, and all the now commonplace accompaniments of primary schooling became more widespread. Cuvier and Noël were surprised to find how many teachers had abandoned corporal punishment and had no qualms about mixing boys and girls together in the same classroom."[127] Van den Ende opposed introduction of the Lancaster/Bell method of mutual instruction which was fashionable in England and France and, to some extent, in the United States at the time, since it reduced the personal influence of the teacher, so important for the moral development of the children.[128]

Most of the Dutch still dwelled in rural areas; in the cities, schooling was somewhat more elaborated, as indeed it had been for several centuries. There were "poor schools" supported by communal and church funds so they could offer instruction without charge, as well as public primary schools of good quality for which middle-class parents paid. In some cases there were also "in-between" schools which charged a moderate tuition. As late as mid-century the city of Leeuwaarden in Friesland provided elementary education through three poor schools, four in-between schools, and two middle-class schools with the highest tuition and level of education.[129]

In 1811, when Cuvier and Noël made their inspection, there were 1,755 fully public schools, 281 endowed schools, and 581 private schools dependent entirely upon tuition. The number of private schools increased rapidly up to about 1850, patronized by parents who wanted a better quality of education for their children; the sort of phenomenon, it should be noted, that the foreign visitors did not notice and that might have tempered their enthusiasm for state action somewhat.

The public schools were required to teach a "general Christianity" which would develop in their pupils "all social and Christian virtues," as the 1806 law put it. The lawmakers had been "thoroughly convinced of the importance of public education for all classes of society and especially for the upcoming generation, whose happiness hangs above all of the early implanting of the fundamental principles of religion and ethics."[130] The confessional neutrality of public schools met some resistance, for example, in Utrecht where Protestant church officials objected to its extension to the schools which they had long maintained for poor children,[131] but it was only decades later that this became a major political and social issue.

The government decided in 1817 to fund some private Jewish schools[132] but—in this period—no private Catholic or Protestant schools. Public schools were intended to be national, bringing together all children whatever their social background, their (Christian) denomination, or their sex. The bad old days had been characterized by special rights and privileges for the different social orders; the new society under creation was intended to be one of equal opportunities based upon talents and accomplishments.[133]

The role of popular education in the nation-forming program in The Netherlands was of critical importance. Schools were intended not simply—or even primarily—to teach literacy and other skills, which were of little economic value to much of the population at that stage in economic development.[134]

> The 1806 Dutch School Law . . . was the boldest and clearest statement of the responsibility of a national government towards the primary education, not merely of the poor but of all children between the ages of six and twelve. It stood in marked contrast to the general emphasis in Napoleonic Europe on placing public resources in secondary and higher technical education to produce the engineers, bureaucrats and military men who were the cogs of the Grand Empire.[135]

The influence of the Maatschappij tot Nut van 't Algemeen on the development of the 1806 law and upon the subsequent development of a more complete and effective provision of popular schooling was widely acknowledged. In Utrecht, for example, the education commission was made up of Nut members and the local chapter was closely involved with all aspects of schooling.[136] Such local effort was all the more essential because, despite the activity of van den Ende and the school inspectors, there was no funding for local schools from the central government until after 1815.[137]

New laws enacted in 1822 and 1824 tightened government control over local public schools, and private schools continued to require authorization by municipal authorities.[138]

BELGIUM

The Enlightenment had little impact in the southern Netherlands until the French occupation and incorporation for some years into France itself. Because what is now Belgium had been incorporated into France, the region was encouraged to send young men to Paris to be trained as teacher-educators at the École Normale established by the French revolutionary government. The response was much less than intended; forty-one "Belgians" eventually studied in Paris, of whom only two were elementary school teachers.[139]

The French administration dismantled completely the existing secondary education provisions, both the royal colleges and the remaining Catholic schools. Nine "central schools" were established in the chief cities of the nine new *départements* into which the southern Netherlands were organized as part of France. The curriculum, inspired by the philosophers, emphasized French, mathematics, and science. These were explicitly government schools, but they remained "more theoretical than real, to the extent that the means to pay the teachers did not exist."[140]

The emphasis upon centralization under the Napoleonic system was so strong that local efforts to train teachers and to improve schools were actually discouraged in some cases. Authorities in Antwerp, where schooling (at least in the city itself) had been relatively adequate during the Austrian period, reported in 1810 that schools had become almost useless.[141]

With the defeat of Napoleon, the allies were concerned to create strong barriers to the revival of French power, and on France's northern border the best solution seemed to be to restore the historic line of Dutch *stadholders* as kings over a new country made up by combining the northern and the southern (formerly Austrian) Netherlands. This externally imposed union was, perhaps, fated to fail; "neither the Dutch nor the Belgians welcomed with any enthusiasm the creation of an artificially United Netherlands."[142]

Van den Ende received reports indicating that schooling in the southern Netherlands were "in the most devastated condition," and in 1816 he began to take measures for its improvement with priority given to the training of adequate teachers. A state teacher training institution, located near Antwerp, opened in 1818; in an attempt to disarm suspicion, the government took care to appoint a Catholic head.[143]

The first years of the new kingdom were a time of substantial progress in the extension of popular schooling, stimulated in part by the financial support of the central government: in 1826, the State spent twelve times as much on elementary schools as did the government of France, disproportionately in the southern Netherlands where the provision was less adequate, and where 1,146 school buildings were built or repaired between 1817 and 1828.[144] Popular schooling in Belgium had been devastated by the French appropriation of church endowments and by the indifference of Napoleon's regime to elementary education. Although the government moved cautiously at first to avoid alarming the heavily Catholic population of Flanders, Brabant, and the other southern provinces, the commission sent to investigate the quality of schooling concluded that it was out-of-date and ineffective.

The measures prescribed by the 1806 Dutch law went gradually into effect (fully by 1821) in the southern provinces, with the establishment of a teacher training institution and a steady pressure to adopt whole-class instruction and other classroom reforms. The government "recognized the principle of educational freedom, but placed it under so much control that there was a danger of a state monopoly."[145] School inspectors—the government took care to appoint Catholics—pressed for continual improvements, and for teaching on a nondenominational Christian basis.[146] More than a thousand public schools were established between 1815 and 1830 in Belgium alone;[147] the Dutch provinces were better provided with schools already, but also saw significant improvements in attendance, school buildings, and qualifications of teachers. In 1825, eighty-nine children were attending school in Belgium for every thousand inhabitants, while in the northern provinces of the kingdom the rate was 123 per thousand. In Belgium's Hainault province, for example, there were twice as many pupils attending school in 1820 as there had been in 1817.[148]

An English observer, commenting in 1840 on the recent "decline of popular education in Belgium," noted approvingly that the government of the United Netherlands had

> required the communes to contribute for the erection of schoolhouses; it provided also from the general funds, or from those of the provinces, for the increase of the salaries, and for the pensions of teachers. A great impulse was consequently given to popular instruction. The number of schools and of scholars was increased; the methods of instruction were improved; the institution of a normal school at Lierre, of model schools, and of courses for instruction in the art of teaching in the principal cities . . . were among the advantages arising from the Dutch system.[149]

The efforts to extend popular schooling in what would become Belgium went reasonably well, despite—or in some cases because of—the traditional indifference of local authorities toward the provision of popular schooling. The government implemented the religious neutrality of public schools in a way that allowed schools to take on the confessional character of local communities, so in effect those in the Belgian provinces became unofficially Catholic. In the majority-Protestant north, Catholics began in 1822 to agitate for permission to establish their own schools, and in Belgium several hundred petitions were presented to the government asking for the same freedom.[150] On the other hand, there was a good deal of resistance in some areas to the extension of public schools, both from parents who saw no need for instruction beyond the catechism and from some (not all) Catholic clergy who were concerned about the effects of an institution sponsored by a Protestant government.[151]

After Belgian independence in 1830 (see the next chapter), a law adopted in 1836 to organize the administration of the new kingdom gave responsibility for public education to local governments, including the inspection of their own schools, in contrast with the principle established in The Netherlands of external inspection on behalf of the national government. Another law the same year obliged the provinces to assist local communities financially with the cost of schools, and gave them authority to inspect schools that they subsidized while also authorizing them to establish their own schools. This is the origin of the present Belgian arrangement under which there are several different types of public schooling under different sponsorship—the local commune or municipality, the province, or the [language] community.[152]

The new government finally adopted an elementary education law in 1842, representing a compromise between Catholics and anticlerical Liberals. Each commune was required to provide an elementary school, giving the local clergy a role in its oversight (as, for example, was the practice in Prussia); the obligation could be met through "adopting" and supporting an existing church or private school, as occurred frequently. Poor children were entitled to free schooling, and training was required before appointment, by the commune, as a teacher. Catholics were relieved of the burden of supporting schools with church funds while satisfied with guarantees of the Catholic character of communal schools through curriculum requirements and clergy oversight. In 1846, a government circular broadened the supervisory rights of the clergy over public schools to all aspects of the curriculum.[153] Under this arrangement the proportion of children attending communal schools increased to 75 percent in 1878.[154] Public elementary schooling came—at least outside the larger cities—completely under the influence of the Catholic Church, in fact if not in law;[155] the great majority of teachers seem to have accepted the oversight of local clergy as unproblematic, either out of conviction or out of practical considerations.[156]

On the other hand, schools in those cities where the liberal bourgeoisie was politically dominant—especially the preparatory sections of secondary schools which served, for children from well-to-do families, as a substitute for elementary schools—sometimes did not provide religious instruction.

In 1843 a regulation was issued spelling out the training to be provided in public normal schools for elementary teachers, modeled on the seven Catholic institutions already in existence, which were also publicly funded. A three-year program was prescribed, with the third year consisting of supervised practice teaching. Training of female teachers, however, remained a Catholic monopoly—ten Catholic institutions were "adopted" by the government in 1848—until 1874, when the first state institution for female teachers was opened.[157] As late as 1855 only 33 percent of the teachers with diplomas had received them from state teacher training institutions; the others had received a Catholic training.[158]

The provision for clerical oversight of public schools was taken to a logical conclusion in 1845 in Doornik, where the leadership of an *Atheneum* (higher secondary school) agreed that a veto would be given to the local bishop over the appointment of any teachers. This arrangement was strongly criticized in the parliament by Liberal leader Charles Rogier, who told his colleagues that

> the clergy should easily be satisfied with what they have; they already have a lot, they have much more than they hoped for before 1830. They called, before the Revolution, for freedom for their education, for the education of clergy, for religious instruction. That's above all what they were asking for . . . Well, since 1830 the clergy have not only taken part in secular education, but it is clear that their pretensions extend to no less than to absorb the entire secular education. They are going too far, and a strong reaction against such pretensions is inevitable.[159]

Regulations were issued for elementary schools in 1846. Article 18 stipulated that "teachers will conform themselves, in the methods to employ in teaching religion and morality, to the instructions issued by the Belgian bishops to the parish priests." Belgian Liberals criticized the way the 1842 law was implemented—distorted, in their view—in ways favorable to the influence of the Catholic Church, including the widespread adoption of Catholic schools to serve as communal schools, but until 1856 they did not press for its revision.[160]

Chapter Four

Schooling Becomes Controversial

BELGIUM

Belgium has the distinction of being possibly the only country in the world whose very existence resulted in substantial part from controversy over education.

Unfortunately for the continued existence of the United Netherlands, the king was receiving his advice on how to handle issues of church and state in his southern provinces from anticlerical Catholics; thus the conflict which would split the pasted-together country was not one of the Protestant North versus the Catholic South, but "disunity in Belgium itself: conflicts between anticlerical liberalism on the one side and ultramontanism [Catholic obedience to the dictates of Rome, 'on the other side of the mountains'] on the other, theological conflicts even within the church."[1]

In the face of the unified opposition from the Catholic bishops, the government was forced to back down, though too late to heal the alienation which had resulted from these measures. In January 1830 the Collegium Philosophicum was closed; in May of that year the government conceded freedom to provide secondary and higher education, though characteristically maintaining control over elementary schooling. But already by March 1829 hundreds of petitions with some 40,000 signatures had been submitted to the Parliament, calling for freedom of the press and of education, and a year later a petition drive organized in large part by the Catholic clergy gathered more than 350,000 signatures . . . or marks by illiterates. Peasants thus signified that they were "supporters of freedom of a press which they did not read, of an education which they did not participate in."[2] By August 1830 the demand for Belgian independence was being expressed by a rather mild armed uprising which provided the pretext for similar demands on the part of much of the civic leadership. When the major European powers decided to support this change, it was clear that the United Netherlands had no future. Although King William I continued to hope that the situation would change, it seems that much of the Dutch population was glad to accept separation from their southern neighbors.

With the declaration of the independence of Belgium on October 4, 1830, the government supervision of elementary schools as developed under the law of 1806 came to an end. Local communities, associations, and private persons once again had the right to manage autonomously the schools that they had established with some government supervision only of those schools which the central government itself helped to finance. Such local decision-making was in a Belgian tradition that went back to the strong role of the emerging cities in the early modern period and would later in the century lead even Socialists to resist central government control, in contrast with the centralizing instincts of their counterparts in France.[3]

A decree issued on October 16 to protect freedom of opinion also gave a preliminary protection to educational freedom (as a form of expression), and the constitution adopted in February 1831 stated that "Instruction is free; all preventive measures are forbidden; the repression of abuses is regulated only by law. Public instruction given at state expense is also regulated by law (Article 17)." That the political alliance between Liberals and Catholics was already weakening at this early point is indicated by the fact that continued state supervision of schools was only narrowly defeated,[4] but the leading Liberal, Charles Rogier, introducing an unsuccessful bill on elementary education in 1834, insisted that its only purpose was to allow the State to establish a small number of model schools, and that otherwise local communes could organize instruction as they wished.[5]

The effect of these measures was dramatic. A contemporary English observer reported that "the revolution of 1830, by proclaiming the principle of freedom of teaching, suddenly snapped the spring which gave life and motion to this system . . . The consequence was, that the [new Belgian] Government of 1830 abandoned the power, together with the moral influence, exercised by the Dutch Government." As a result of "the unlimited freedom of teaching, which allows any individual, the ignorant as well as the instructed, to open a school in the same manner as a shop," the number of schools and pupils increased significantly, while the quality of instruction declined.[6] The efforts of the government of the United Netherlands to promote teacher training largely collapsed under the new regime, and it was more than a decade before legal and other provisions were in place to begin to rebuild the educational system.[7] Some two-thirds of the new schools established, another historian claims, were the result of initiatives by the Catholic Church.[8]

Catholic leaders argued that instruction always implied education in the broader sense, which in turn, rested upon moral convictions; religion was thus not simply a subject, but must permeate all instruction in a school.[9] A neutral state was thus not competent to open or to operate schools.[10] Many new Catholic schools were established, with their total enrolment nearly doubling, and education became a priority of the bishops, while on the other hand many local governments reduced their efforts in support of elementary schooling. Good teachers in droves left public schools and went to work under the better conditions in Catholic schools. The proportion of pupils attending "free" (private) schools increased from 36 percent to 57 percent when the first Belgian elementary education law was adopted in 1842.[11]

Rather than seeking to remove religious instruction from the curriculum, Belgian anticlerical Liberals promoted the idea that morality could be taught separately, on a secular, universalistic basis, inspired by the "eclecticism" of French philosopher Victor Cousin. As successor to Guizot as minister of public instruction in France, Cousin had had a considerable influence on the development of the curriculum of French schools in the 1830s and 1840s, promoting "a sort of secular religion . . . claiming for the State the rights which the [advocates of papal authority] demanded for the Church."[12] This theme of secular morality was especially important among the many Liberals who were Masons. As one put it, "there is a moral law which governs the whole universe; this law is the same among all peoples, on every continent; it is the moral law which forms the true religion of the people."[13]

If the Catholic clergy refused, as sometimes occurred, to enter public schools to provide religious instruction, Liberals pointed out, it would be sufficient to say to the children: "There is the church; go there to receive religious instruction!"[14]

The founding congress of the Belgian Liberal party was held in 1846, intending to provide a united front against Catholic power. Among its demand was "the organization of public instruction at all levels, under the exclusive direction of the civil authorities . . . and in rejecting the intervention of the clergy, ex officio, in the schooling organized by the civil authorities."[15]

It was several years later, in 1850, that proposed legislation to create an alternative state system for secondary education gave Liberal Prime Minister Rogier another opportunity to address this issue. "I have a great deal of respect for educational freedom," he said, "but we do not want you, under the form and the banner of freedom, to extend a vast monopoly over the country. When we defend state education, it is out of love of freedom that we do it, for to suppress the instruction given at state expense, under present conditions, would be to confirm the monopoly in the hands of the clergy."[16] In East and West Flanders, for example, sixteen of the nineteen secondary schools were managed by clergy.[17]

In response, a Catholic legislator said,

> If we want a conciliatory law, a law which would unite all opinions, it is indispensable that this offer religious guarantees to fathers of families. Without such guarantees, you will only succeed in producing a partisan law, violent as are all measures of that sort. Why? Because the State, as State, has no religion, has no morality; and the people, by contrast, must have a religion, a morality . . . What is the morality of the State? It is the Penal Code. The State has no other priests than judges, and for carrying out its morality, the high priest of the State is the executioner.[18]

Despite this opposition and many other dire warnings, the Liberal-inspired legislation passed. Secondary instruction would include religious instruction, given by or in consultation with the clergy, but schools would be under the control of the government, which would name all the staff and inspect regularly. The way was opened for "mixed" schools in which Protestant and even Jewish religious instruction would be provided alongside Catholic. In effect, in place of collaboration between Church and State, the new law instituted— for secondary though not as yet for elementary schooling—a clear separation under which each was free to maintain its own system.[19]

At first the bishops refused all cooperation with this new law and forbade the clergy to provide religious instruction in state secondary schools, but an agreement was worked out in Antwerp in 1854 and then adopted by royal decree as a model for other secondary schools: it provided that two hours a week of religious instruction was a regular and required part of the program for Catholic pupils; it would be taught by clergy nominated by the bishop and approved by the government. Non-Catholic pupils would be excused from this instruction. No books would be used in other courses which were in contradiction to the religious instruction. In exchange, the Church gave up its claim to an official role in the appointment of teachers.[20] In most parts of the country, this compromise proved acceptable, though one bishop sought to impose such drastic conditions—the right to teach that Liberalism was a heresy, for example—that no agreement could be reached.[21] Despite generally accepting the Antwerp Convention, however, the bishops became more determined than ever to promote private Catholic secondary schools.[22]

A number of controversies during this period seemed to warn of a danger of Catholic reaction, parallel to that which had helped Napoleon III to come to power in France in 1852. Liberals were encouraged to continue to press the claims of secular instruction—and to call for revision of the law of 1842 governing elementary schools—by their gains in the elections of 1857 (they would remain in power for thirteen years), and there was a heightening of political tensions over the issue of education. Church influence through schools was seen as a threat to "the diffusion of Liberal notions among future generations of Belgian voters."[23] In turn, efforts to reduce that influence were quite naturally resisted by Catholic leaders. "The Liberals' school policy shattered the complacency of the elite that had traditionally led the Catholic party. By trying to create a completely government-run educational system and demote church schools to second-class status, the Liberals appeared to be going beyond anticlericalism and upsetting the foundations of the Belgian constitution."[24]

It was in this period, in fact, that "the secular [laïc] spirit took its first significant steps," corresponding to the rise of a new generation of more radical Liberals, lawyers and doctors, engineers, teachers, and journalists, small businessmen, and placing great confidence in popular schooling. "Retirement or death removed each year several of the men who had, in cooperation with Catholics, made the Constitution [of 1831]. They were replaced among the [qualified] voters, in the administration, and in the legislature by a new generation, grown up in the religious conflicts and more and more hostile to the traditional faith of the Belgian people."[25] It should be noted that until 1893 voting remained very much an elite monopoly, involving only about 10 percent of adult males in Belgium.

Evolution of society and government also had its effect, as elsewhere in contemporary Europe. "The central apparatus of the State, in the hands of and in service to the liberal bourgeoisie, demanded more than ever a rational and differentiated approach, which was mirrored in the expansion of ministerial departments and in the formation of great bureaucracies," which in turn required more government officials at all levels who tended to be anticlerical and to seek to expand the role of the State at the expense of that of the Church and other civil society institutions. Parallel with this was a growing demand for "enlighteners" (voorlichters) in journalism, teaching, publishing, bookselling and other occupations concerned with the dissemination of ideas. At the same time, the social status of intellectuals was declining in comparison with the first part of the century, when most were drawn from the bourgeoisie and were university educated. This evolution helps to explain the development of a radical tendency within Liberalism, and the eventual development of a separate Socialist party.[26]

An influential book published in 1865, *L'enseignement du peuple* (by P. Tempels) would sum up the liberal program. Through the right sort of schooling—under State auspices—the common people could be shaped into virtuous citizens who would not be open to the sort of reactionary influences which had led in the France of the Second Republic (1848–51) to disastrous results when universal male suffrage was introduced. Universal state schooling would, the Young Liberals claimed, achieve a moral regeneration of the peasantry and working class.[27]

There were several new organizations of free-thinkers founded in the 1850s, and the 1860s in Belgium, as in The Netherlands, was a period when "liberal" forces, characterized more by their positive valuation of most aspects of modernity and their hostility to traditional religion and its institutions than by concern for social justice, were gathering strength and confidence. The limited electoral franchise, under which the predominantly rural common people in both countries were not able to vote, benefited the urban middle class groups among which this liberal viewpoint was dominant. Popular education, guided by liberal principles in the interest of the enlightenment of the people, was a priority for these groups.

L'Affranchissement (emancipation) was founded as an antireligious association in Brussels in 1854 by skilled workers and political exiles from the France of Napoleon III; the primary purpose of this and similar groups was to arrange for nonreligious funerals so that the last wishes of "free thinkers" could be respected. In 1863, however, a more middle-class and thus more influential group, Libre Pensée (free thought), was founded and moved with some effectiveness to promulgate a "free thinker behavior and mentality" (*vrijdenkersgedrag en -mentaliteit*) among a broader public.[28]

The following year Libre Pensée was instrumental in establishing the Ligue de l'Enseignement in conscious imitation of the Maatschappij tot Nut van 't Algemeen in The Netherlands. It had been at a meeting, in Amsterdam, of the International Association for the Progress of the Social Sciences that the founder of the Ligue had met members of the Nut and taken the opportunity to visit some of their elementary schools where he was impressed by their progressive pedagogical methods and their nonconfessional character. The Ligue promoted what has been called a "true 'religion of humanity'" through publications, lectures, libraries, and other efforts to emancipate the Belgian people from Catholicism.[29]

The Belgian Ligue de l'Enseignement was the inspiration for the similarly named group, founded by Jean Macé in 1864, that would have such a great influence over the development of education policy in France. The Ligue called for the complete secularization of schools, which would make them—it claimed—truly neutral.[30] The 1842 law must be changed, the Ligue insisted, since the authority which it seemed to give to local communities to operate schools was an illusion; it was entirely subject to the demands of the government and especially of the clergy who, "by complicity or by weakness of the government," had made themselves the masters of communal schools. Belgium must create a true system of educational freedom, on the model of England, the United States, and of The Netherlands.[31]

As this implies, the Ligue was not, in its early years, an advocate of an expanded state role in education. "They have not failed to accuse the founders of the Ligue of being devotees of the god-State," the president pointed out at its first public assembly, "but everyone should be aware that the ideal which they pursue is the awakening of private initiative in all matters which have to do with education." Some of the founders, in fact, hoped that the State's role in education would grow less and less important, and would finally disappear altogether. Soon, however, they became convinced that only the State could overcome the resistance of local communities to providing appropriately for schooling, and (especially in Flanders) keeping schools free of clerical influence.[32]

The reliance upon local initiatives still dominated, however, in an interesting legislative proposal developed by the Ligue in 1871: the *Projet d'organisation de l'enseignement populaire*. Making explicit reference to the example of school committees in Massachusetts, the Ligue called for directly elected *comités scolaires* in each community with authority over the schools funded by local and national government. The State would organize the inspection of schools, but this would be limited to confirming whether the law was being carried out and funds used appropriately, not whether the instruction was effective. The State would also provide teacher training institutions, but teaching certificates would be granted by boards not under the control of the State. It would be up to the local school committee to appoint teachers and to ensure the quality of schooling; the State would in fact have a less important role than under the 1842 law already in effect.[33]

This proposal met with almost complete indifference if not hostility on the part of the public, though some of its elements influenced the school law enacted by Liberals in 1878.[34] The Ligue's more direct influence, however, would be through its model school in Brussels (see below).

The presence in Belgium of a number of distinguished refugees from the France of Napoleon III heightened the sense, among Belgian Liberals, that liberty was under siege. An influential brochure by exile Eugène Sue, *Lettres sur la question religieuse* in 1856, warned that the Catholic clergy were seeking to gain control of the minds of youth through the education system, and so to shape them "to believe without reasoning, to submit without questioning." To defend against this threat, Sue urged the establishment of a rationalist organization to preach a secular understanding of life, and the secularization of schooling. Schools should provide nontheistic moral instruction, and the clergy should be forbidden to open schools.[35]

Liberal anticlericalism and focus upon popular schooling was only strengthened by the papal encyclical *Quanta Cura* and its *Syllabus of Errors* (1864). Article 47 of the latter condemned the idea that "the best theory of civil society requires that popular schools open to children of every class of the people, and, generally, all public institutes intended for instruction in letters and philosophical sciences and for carrying on the education of youth, should be freed from all ecclesiastical authority, control and interference, and should be fully subjected to the civil and political power at the pleasure of the rulers, and according to the standard of the prevalent opinions of the age." This official statement confirmed the worst fears of the anticlerical Liberals, "with the shrewd and ruthless Frère-Orban as their chosen leader," who were determined to limit the influence of the Catholic Church.[36]

On their part, there was a growing mobilization among Catholics over the school question, which found expression in a congress held at Mechelen in 1863 with more than three thousand participants; among the resolutions adopted was that instruction cannot be separated from education, and that education is always in its nature religious. State schooling should only be supplementary to free schooling, and Catholics should do everything possible to make state schooling unnecessary. The congress "roundly denounced both clergy and congregations [religious orders] who could not or would not face up to the political realities of changing times and circumstances."[37]

A second Catholic congress the following year, with over five thousand participants, adopted a series of concrete action steps to strengthen Catholic schools and their legal position;[38] there was a third in 1867, which proposed a variety of measures designed to counter the growing influence of the anticlerical Ligue de l'enseignement with Catholic publications, lectures, libraries, and popular conferences. At first it was proposed to create a Ligue de l'enseignement primaire catholique et libre, but it was then decided to promote diocesan Saint Francis de Sales associations, "to combat infidelity" and to oppose schools "where, under the pretext of an equal respect for all religions, they are obviously confused in an equal disrespect, not discerning in anything the work of God in human efforts, adoring nothing but the human spirit."[39]

As a result of the strong Catholic influence on communal schools—which had official diocesan as well as government inspectors—and the widespread practice of "adopting" private schools as communal institutions, the share of entirely private elementary schools declined from 44 percent in 1840 to 16 percent in 1878.[40] After 1859, a further impetus was given by "firm, attentive, and constant administrative action"—in the absence of a revision of the 1842 law—to assert the state's role in elementary schooling. Municipalities were pressured to provide their own schools rather than to "adopt" Catholic schools. While 51 percent of pupils attended communal schools in 1845, the proportion rose to 73 percent in 1869.[41] These administrative measures were part of a broader effort to secularize cemeteries and other aspects of public life.

The growing industrialization of Belgium, second only to Britain as an industrialized country until the 1880s,[42] did not lead, as might have been expected, to political conflict along the lines of labor policies and a social safety net—that would come only toward the end of the century—but rather continued along the traditional lines of liberal anticlericals against loyal Roman Catholics. Education at all levels was a primary focal point of these conflicts.

"What a splendid task we have to fulfill," wrote the liberal *Revue Nationale* in 1840. "Everywhere in Europe there is malaise, but we dedicate ourselves to the noblest work to which the human spirit can be committed: the creation of a people."[43] Still too weak to impose their agenda of secular schooling, Liberals had been forced to compromise with Catholics in the enactment of the 1842 school law, which would be in effect for elementary schooling until replaced by the much more controversial law adopted in 1879. By the 1860s, however, they were insisting that elementary schooling was not an exclusively local concern, but one which the State should consider a matter of "national necessity." Since many local governments were indifferent if not hostile to the extension of schooling, that came to be considered an "obligation," a "duty," even a "mission" of the State.[44]

During the 1860s, the Catholic portion of the Belgian population, especially in the Dutch-speaking areas, was gaining institutional strength; in the diocese of Ghent, between 1839 and 1895, a new parish was established almost every year.[45] Just as in contemporary France under the Second Empire, the number of religious orders and members of those orders increased sharply, and there were new institutions of every sort to serve Catholics. Some Catholic leaders went so far as to contend that state education as such should be condemned, "first because it is contrary to the fundamental principles of our political organization and to the notion of the State, as we understand it today, and then because it is by nature invasive, fatal to freedom and also dangerous both from the point of view of the children which it shapes and also from that of the teachers which it employs." Recognizing political realities, they were prepared to compromise to make it more limited and thus less objectionable,[46] but the stage was set for the *lutte scolaire* that created the present system of structural pluralism.

THE NETHERLANDS

In The Netherlands, efforts to impose the model of "general Christianity" on elementary schools and to bring the training of clergy within the public system of secondary and higher education aroused growing resistance on the part of both Catholics and orthodox Protestants.[47]

After the loss of its Belgian provinces, the government became more sensitive to the grievances of Catholics. Local authorities must ensure, the king ordered in 1830, that the religious convictions of any pupils not be offended; in 1842, school inspectors were required to check whether any books or songs used in schools could be offensive.[48] Already in 1822 the Catholic journalist Le Sage ten Broek, a convert from Protestantism, had called on Catholic pastors to start parochial schools, and there were growing complaints that the public schools were too Protestant. Singing religious songs, reading from the Bible, and the lack of crucifixes on school walls were all considered dangerous for the spiritual well-being of Catholic pupils. The efforts of the Nut and of the government, some Catholics charged, were spreading religious indifference through the schools.[49]

The more "advanced" pastors of the Hervormde church, on the other hand, tended to be closely involved with local schools as well as with Nut-sponsored popular libraries and other vehicles of *volksverlichting* (popular enlightenment). Thus Petrus Hofstede de Groot, as a young pastor in the village of Ulrum (where, under his successor, the congregation would break away from the Hervormde church), helped to organize a discussion group and gave the first lecture in December 1828 on "the origin and value of the popular enlightenment of our days." He also bought himself a copy of Pestalozzi's didactic novel *Leonard and Gertrude*, and reported years later that he had learned from that book "what education is, how education must serve upbringing, how our life on earth must become an upbringing to a higher life."[50]

The 1830s and 1840s saw developments in The Netherlands whose working-out, over the next half-century would give Dutch education its distinctively pluralistic form. In the 1830s conservative Protestants began to separate themselves from the Hervormde church, which had long since lost much of its Calvinistic distinctiveness and—at least among its leadership—had adopted a "rationalistic supernaturalism," which had little in common with the formulations of the Synod of Dordt (1618–19), the traditional standard for Calvinist faith and practice in The Netherlands. "The concept of the church on the part of the ruling and tone-setting bourgeois, political, theological, and denominational class is difficult to describe. Its strength lies in its vagueness. In the subjectivity of a generalized religious feeling . . . The craving for universality of salvation and reconciliation without conversion, without repentance."[51]

This concern for tolerance was not, however, extended to their opponents among the orthodox Protestants; as Nicholas Schotsman pointed out at the time, "experience throughout the ages has shown that those who esteem tolerance in matters of faith most highly are the most intolerant toward any who speak up for the truth."[52] Among the dissidents from the religiously liberal consensus were intellectuals like Isaäc da Costa, a Jewish convert to orthodox Protestantism, whose Objections against the Spirit of the Age (1823) challenged the complacency of a self-consciously "modern" bourgeoisie in the name of traditional Christian teaching. True tolerance was based upon a recognition of the reality of human sinfulness and helplessness before God, not upon "a proud human spirit raising itself up in judgment upon God's ways."[53]

For Hofstede de Groot and other liberal Protestant advocates of the religiously neutral common school, such "fanaticism" was "a great evil which spreads contagiously from city to city and from village to village and, like an undermining sickness, drains away the noblest strength."[54]

More significant than the spiritual renewal and the controversies in elite circles, however, was a movement of separatism from local parishes on the part of a growing number of the common people, led by a few pastors who had rediscovered Protestant orthodoxy. Some who believed that only the metrical psalms should be sung in church, for example, objected to the requirement adopted in 1807 that at least one selection from a new hymn book be sung at each service.

In 1841 nearly nine thousand members of the Hervormde church sent a petition asking that the church be restored "on her old and solid foundations" through maintaining the various doctrinal statements and the decentralized church organization which had been established at the Synod of Dordt. When this was ignored, seven distinguished lay members, including the historian Guillaume Groen van Prinsterer, published a detailed critique of the ways in which the church had deviated from its traditions.[55] One of its failings, they charged, was in showing too little interest in schooling—despite the very specific injunctions in that connection of the church leaders at Dordt two centuries before—and for allowing the Nut, with its vaguely undoctrinal Christianity, to take the lead in creating private schools.[56]

Some of the dissenters—"simple people to whom the spirit of the Enlightenment had not penetrated [and who] could not find any more in the church what their spiritual lives required"[57]—had been meeting for decades in conventicles for prayer and study of the Bible and Pietist devotional literature where the traditional doctrines of human sinfulness and the need for a redeemer were still taught. The authorities considered these gatherings unlawful and a source of a disturbing fanaticism.[58] A law adopted during the French occupation had—for political reasons—forbidden gatherings of more than twenty persons without government permission, and this was now applied to these religious gatherings with prison terms and heavy fines. The dissenters were condemned as "hotheads, fanatics, heretics, and disturbers of fraternal harmony."[59] For the government, anything which created divisions within society was to be opposed; the Hervormde church was valued for its preaching of virtue and concord as well as love for the Fatherland and the royal family.[60] The king felt especially strongly about this, and had taken a personal hand in the church's reorganization; he was thus not receptive to the position of the dissenters. For him, and for the denominational leadership, "a first requirement for the preacher was to give no offence at all to the supporters of other Christian denominations. That meant that controversial matters must not be handled and that any form of unseemly enthusiasm for religion must be avoided"; civil peace would be ensured through religious peace.[61] Rumors circulated that the separatists had been incited by Jesuit envoys from Belgium,[62] seeking to weaken The Netherlands!

Many Protestants who continued to hold to the orthodox Calvinism that had flourished in the sixteenth and seventeenth centuries objected to the liberal, nondoctrinal version of Christianity promoted by the public schools. Although there were daily prayers and Bible reading in the schools, the instruction—especially that concerned with morality—rested upon an anthropology which denied the power of sin and the need for a redeemer, considered by the orthodox as essentials of the Christian faith.[63] In protest, some kept their children home, or sent them to illegal schools; fathers were in some cases sent to jail for that reason, even though school attendance would not be compulsory for another half-century.[64]

This resistance reflected a revival (the so-called *Réveil*), spreading from Switzerland and related to contemporary "awakening" movements in the English-speaking world, which was occurring among Dutch Protestants and led to an increased stress upon religious experience and the preaching of sin and redemption. There was in fact an evangelical upsurge at this time throughout Protestant Europe with which the separatists were in close contact,[65] and parallel developments in Catholic countries, both related in a complex way to Romanticism and an emphasis upon truths of the heart and "authentic experience." While largely discounted in elite circles, this emphasis found an eager response among the common people, many of whom had long nurtured the tradition of orthodox piety in "conventicles" with lay leaders. The socially conservative but theologically liberal denominational leadership deplored the criticism of liberal pastors by members of their congregations, and condemned "unlawful gatherings" in which "ignorance and fanaticism go hand in hand."[66]

In scores of villages and towns a deep cleavage developed between the "enlightened" landowners and local notables, often members of the Nut, and their humbler neighbors who held to traditional religious convictions. The latter, whom their later political and theological leader Abraham Kuyper would refer to as the *kleine luyden* (little people), resisted the benevolent program of their social superiors to "raise the children above the condition [and backward convictions] of their parents." They were, in turn, considered bigots, fanatics, hopelessly mired in superstition.

It was in 1834 that matters came to a breaking-point, and groups of separatists (*Afgescheidenen*) rejected not only the parish churches and the central authority of the Hervormde church, but also the public schools which sought to teach a generalized Christianity unsatisfactory to those parents with strong convictions about orthodox Protestant doctrine. "We began to keep our children home," one wrote. "Here and there father and mothers began to teach their children themselves. A neighbor would ask her neighbor, 'Can I send my children to you? You can surely teach four as easily as two.'"[67] The most important thing for the *kleine luyden* was to pass on their own beliefs to their children; a generalized Christianity which had no place for teaching about sin and redemption was not acceptable as the basis for educating their children.[68]

In doing so, they were subject to prosecution. In 1834, for example, the very day after a group of Protestants in Smilde separated themselves formally from the Hervormde church, establishing the Old Netherlands Reformed Church, a teacher began to give instruction in the orthodox teachings in a barn "full of turf, animals, and children." Before the end of the week, the school inspector had informed the mayor that this was a "rebellious movement against the existing order of things" and should not be permitted. In 1837, a woman was condemned to three days in jail and a hefty fine for teaching some children in her husband's *klompenmakerij* (workshop for making wooden shoes). Fines and imprisonment did not succeed in suppressing this grass-roots movement, and new congregations were formed in many communities.

The efforts of the separatists to provide an alternative education for their children ran afoul of the law enacted in 1806 and strengthened subsequently. In 1845, the mayor of another community ordered the closing of a school where forty-two children were being taught from the Bible and the (Calvinist)

Heidelberg Catechism. A group of separatists wrote to the king in 1846, asking him to keep in mind that "everything offends us that does not reveal or point to the narrow path to life, which is commanded by God for us and our children: Seek first God's kingdom and His righteousness. Sire, do not deny us any longer the affectionate concern for our children. We would rather see our goods wasted than to see our flesh and blood spoiled." They were willing "to provide teachers and schools for ourselves without a burden on the nation or the community's treasury," if they could be given approval to establish schools.[69]

These "grass-roots" developments might have produced no more significant results than countless other movements of religious protest, renewal, and division in the nineteenth century were it not for the interpretation given to them by Groen van Prinsterer. In his widely noticed *The Measures against the Separatists Judged by Constitutional Law* (1837), Groen pointed out that Church and State had been separated in 1796, but the government was still behaving as though dissent from the former state church was a form of public disorder. The Hervormde church was being treated as though it were part of the state machinery. That church had driven the separatists out by not responding to their concerns, and now was seeking, with the help of the civil authorities, to drive them back in again, as though they were runaway serfs. Groen's defense of the separatists attracted positive attention even from some Catholics who saw that the measures taken against orthodox Protestants might next be directed against them as well.[70]

The public elementary schools, Groen charged, had "fallen prey to the principles of the French Revolution," a theme he would return to a decade later. "Freedom of conscience, freedom of worship, freedom of education," he wrote, "between these there exists an indissoluble connection." The provision of the 1814 Constitution, that schooling was a matter of "continuing concern for the government," had been misinterpreted as mandating continuing control, in the supposed interest of national unity. Because of a "longing for quiet and unity," the common schools were teaching "a general religion, a Deism without Christian vocabulary and coloration," which would always be unacceptable to Christians for whom there was "only one source of true godliness and virtue, for whom God could not be known apart from Christ, for whom there was only one way to salvation."[71]

In 1840 in a speech in Parliament Groen charged that public schools, to avoid offending any conscience, had become not only "un-Christian" but "anti-Christian," since "overlooking the unique Mediator, [schools teach] a Supreme Being, overlooking the chasm that sin has produced, [they teach] a general Father of Mankind . . . Thus they preach to youthful hearts a god who is a fantasy of human wisdom, an idol set up through renunciation of the living God of Revelation."[72] He insisted that

> parents who, with or without adequate grounds, are earnestly convinced that the tenor of education at existing schools is un-Christian must not be hindered, directly or indirectly, from providing their children with the kind of education they believe they can justify before God. This coercion . . . is intolerable and should be terminated . . . It is an arrogance sprouted from the Revolutionary theory, which, while ignoring the rights of parents, views children as the property of the state.[73]

The separatist movement spread rapidly through the existing network of Pietist conventicles: by 1849, there were more than 40,000 and twenty years later more than 100,000 *Afgescheidenen* (separated), not counting the thousands who had emigrated to the United States—especially to Michigan and Iowa—for religious as well as economic reasons.[74] There they founded Christian schools as well (eventually) as colleges like Calvin in Grand Rapids, Michigan, and Dordt in Sioux Center, Iowa.[75] Although the *Afgescheidenen* represented only 1.4 percent of the Dutch population in 1847, the top year for Dutch emigration, they were 35 percent of the emigrants.[76] The movement remained largely confined to the lower social orders; orthodox Protestants in elite circles like Groen and Da Costa remained within the Hervormde church and continued to press for its return to traditional beliefs. Groen wrote to a friend that he found it almost impossible to attend those services where the great majority of ministers presided, but that he was opposed to abandoning the Hervormde church and hoped that the controversies could be the means of reforming it.[77]

Liberal Protestants dismissed the concerns of the *Afgescheidenen*. Petrus Hofstede de Groot, now a professor of theology at Groningen and a school inspector, published a little book asking *Are Separate Schools for the Various Church Fellowships Necessary or Desirable?* He insisted that the goal must be a single common school, a "people's school for the entire people." Such schools were, in fact, authentically religious, he stressed, teaching "common Christian principles" with which every parent could be comfortable. The demand of Groen van Prinsterer and other orthodox Protestants and Catholics for schools—whether public or private—with a denominational character was completely unjustified. After all, God had created not only the Family and the Church, each with its own rights and duties, but also the State, with its rights and duties, one of which was to control the education of all children, to prevent the spreading of destructive doctrines, for example, of Jesuits or Communists. Imagine if a school could be established "where perhaps the children learn to write well, to do sums rapidly, to read accurately, but are also taught that the Dutch were wrong to rise against Philip II, that they should have obeyed the fatherly discipline of Alva." This would be a disaster for The Netherlands where all children, "Romish and un-Romish," seated "next to each other on the same school benches, offer a single prayer to the same God . . . But if schools should come for the various communions—*Ach, mijn Vaderland!*" The Netherlands would in an instant return to the conditions of the 16th century: "Church quarrels would tear us apart again; fanaticism would be injected into the receptive hearts of children, and the gentle nation would become a prey to the most horrible of evils: religious hatred."[78]

The government persecution of the separatists was moderated, however, in response to the criticism that came both from Groen and other Dutch intellectuals and also from abroad. In 1841, the new king, William II, ordered that military force no longer be used to disrupt the meetings of the separatists.[79]

This was also a period when the long-disadvantaged Catholic population of The Netherlands began to develop a higher profile in social and political life. In 1840 Catholic leaders presented the king with an address lamenting what they considered the religionless character of public schools and asking for religious freedom. Concerned about growing tensions over public schools (especially in view of the Belgian revolt ten years earlier), a few months later he appointed a commission consisting of two Catholics and an orthodox Protestant, Groen van Prinsterer, to look into these complaints. While Groen urged that private religious schools be allowed, the Catholic leadership, at this point, was still inclined to see its minority position protected by a predominant state role in education.[80]

The government issued a decree in 1842 "against any offending of the different feelings" that responded to many of the concerns of Catholics, though at the price of further alienating orthodox Protestants from the public schools. In filling teacher vacancies, officials were instructed to take into account the religious identity of the local population. All public and private schools were required to report on what "books, songs, and writing" they were using so that it could be determined by religious authorities whether any were offensive to them; if necessary, offensive passages could be removed. School facilities were to be made available for an hour each day for doctrinal instruction given by the local church, whether Protestant or Catholic.[81] The Calvinist Heidelberg Catechism vanished from the public schools in Catholic areas, and books approved by the Catholic hierarchy were introduced. Teachers in elementary schools and in normal schools for teacher training were "strictly forbidden to give instruction in the doctrines of any denomination, or to give any expositions or expressions through which offense could be given to one or another religious conviction."[82] What was to be understood as "general Christian education" was gradually less and less clear, and teachers didn't know how they should approach it;[83] in fact, the "de-Christianizing" of the schools gathered momentum out of this effort to avoid religious controversy, just as occurred in the United States about the same time.

These measures were greeted with some satisfaction by Catholics, but they did not prove a lasting solution for those who wanted explicitly Catholic schooling. While "for the Protestant part of the people the break with the past was too radical, from the Catholic point of view it was not radical enough, since the school retained a Protestant character, was not neutral, and certainly not Catholic."[84]

In 1848, about 38 percent of the population was Catholic, but they represented only 4 percent of central government and 15 percent of local government officials. During the first half of the nineteenth century, Catholics saw their best allies as the Liberals who supported individual freedom, but after about 1860, in a fateful realignment, they instead entered into an effective alliance with orthodox Protestants in support of their faith-based group interests. In the earlier period, it had only been a small elite among Catholics—some 2.5 percent of them were qualified to vote—who were politically active, and naturally their concerns were in large part to remove barriers to opportunities for themselves. Catholic elite opinion at this point supported the "neutral-Christian" character of public schools on the grounds that private confessional schooling would lead to intolerance. After 1860, however, there began to be a mobilization of the broader Catholic population, largely organized by the clergy, around such issues as public funding for Catholic schools.[85]

That the religious and social ferment in Dutch society led eventually to a distinctive manner of organizing education had much to do with the conscious effort by Groen van Prinsterer and a few others to shape a distinctively different worldview—Abraham Kuyper would refer to this as the "antithesis"— in contrast with that associated with the Enlightenment and the French Revolution. In a series of private lectures given in 1845–46 and published in 1847, Groen stressed that it was not the external events of that Revolution— the confiscations, the Terror, the overturning of traditional relationships— which were the real evil, but rather the set of ideas upon which the revolution, and all revolutions, rested: the replacement of the sovereignty of God over human affairs by the sovereignty of man. "By Revolution," he wrote, "I do not mean one of the many events by which public authorities are removed, nor only the storm of upheaval that raged in France, but rather the reversal of ways of thinking and conviction which has become evident in all of Christendom." The results of rebellion against God's sovereignty could, Groen argued, be predicted to include revolutionary dictatorship and the loss of liberty. "Man wanted to retain the consequences [of the biblical worldview], while discarding the principles . . . The result is the opposite of what was anticipated. For justice, injustice; for freedom, compulsion; for tolerance, persecution; for humanity, inhumanity; for morality, corruption of morals."[86]

Forty years later the newspaper of the now-flourishing Anti-Revolutionary Party (ARP) observed the centennial of 1789 by pointing out that "what we reject is not that 1789 put an end to many abuses, nor that it used force to do so, but that it had no better principle to put in their place. Over against 'the Revolution' we put, not the 'ancien régime,' but the Gospel."[87]

When he took his seat in the Parliament in 1849, Groen announced "I have been sent here by a religious party."[88] It was, however, not until 1878 that the ARP was founded as a nationwide political organization, defining its identity by opposition to events already nearly a century in the past (though there had, of course, been several intervening revolutions in France, which were duly noted). Unlike political movements established to promote particular economic or social goals, the ARP had a fundamentally cultural concern, to seek to restore Dutch society to the commitments which—they believed— had been the basis of its seventeenth-century flourishing.[89] The original French Revolution continued to serve as a powerful symbol for what orthodox Protestants considered

> a mentality characteristic of liberal politicians and theologians, taking as their norm human reason rather than God's Word. The orthodox felt disadvantaged in both church and society, since the disrespect for the beliefs of the "little people" was associated with a lack of appreciation for the contributions of orthodox Protestants since the [rebellion against Spain] to the spiritual and material strength of Republic and Kingdom. Their movement was thus directed toward emancipation across a broad front: church, education, social organizations, government, and economic life.[90]

With respect to schooling, Groen initially called for confessional public schools on the Prussian model, with some explicitly Protestant and others explicitly Catholic, in place of what he considered the vain attempt to provide a nonconfessional and primarily sentimental and moralistic Christianity to which no one could possibly object. Such a thin gruel could not actually satisfy anyone who took religion seriously. The proposal for *een naar gezindte gesplitse staatsschool* (religiously divided public schools), as in Prussia and most other German states, was fiercely resisted by Dutch conservatives, who believed that the common public school was the institution which should knit the nation together. It was only grudgingly that Groen eventually came around to what became the position of the ARP: that private confessional schools should be funded on the same basis as secular public schools. It was difficult for Groen and other orthodox Protestants to abandon the hope that somehow The Netherlands could be persuaded to return to the theological certainties of the seventeenth century, and by the early 1870s there were only about 200 orthodox Protestant schools among the 3,800 elementary schools countrywide.

The first of these was established in Nijmegen—in a predominantly Catholic part of the country where the public schools were especially undesirable from an orthodox Protestant perspective—by the initiative of J. J. L. van der Brugghen, a judge who would later be the primary shaper of the 1857 education law. This law would open the way for an expansion of private schooling while affirming the religiously neutral character of the public schools and putting an end to Groen's hope that public schools could, as in Prussia, have a denominational character. It was also in Nijmegen that the first orthodox Protestant teacher training institution would be established, to prepare teachers for the growing network of alternative Protestant schools.

PRUSSIA

The developments in Prussia were very different from those in The Netherlands: rather than Protestant and Catholic families and pastors demanding the right to provide schooling that was more religiously orthodox than the lowest-common-denominator Christianity promoted by the public schools, the main source of agitation over popular schooling in Prussia was on the part of teachers objecting to the supervision provided by the clergy, both Protestant and Catholic.

In 1840, with the death of Altenstein, the new Prussian king, Friedrich Wilhelm IV, appointed a more conservative minister who moved at once to rebuke the agitation among teachers for greater independence from the oversight of the churches. Friedrich von Eichhorn issued a ministerial circular charging that the teacher training *Seminare* were providing more education than future elementary teachers required, and were thus creating ambitions that would inevitably be frustrated by the humble work of village schoolmasters. Teachers trained in this manner would, in turn, tend to convey to their pupils a sense of discontent with the existing social order.

"I am convinced," he wrote,

> that, as is true of all schools, but especially of the *Volksschulen*, they must concentrate their efforts first upon the revealed truths of Christianity, and then upon modesty in the demand for the enjoyments of life, upon fidelity to their

vocational duties, and upon the virtues which result from neighborly affections, and, finally, upon that knowledge which is a part of human culture and which advances and enobles existence. Upon those conditions they will be able to form a sound and contented generation.[91]

That government concern about discontent among teachers was not altogether unjustified became evident in 1848, when revolts throughout the German states were ignited by the success of the February revolution which had overthrown Louis Philippe in France. "It was but natural in the revolutionary forties that schoolmasters, who had in large part come from the lower social and economic classes, should play an important part in the effort of those politically submerged portions of the population to gain political recognition. They were able to write and to speak and they made large use of the position of advantage which they thus held in forwarding the cause of liberalism."[92] Nipperdey, in his general history of Germany between 1800 and 1866, suggests that in the decades before 1848 village schoolteachers were a force for popular emancipation, "an element of unrest and opposition. They were new Men with the task of civilizing Society and broadening Humanity, but their social status—they could scarcely marry a land-owning farmer's daughter, and people still addressed them with 'thou'—like their salaries, was miserable; they were controlled and disciplined by the State, but without the privileges of civil servants, upwardly mobile without social integration . . ." Despite this uncertain and uncomfortable position, however, "the teacher was in the village a new authority, next to the pastor and against him, next to and against tradition. The competition of interpretations of the world and of forms of relationships promoted a position critical of tradition that could stretch to political and social institutions."[93]

Adolf Diesterweg, perhaps the best-known advocate of the role of popular schooling, endorsed the call for the national convention in Frankfurt where delegates from all parts of Germany gathered—they hoped—to create a new, liberal German nation. In September of that year teachers gathered in Eisenach to found the first Germany-wide federation of teachers, and there were many regional gatherings where teachers expressed their frustration and demands.[94]

Other historians question whether teachers played such a significant role in the revolutionary ferment, suggesting that the great majority of them remained passive. Douglas Skopp, for example, contends that elementary school teachers "were typically neither atheists nor radical democrats nor even revolutionaries but rather aspiring members of an enthusiastic, self-acclaimed educational *Berufstand* [profession]" and were easily satisfied "as their demands for higher salaries and improved teaching conditions were met."[95] Steven Welch, in his study of teachers in Bavaria in 1848, takes an intermediate position while noting that teacher activism varied significantly between different areas and typically focused on complaints specific to the position of teachers—especially their subordination to the clergy and their meager salaries—rather than on political change.[96] Perhaps Tenorth puts it best: teachers were not central in the ferment of 1848, but their role should not be overlooked.[97]

Chapter Five

Consolidation of State Control 1880–1930

GERMANY

The wave of revolutions, which threatened the existing order in most of the countries of Europe in 1848, was followed by a period of reaction in France, Italy, and the various German states. Golo Mann summarized the March 1848 events and their consequences as "a few thousand beautiful speeches, a few thousand deaths, and a few thousand trials, that was the harvest of the years 1848 and 1849. From the great hopeful unrest nothing seemed to remain behind but disappointment."[1]

Reaction was already evident in the years leading up to 1848, in response to the early growth of Socialism and other challenges to the social, economic, and political order, and indeed reactionary measures helped to precipitate the violent upheavals of that year. Teachers were well represented among the progressive elements, and as a result were a particular target of those determined to maintain the existing order; "it was an irony of eighteenth-century school reform that schoolmasters, originally trained to be an arm of the state, were by 1848 among its most vocal critics." It has been suggested that this situation resulted from the disparity between the rhetoric about the high mission of teachers and their actual poverty and subordination to local clergy and notables.[2]

After the fall of Eichhorn as a result of the political disorders of March 1848, more than 500 teachers, responding to a summons from two teacher educators, gathered at Tivoli, near Berlin and adopted a series of resolutions to the Prussian National Assembly on educational reform.

The teachers proposed the appointment of secular school inspectors [in place of local clergy], the reorganization of the elementary schools with the state assuming complete responsibility for school maintenance and the appointment of teachers, the integration of schools at all levels of learning into a single system with the comprehensive school as the foundation of the system (*allgemeine Schule*) educating the youth of all social classes, and the elevation of the *Lehrerseminare* [teacher-training seminaries] to a branch of the university with the same admission requirements.[3]

They also called for the creation of a separate ministry of education, no longer combined with the responsibility for overseeing the churches, and the establishment of a minimum salary schedule. "It was not until 1919 that many of these recommendations were accepted in the Constitution of the German Republic."[4]

One striking characteristic of the petitions and proposals by teachers during this time of intense ferment was the frequent use of the phrase "the school is a state institution [*Staatsanstalt*]."[5] Eager to be freed from the galling supervision of local clergy, activist teachers put faith in the State as their liberator. Together with this misplaced confidence that the State would leave them free in a way that the Church did not, teachers also hoped that, by becoming civil servants, they would improve their financial situation and prestige.[6] More radical elements in the teacher movement, like Karl Friedrich Wilhelm Wander (1803–1879), called for teachers to be the avant-garde of fundamental change. "To awaken the right spirit among the People where it is sleeping," Wander wrote in 1848, "to strengthen it, where it is lying supine, to lead it, where it is erring in false paths: that is the task of German popular education, which lies primarily in the hands of German teachers."[7] Most historians agree, however, that to the extent that rank-and-file teachers became involved at all in the events, it was to advance their professional interests. There was in fact Liberal criticism that teachers were placing their interests above those of society and of parents.[8]

The Prussian National Assembly, during the brief period of Liberal ascendancy, decided that the new constitution which it was drafting would have a section about schools. Articles were proposed, which defined the *Volksschule* as a state institution under the supervision of public officials and supported with public funds explicitly "free of any church supervision" (Article 24). Children of all faiths would be educated together in interconfessional schools, and the curriculum would include no confessional instruction. There were strong reactions to this proposal on the part of Catholics, warning that it would lead to the establishment of many private confessional schools. One petition to the assembly warned that "the inevitable outcome . . . would be the sad experience that, like the example of Belgium, we would see confessional parochial schools established independently beside state schools and such a host of problems arising." The scale of this protest convinced the government that there was limited popular support for the proposals advanced by the Liberal teachers.[9]

In December 1848 the Prussian government dissolved the National Assembly, but continued work on a constitution. State officials were "convinced that the state's interest in the education of its citizens were too vital to permit an unrestricted liberty for private instruction," and recommended accommodation of Catholic concerns. One advisor predicted that "this confessional school, against whose power of religious conviction the school without religious instruction would have no similar power to match, would carry away the victory in the embittered conflict breaking out in families and communities." The constitution promulgated in January 1850 reflected this concern by providing that "confessional conditions are to be considered as much as possible in the organization of the public elementary schools."[10] Guarantees were provided for the religious character of schooling, and the constitution called for adoption of a comprehensive school law; this was not forthcoming, however, for the government chose to act through ministerial regulations.

If teachers played a role in the political agitation, which came to a head—Europe-wide—in 1848, this role was exaggerated in retrospect, when they served as a convenient target during the period of reaction which followed in the German states as in France. Prussia's King Frederick William IV made a personal appearance at a conference for faculty of *Lehrerseminare* in 1849 to express his displeasure:

> All the misery which has come to Prussia during the past year is to be attributed to you and only you. You deserve the blame for that godless pseudo-education of the common people which you have been propagating as the only true wisdom and by means of which you have destroyed faith and loyalty in the minds of my subjects and turned their hearts away from me. Even while I was yet Crown Prince, I hated in my innermost soul this tricked-out, false education strutting about like a peacock, and while I was Regent I made every effort in my power to overthrow it. I will go ahead on this beaten path without allowing myself to deviate from it. First of all, these [teacher] seminaries must every one be removed from the large cities to small villages, in order that they may be kept away from the unholy influence which is poisoning our times. And then everything that goes on in them must be subjected to the closest supervision. I am not afraid of the populace, but my bureaucratic government in which up to now I have had proud confidence, is being

undermined and poisoned by these unholy doctrines of a modern, frivolous, worldly wisdom. But as long as I hold the sword hilt in my hands, I shall know how to deal with such a nuisance.[11]

Similarly, in 1851 the journalist and social critic Wilhelm Riehl charged that elementary schoolteachers had been the ringleaders of rebellion in their local communities, inspiring the people to rise against the established order. King Maximillian of Bavaria read his account and was so impressed that he invited Riehl to Munich to become one of his advisors in restoring order.[12]

In Prussia about 500 of 30,000 *Volksschule* teachers were disciplined, as were 50 of 3,000 in Saxony. During the period of reaction in Prussia, Ferdinand Stiehl, responsible for the *Volksschule* from 1844 to 1873, established detailed regulations in 1854 to ensure that they would have the most modest goals, and that their teachers would be kept in order and not educated above their calling. He would later justify these by insisting that it was necessary to put an end to the emancipation of schools from the churches and of teachers from the government; the school should be the daughter of the church and the helper of families.[13] Rejecting the goals associated with Humboldt and Suevern, Stiehl insisted that the idea of a general humanistic education had proven through experience to be mistaken. What the People needed was an education that built upon and served family, occupation, local community and the State in the closest association with the churches; only in this way could it prepare pupils for the actual life they were fated to live. Stiehl rejected the Pestalozzian and Herbartian emphasis upon "method" as a distraction from the practical lessons which pupils required.[14]

Unauthorized teacher conferences were forbidden; teachers were forbidden to belong to associations that discussed matters of public policy,[15] and *Lehrerseminare*, whose primary purpose was to shape the mind and the conscience of future teachers, were required to follow a government-defined curriculum which included only those subjects which teachers would be expected to teach. Some located in urban areas were moved to the countryside to reduce the risk of infection by dangerous ideas. The very limited curriculum of the *Volksschule* was to serve as the absolute priority for teacher training, and it should not go further until such time as the future teacher had mastered the skills needed to teach effectively. "The unconditional achievement of this goal must not be put into question or hampered through an attempt at a scientific approach to disciplines which do not stand in the closest relationship to the most immediate tasks of the teacher trainees; though these [studies] might be indeed desirable and useful for more general educational goals, they are not strictly useful for elementary school teachers." The practice school was the center around which all the work of the *Seminar* should be organized.[16]

Parallel regulations were issued for Prussian elementary schools, stressing that "for the inner and mental activity of the school, an important turning point has arrived recently." The time had come to eliminate whatever was unjustified, excessive, and misleading and, in its place, to put that which would meet the need to provide a real Christian popular education (*Volksbildung*). "The idea of providing a general education through a formal development of mental abilities on the basis of abstract content has been demonstrated by experience as ineffective or harmful." The elementary schools, "in which most of the people receive the foundation, if not the completion, of their education," should provide them with what would prepare them for life, rather than offering them an abstract system.[17]

These and other regulations were intended to make the schools attended by the children of the common people suitable to "support, build up, and permeate family, vocational, community, and national existence,"[18] and with some modification from time to time they served as the basis for popular schooling in Prussia for the next sixty years, though it should be noted that very significant advances were made in the quantity and quality of elementary schools under conservative governments.

Although Stiehl's 1854 regulations (known as the *Regulative*) have been much criticized by historians, some have recently pointed out that the low level of instruction that they prescribed for rural schools was in fact pretty much what was possible under those circumstances, and that the regulations were generally not implemented in the cities. Such modest and perhaps reachable goals may have promoted the actual development of rural schools more than had the earlier ambitious claims that they would transform humanity.[19] There were three general types of public elementary schools at the time. The schools in the countryside often had only one teacher, a situation which continued into the twentieth century; they were generally equivalent, in their low quality and the low pay and status of their teachers, to the free schools for poor children in cities. Then there were tuition-charging urban schools (usually with some free places) that served children from middle-class and skilled working-class families. Finally there were higher-level urban elementary schools patronized by families whose own positions depended in part on the educational attainment of the fathers and who intended that their children continue their education in the *Gymnasium* and perhaps a university. There were also urban private schools of all three types. Through local government efforts between 1865 and 1880 many new schools were built in urban residential areas.[20]

Similar measures were taken in Bavaria, where the king insisted in 1851 that the highest goal of elementary schooling should be the development of Bavarian patriotism.[21] New regulations were issued in 1857, warning about the widespread "moral corruption" of society and attacking "the arrogance of the young schoolteachers [with] their vain conceit and haughtiness, their shallow liberalism and pitiful sciolism [superficial and pretentious knowledge] . . . their intractability and obstinacy against all higher authority, their irreligious and worldly attitude, their independence and lack of moral self-discipline . . . their discontent and disaffection with their material situation in life." This condition was blamed in part upon the laxity of the *Seminare*, but even more upon the recruitment of teachers who were "degenerate" with regard to "religion, morals, and attachment to the church," drawn from among those who were "physically or mentally incapable" of exercising any other craft or trade. A new generation of teachers must be recruited and trained to possess "contentedness, moderation, love of order, fear of God, obedience and humility." *Seminare* should focus on building the character of future elementary teachers rather than cultivating their intellect.

> Proper moral character and correct religious belief, not knowledge, became the key prerequisites for the model teacher, whose primary purpose was "to exercise in word, deed and example an effective and fruitful influence on the religious, moral, and spiritual welfare of his pupils." The image of the teacher was in effect redefined: the enlightened *Kulturtraeger* (agent of high culture)—always more ideal than reality—was replaced by the humble, spiritual aide-de-camp to the local priest or minister. Seminar training was designed to produce teachers who could be "partners and assistants in the development of human education for a higher world."[22]

Only in this way could the government ensure that popular education would not be the vehicle of "a dangerous incursion by the Spirit of the Age."[23]

For more than a half-century in Prussia there were repeated attempts to enact a school law that would give specific content to the general principles expressed in the 1850 constitution, but these were frustrated again and again by the mutual mistrust between Liberals (joined later by Socialists) on the one hand, and Catholics with their conservative Protestant allies on the other.

It has been observed that "through most of the nineteenth century the public elementary school in Prussia was de jure an institution of the state but de facto an institution of the church through the clergy's virtual monopoly of school inspection offices and the precedence given to confessional religious instruction in the curriculum."[24] Despite continual demands from teacher organizations for an end to clerical supervision, this continued in most of Germany until 1918, in part because of the cost implications of providing an alternative system of lay inspectors. It seems that in rural areas there was often a friction between the pastor and the schoolteacher,[25] as was the case in France during the same period.

Religious instruction was, on the one hand, seen as a primary instrument of the state's policy of shaping the hearts and loyalties of the people, but on the other hand it inevitably created the possibility of competing value systems. This was particularly the case in Catholic schools, given the international character of the Catholic Church and—during the second half of the nine-teenth century—the heightened tensions between that Church and many aspects of modernity, including especially the claims of nationalism which were undermining the temporal position of the Papacy in Italy. The fact that Germany was being united behind the leadership of Prussia at the same time that Italy was being united, at the expense of the Papal States, behind that of Piedmont created the potential for conflict over popular schooling.

Meanwhile, what seemed to be a workable compromise—though arguably it retarded the professionalization of elementary education—was what Prussian and other German government officials recognized as the right of the churches to collaborate with public authorities (*Mitwirkungsrecht*) in the provision of schooling.[26] This collaboration was not, however, on equal terms. The Bavarian government might stress repeatedly the religious mission of its schools, and its desire for teachers who were sincerely attached to their church, but when, in the wake of the 1848–49 disturbances, the Catholic bishops presented a set of requests to solidify their oversight over the Catholic character of the schools, these were rejected. "The state, which desired and valued the church's support, had no intention of yielding any of its authority over the *Volksschule*. It sought to press the church into service for its own goals but was unwilling to com-promise on the issue of superiority and control. The church was to be a servant and an ally but not a full-fledged partner, much less the master, in the field of education."[27]

With the establishment (theoretically the re-establishment) of the German Empire in 1871, the organization of schooling took on added importance to overcome the differences among the many territories which had been brought together, although the constitution adopted (like the American Constitution) did not include education among the national functions but implicitly left it to the various states.

Considerable progress was made in strengthening popular schooling during the second half of the nineteenth century. The proportion of total expenditures for schooling in Prussia increased from 4 percent of the state budget in 1867 to

12.2 percent in 1878;[28] of course, most expenditures were local. By the 1880s, nearly 100 percent school attendance had been achieved in Prussia, and the number of pupils had grown from 1.4 million in 1822 to 4.3 million sixty years later.[29]

During the second half of the nineteenth century, Prussian cities developed comprehensive systems of public schooling; elementary education was free of tuition from 1870 in Berlin, and in all of Prussia from 1888, though most other states retained tuition. This was not the result of the assumption of the costs of schooling by the Prussian state; in the middle of the nineteenth century local communities paid on average 75 percent of the cost of schooling, and parents another 20 percent. Tuition (*Schulgeld*) was reduced as local authorities took over more of the cost, and it was not until the twentieth century that the state began to make more than supplemental grants to schools.[30] An American observer, writing in the early 1920s, noted that

> the history of the development of a national system of education in Prussia exhibits an apparent inconsistency in that, whereas the state very early secured extensive control, only in the most recent times has it contributed substantially to the expenses of public education. Even as early as 1716, the state prescribed compulsory attendance at school. . . . By these various developments, the state had acquired a very complete control over all phases of education. It has established standard qualifications for teachers, uniform curricula, and uniform administration. . . . By the law of 1888 school fees in the primary schools were abolished and the state undertook at the same time to pay a portion of the salary of every teacher . . . [but] up to 1906 no thoroughgoing reorganization of the maintenance of the primary schools had occurred. . . . As a result of all these state aids that have resulted from legislation during the last sixty years— mainly during the last fifteen years, before the Revolution of 1918—the central authority was paying in Prussia a little less than one-third of the total cost of primary education. The same proportion of state to local contributions was true for Germany as a whole.[31]

Social Democrats like August Bebel (1840–1913) pointed out the fundamental inequities in the allocation of public funds for schooling. In 1875, Bebel wrote, Saxony expended more for the privileged 4 percent of its youth who went on to secondary and higher education than for the 96 percent who attended only elementary school.[32]

The situation changed only gradually. In 1900 Prussia paid 27.1 percent of *Volksschule* costs; Bavaria, 35.7 percent; Wuerttemberg, 30.6 percent; Baden, 21.8; percent; and Saxony, 19.9 percent.[33] By comparison, thirty years later in the United States, the states on average still contributed less than 17 percent of the cost of schools.

In 1906 a school law was finally enacted in Prussia to carry out the provisions of the 1850 constitution. This law recognized confessional schools as the norm and interconfessional schools as exceptions under special circumstances, although for decades leading elements among German educators had argued for interconfessional schools with a religiously neutral curriculum and separate religious instruction classes for Protestant and Catholic and—where numbers warranted—Jewish pupils. "They saw it as a means of diminishing church influence in the schools as well as promoting tolerance and social harmony in a confessionally segmented nation" while taking care to distinguish their position from that of Socialists who called for completely secular schools. The latter had taken that position in their party congress in 1904, which made "the separation of the school from the church, the removal of religion from the school curriculum, and the establishment of comprehensive schools for the education of all social classes from the age of six to fourteen, the focal point of Social Democratic Party agitation in school politics."[34]

A study in 1906 found that, "of the 37,761 public elementary schools attended by 6,161,378 children, there were only 900 *Simultanschulen* with 370,079 children," concentrated in a few areas.[35] In fact, between the Socialists on one hand and the denominational forces on the other, "by 1906 the partisans of the interconfessional school were reduced to a small coterie of the Liberal leadership of the Prussian Teachers Association, the advocates of school reform in the two progressive parties, and the interest groups representing the Jewish community in public life. These groups had no influence on the government's school policy or on public opinion." There was little popular support, in part because the "circumstances in which the interconfessional schools were opened in the 1870s gave them the reputation of being a '*Kulturkampf* institution.'" As a result, the 1906 "school bill was a bitter disappointment to the teaching profession," or at least to its anticlerical leadership.[36]

For those concerned about the role of religion in education, the interconfessional school threatened to marginalize it into "merely one subject in the curriculum [which] would no longer penetrate and inspire the entire instruction." "The fight for the interconfessional school, which raged a generation ago," Minister of Education Studt wrote in 1903, "no longer stands in the foreground of the activities and interests" of the parties at the dominant center of the political spectrum. "People have recognized that the interconfessional school carries with it disadvantages insofar as it is apt to impair not only religious and moral education but also the cultivation of patriotism."[37]

Hopes that interconfessional schools would have a unifying influence on a religiously divided society were disappointed; in cities where they were imposed by a Liberal elite, "the results were political strife rather than social integration and mutual respect between the religious groups."[38] In another sense, of course, the threat of their imposition did promote Catholic and Protestant cooperation in opposition to secular liberalism.

A marked characteristic of the elementary schools which, by the end of the nineteenth century, more than 90 percent of German children attended, was that they were organized on a Protestant/Catholic confessional basis. This was true not only in Prussia but in most of the German states; in 1900, in Bavaria, 70.6 percent of the schools were Catholic; 26 percent, Protestant; 1.2 percent, Jewish; and only 2.2 percent, neutral. Jewish public schools were provided where sufficient demand existed from the 1820s in Wuerttemberg and from 1847 in Prussia.[39]

In 1861, 99 per cent of Protestant children were attending Protestant schools, and 97 per cent of Catholic children attended Catholic schools, though most Jewish children went to a Protestant school, while having separate religious teaching . . . In 1906, 95 percent of Protestant children and 91 percent of Catholic children, though only 27 percent of Jewish children, were being taught in schools of their own confession.[40]

The effect of accommodation of religion within the *Volksschule* was to maintain state monopoly of popular schooling, since it made it unnecessary for Catholics and orthodox Protestants to create their own schools, as occurred in The Netherlands. "Teaching religion as a required subject in the public schools guaranteed that the instruction remained under the state's oversight and served the state's interests."[41]

The apparent stability of this situation, however, conceals decades of political conflict over the relationship of—in particular—the Catholic Church with popular schooling. In 1864 Pope Pius IX issued his encyclical *Quanta Cura* and the *Syllabus of Errors* which accompanied it, condemning many features of contemporary life, including notably the efforts of governments to extend their authority over all aspects of society within their boundaries. There was also opposition in the Catholic Rhineland to Prussia's war of aggression against Austria in 1866, which led Bismarck to question the political loyalty of Catholics, as did the support of Catholic legislators for federalism and opposition to his plans to create a strong central government.[42] The declaration of the infallibility of the popes on questions of doctrine by the Vatican Council in 1870 was further evidence of the counterattack of the Papacy against the secular forces which, especially in Italy, were pressing it hard; in September 1870, in part as a result of the withdrawal of French troops because of the Franco-Prussian War, the Italian army entered Rome and the temporal power of the Papacy was at an end. Pius IX, in response, became even more intransigent in his opposition to modernity.

In the 1870s, having defeated France and established the German Empire through the voluntary unification of existing German states (except Austria and—arguably—Switzerland), Chancellor Bismarck began to challenge the influence of the Catholic Church and especially of the Papacy. The campaign of the Catholic Center Party in the 1871 Reichstag election seemed a challenge to his project of national unity, and an even more direct challenge was the support of Polish Catholic clergy for the maintenance of their language. At the same time, the creation of an empire in which Catholics were in a distinct minority because of the exclusion of Austria was seen by German Liberals as a victory over "Jesuit intrigue and domination." The struggle against the pretensions of the Papacy, one distinguished historian declared at the time, was "a more important and more difficult battle than that of 1870" against France.[43]

The *Kulturkampf* began when the Prussian parliament adopted a series of measures directed against Catholic institutions, including state oversight over seminaries training priests. "In the course of the 1870s Bismarck broke off diplomatic relations with the Vatican, expelled the Jesuits, tampered with the discipline and education of other religious orders and parish priests, instituted civil marriage, and jailed resisting priests and bishops."[44] Eventually, half of the Prussian bishops were imprisoned for violating various laws, and one was exiled. Liberals rejoiced as the religion article of the Prussian Constitution, which guaranteed the right of churches to freedom of self-government, was abolished, and the management of Catholic properties was turned over to local congregations, on the Protestant model.[45] This was, it might be noted, the arrangement imposed by the French Republic thirty years later.

The School Inspection Law of 1872 made the supervision of schools—including private schools—an exclusively civil function, though in actual practice many clergy continued to carry out this function and until 1918 about three-fourths of the district school inspectors in Prussia were clergymen.[46] Petitions in opposition with more than 326,000 signatures were submitted to the Prussian legislature, mostly from Catholics.

The primary agent of the effort to limit the influence of the Catholic Church was Adalbert Falk, appointed to head the Prussian ministry of education in 1872. The Elementary Schoolteachers Association urged him to press local authorities to create interconfessional schools, and to appoint experienced teachers rather than local clergymen to inspect schools. By June 1875, 373 Catholic priests, but only nineteen Protestant ministers, had been removed from school inspection.[47] It was primarily in Polish regions that such full-time school inspectors were appointed because of doubts about the loyalty of the Polish Catholic clergy; a similar policy was adopted in recently annexed Alsace-Lorraine for similar reasons. The *Kulturkampf* was extended into this newly acquired territory; the German administration "expelled members of French teaching orders, required teachers' certificates for nuns, curtailed religious and particularly catechism instruction, and ended the strict segregation of the sexes practiced in French schools. He also succeeded in alienating the powerful Catholic clergy and the Catholic rank and file, creating resistance to German schools" in Alsace and Lorraine.[48]

Ironically, however, German rule shielded the religious character of schools in Alsace-Lorraine from the more extensive secularization that would occur in France during the 1880s. In 1871, the authorities established a curriculum for primary schools that continued their religious character: five hours a week of religious instruction; different textbooks for Catholic, Protestant, and Jewish schools; "and, initially, even different arithmetic books." Over the next several years, government control was extended over the appointment and dismissal of teachers in these schools, and this was used to purge them of teachers—especially members of religious orders—who were not considered loyal to German rule.[49]

The measures taken in Prussia in 1872 had the effect of undoing to some extent the regulations adopted in 1854, which had stressed the moral and religious function of schooling at the expense of academic instruction. The confident government of 1872 extended the curriculum of teacher-training *Seminare* to include more mathematics and science, though without neglecting religion. It continued to be "as much a matter of course that the German child should be taught in the public schools the religion of his parents as that he should be taught the German language or arithmetic."[50]

Falk was determined, however, that the influence of the Catholic Church would be reduced in this area as well. In 1876 he issued regulations on Catholic religious instruction, and altogether during his administration 2,848 priests were prohibited from giving and directing religious instruction in schools. Henceforth, he insisted, the government alone would select and appoint teachers of religion. As might be expected, Catholic leaders "argued that the government had neither the right nor the competence to appoint religion teachers and to decide what was authentic Catholic doctrine."[51]

Partially to gain some political advantage in response to these government measures hostile to Catholicism, the German Socialists adopted, in 1875, the

Gotha Program, which sought to widen their base of support by insisting that religion was a private matter and—contrary to much earlier rhetoric—was not opposed by Socialists so long as it did not serve as a tool of domination. In effect this was a recognition that, despite Marxist orthodoxy, "cultural goals and religious loyalties determined political behavior as much as material interests,"[52] and it would not be wise to alienate a large group of potential supporters.

German Liberals saw the *Kulturkampf* as essential to the nation-building to which they were committed, and educational reform in the direction of the interconfessional school as "the logical accompaniment of political unification" was accomplished in 1870. "Their fight against a confessionally divided school system under clerical supervision was waged with the intention of using education to break down religious particularism, to foster cultural integration, to establish the primacy of the citizen's loyalty to the nation-state, and to nationalize the consciousness of the German people." It was because their reform program enjoyed little popular support that "they were maneuvered into a repressive campaign against the Catholic clergy," a campaign whose effects were still very much felt a generation later and made the preservation of confessional schooling a key element of Catholic political mobilization.[53]

A crucial aspect of this mobilization was that it involved Catholics at all levels of society and had a broad agenda of which education—both in confessional and in state schools—was only one aspect.[54] As a result, the Catholic presence in German politics would be significant for half a century. By the mid-1870s it was clear that

> the strength of the Catholic church had not been broken in Germany (it was, in fact, getting stronger), and the emperor, crown prince, and Conservative party had all lined up against Bismarck on this issue. Never one characterized by self-delusion, Bismarck thus resolved to cut his losses. With the death of the stubborn Pope Pius IX in early 1878 and the election of the conciliatory Leo XIII as his successor, Bismarck succeeded in disengaging himself and abandoning the *Kulturkampf*. Unfortunately, this controversial political campaign had resulted only in a deepening of confessional divisions in Germany.[55]

No doubt Bismarck was motivated in part by his need of an alliance with the Center Party. In any event, during the 1880s all of the laws adopted to limit the influence of the Catholic Church were repealed or modified except that banning the Jesuits, which remained until 1917.[56]

Although opposed to denominational schooling, Liberals were not calling for the exclusion of the teaching of religion in the schools since this "guaranteed that the instruction would be given in the state's interests and under the state's supervision," and the alternative seemed to be the danger that a parochial system of schools would be created. They warned that if the State "permits private schools freely in order to satisfy special confessional interests, then it is only serving the ambitions of the clergy to dominate [education], as the example of Belgium proves." Government officials were concerned that removal of religion from the *Volksschule* would lead to establishment of private church schools not under direct state control; they "doubted that religiously neutral communal schools would compete successfully with Catholic private schools and thought that a large part of popular education would soon be removed from the control of the state. The surest way to preserve the state's monopoly of education was to have the public schools serve the purposes of the church as well as the state."[57]

Despite the ill will created by the *Kulturkampf*, it did not in the long run have a major effect on the role of the churches in relation to popular schooling in Germany; "as late as 1901 nearly 20 percent of the male teachers were still in offices that required them to fulfill the duties of a church organist."[58] Efforts to promote interconfessional schools (*Simultanschulen*) failed in the face of resistance from both Catholics and Protestants.

The *Kulturkampf*, which began in Germany in the 1870s, did not die away altogether; Liberals continued, at every opportunity, to express their conviction that interconfessional schools, "providing a moral education free from religious dogmatism and prejudice," would help to build a united Germany. However, "the weakness that the National Liberal and Progressive Parties could not overcome was the lack of popular consent to their program of school reform." As a result of this lack of popular support, "convinced of the moral righteousness of their cause, the liberals were willing to rely on the coercive arm of the state government," if they could only manage to gain its support as was briefly possible during the *Kulturkampf*.[59] During this period, the German Social Democratic Party

> became something like another, though large and well organized, voluntary association, with its own ethos and culture of popular education, with reading rooms, publications, lectures, not necessarily on directly political subjects. Marx had called on the revolutionary working class to organize and educate itself for its historic role, without perceiving that the more organized and educated it became, the less like the utterly alienated proletariat with nothing to lose but its chains, and therefore the less revolutionary, it also became.[60]

The "reformism" of Edouard Bernstein led the Socialists to become participants in the political process, negotiating and bargaining, and entering into alliances of convenience with other parties, including the Catholics, around specific issues, in a manner that softened the confrontation, which was still so virulent in Spain, Italy, or France. Though anticlerical in principle, the German Socialists did not allow that to become their dominant theme.

The breakthrough of the Social Democrats and of the labor unions to becoming a mass movement began in 1890, and by 1914 there were 1.1 million members in the party and 2.6 million in the unions.[61]

Socialist theoretician Karl Kautsky argued in 1892 "that the industrial order had destroyed family life for the working class, just as Marx had predicted. The deterioration of the home environment placed a new responsibility on the school. Rather than simply supplementing the educational functions of the family, schools in mature capitalist societies had to act as surrogate parents." Properly financed and oriented, Kautsky contended, the school could create the necessary preconditions for revolution through the development of popular enlightenment. This would require that religion be banished from the classroom and that schools lose their confessional character and clerical oversight.[62]

A decade later, the educational ambitions of the Social Democrats had expanded; either the school should be transformed to teach the young values consistent with Socialism, or institutions should be created outside of the school. Thus they sought "greater socialist influence on school practices at the local and national levels, education by the party and by parents at home, in the youth movement, and in adult classes. Thereby education became an integral part of the Social Democrat's political activities."[63]

A recurring theme of Liberals and Socialists was the necessity of eliminating the divided organizational character of German schooling.

> The principle of a unitary national school had, though in differing intensity and at no point in time with a chance of realization, preoccupied the whole 19th century. Humboldt and Suevern had put it on the agenda of educational policy at the beginning of the century; it was renewed by the leading forces of the middle-class Revolution of 1848 and formulated in its pedagogical application in an exemplary manner by Adolf Diesterweg.[64]

This belief in the common (i.e., nonconfessional, but not necessarily nonselective) school became a deeply held article of faith of Liberals; it would be reflected in the Weimar Constitution and, in a crisis over school legislation in 1927–28, caused the government to fall and fatally alienated the Liberal and Catholic political parties, contributing to the political victory of the National Socialists several years later.

In his discussion of how that crisis played out in Baden, Fritz describes how

> Liberals emphasized the destructiveness of class and religious divisions and argued that all segments of society had to cooperate in rebuilding the German nation. "The state," they asserted, "must be filled with *Volksgeist* [spirit of the people]; the *Volk* must be filled with *Staatsgeist* [state idea]." Such pleas for unity betrayed a deeply held belief in the value of social synthesis. Indeed, German liberals traditionally had focused on an allegedly nonpartisan common good rather than on partisan interests. Moreover, the German bourgeoisie in general strongly preferred the notion of "community as a whole" to pluralistic ideas . . . bourgeois liberals tended to view common schools as a counterweight to political factionalism and social particularism, as an invaluable tool for integrating all Germans into the state. Furthermore, common schools, liberals asserted, would contribute to the "ethical character-building of youth on German *voelkisch* foundations" because such schools were rooted in the people. Common schools, then, rooted in "the essence" of the *Volk* and idealistic, were viewed as a vital spiritual component of a democratic state. Common schools thus illustrated liberal concern for the well-being of the people. Indeed, as a unifying element in German society, common schools could be seen as a basic neighborhood unit of the *Volksgemeinschaft*.[65]

As we will see, it was the Nazis who finally implemented the nonconfessional common school, employing much the same rhetoric that had defined the Liberal position for many decades . . . and precisely the same themes of social unification through the common school became a mainstay of Communist educational policy in the German Democratic Republic (DDR).

By the time in the last third of the century when the vertically structured system of schooling with its three distinct branches (*Gymnasium, Realschule, Hauptschule*) had been implemented, the movement for the unitary school defined the self-understanding of teachers working in *Volksschule*. It is easy to understand why. After all, it would have raised their status considerably to be providing the first stage of an instructional sequence running all the way up to university for the most gifted (as was, for example, the case in Scotland), rather than essentially dead-end instruction in schools to which no middle-class parents would entrust their children. Thus the Deutsche Lehrerverein (founded 1871), which eventually enrolled three-quarters of the male elementary teachers, agitated for an organizational model of schooling, which would be vertically integrated from kindergarten on;[66] Johannes Tews, in particular, argued that elementary schools had come to have the image of charity schools for poor children, and should be converted into common schools, which all children would be obligated to attend.[67]

There was also a large Catholic teachers association, and a smaller Protestant one; by 1914, 90 percent of teachers belonged to such organizations, a much higher proportion than among industrial workers or employees.[68]

When, in 1890, the Prussian government introduced a school bill intended to implement at last the provisions of the constitution of 1850, the National Liberal Party praised it for upholding "the principles that the school is a *Staatsschule* [school of the State] and that neither out of consideration for the rights of the churches nor out of consideration for the self-government of the communes should the state be restricted in respect to its right to appoint teachers and to exercise school supervision."[69] That law failed to pass, in fact, because it did not satisfy the demand of Catholics and Protestants for guarantees of the confessional character of elementary schools.

Despite all the discussion of reform, and widely noted radical criticism of German schooling by Friedrich Nietzsche, Jacob Burckhardt, and Julius Langbehn (whose *Rembrandt as an Educator* went through forty editions after it was published in 1890), the system proved remarkably difficult to change, even when the new kaiser, Wilhelm II, called an imperial school conference to demand reform.

The most important factor in favor of retaining the status quo was the bureaucratic structure into which German education had been totally integrated. All paths of preferment led through German schools. Every profession, every bureaucratic post had its educational requirements. Each state examination, whether entitling its examinee to enter a trade, to serve [only] one year in the army, or to bear an exalted title was geared to the school system . . . The teachers themselves were part of the bureaucracy. Their own status depended on their state titles—and in the case of the university and gymnasium professors, their status was very high. Is it any wonder that even the Kaiser could not dent this impenetrable apparatus . . . the Cultural Minister received fully developed plans for reform almost daily, all of which he managed to ignore.[70]

Under this profoundly rooted system, many middle class boys "between the ages of ten and twenty spent the greater part of their youth learning classical Latin and Greek, nine years of the former and six of the latter . . . Without attending a classical Gymnasium they could not attend a university or become doctors, lawyers, ministers, or professors. Nor could they enter the highest ranks of the bureaucracy."[71] On the other hand, a *Gymnasium* education was by no means essential for a good career in business or industry, nor was it apparently an important element in the rapid growth of the German economy in the last decades of the nineteenth century, when

> less than 13 thousand Prussian secondary graduates intended to enter business and the technical professions. During the same period, the *Gymnasium* alone produced about 63 thousand aspiring judges, lawyers, officials, theologians, doctors, officers, and secondary or university teachers . . . the Prussian secondary system clearly was designed to prepare for the "learned," noncommercial professions, including the high civil service.[72]

Obtaining a passing grade on the official examination (*Abitur*) at the end of secondary schooling was a vital step in this process, and few ambitious parents from the "educated classes" would risk the future success of their sons by sparing them the torments, which Thomas Mann described so vividly in *Buddenbrooks*. On the other hand, the growing class of entrepreneurs often had little use for the classical education provided by the *Gymnasium*. During this period,

> new educational institutions and curricular options began to play a significant role as "modern" alternatives to the traditional forms of secondary and higher education . . . Almost invariably, however, the newer programs failed to attain the prestige of the older ones, and their status inferiority was associated precisely with their practical bent, their positive orientation toward commerce and technology.[73]

This was a period, also, of reaction among bourgeois youth against the regimentation of the extended education to which they were subjected. There were many organizations for youth, mostly oriented toward the adult world and organized by adults—the Catholic youth movement had more than a million members—but the one which has acquired almost mythic status is that of the *Wandervogel*, made up primarily of young men from the upper middle class who were attending *Gymnasien*. It was an urban movement which rejected the city for the joys of hiking and camping, with a well-educated membership who discounted the value of their education and venerated the wisdom of the German *Volk*.

The movement began in 1896 and developed over the next years, ostensibly led exclusively by youth (they seem to have invented the phrase, "Trust no one over twenty"![74]) but with encouragement from many of progressive educators. Although their excursions were joyful—once young women were allowed to join, these included folk dancing—the movement was closely tied to the cultural pessimism of intellectual circles in the period. The *Wandervogel* believed that, rejecting the values and goals of the older generation, and substituting for them the cultivation of their own free personalities and getting in touch with the essential qualities of the German people, they could become *neue Menschen*, a new sort of human being. Much as they exalted the *Volk*, however, they were skeptical about democracy and saw themselves as a leadership elite with access to superior understanding. What is more, the exaltation of comradeship on long hikes and singing around campfires only increased the frustration experienced when it became necessary to face the constraints of careers and a political system unresponsive to their vision for a renewed Germany. After World War I, some of the former *Wandervogel* found attractive the Nazi emphasis on youth and on creating a new personality type incorporating the best of what it meant to be German.[75]

Some of the earmarks of the *Wandervogel*, such as the principle of following the leader (*Fuehrer-Gefolgschafts-Prinzip*) and the greeting *Heil!* would take on a sinister resonance when they were adopted by the Nazis in their mobilization of German youth.[76] Many of its members were deeply influenced by a book published anonymously in 1890, *Rembrandt as an Educator*, in which Julius Langbehn charged that German culture was being destroyed by rationalism and could be renewed only by the leadership of artistic individuals who would teach Germans to value the instinctual and would create an education in which the intellect would take second place. "The new intellectual life of the Germans," Langbehn concluded in his immensely popular book, "is not a matter for professors, but for the German youth, especially for the uncorrupted, un-miseducated and uninhibited youth. Right is on its side."[77]

With the revolution of 1918, it appeared for a time that German schools would become structurally unitary—at least until adolescence—and also lose their confessional character. A political struggle developed during the writing of a constitution between those supporting confessional schools and those who wanted to use education as a means of developing common loyalties to the new political system, what they referred to as a "school of national unity." Prussian Minister of Culture Carl Heinrich Becker stated in 1919 that Germany needed a cultural policy consisting of "the conscious employment of spiritual values in the service of the people and of the state to achieve internal consolidation and strength for external competition and struggle with other peoples."[78] The idea of using education as an instrument of state policy thus continued to be a central element in the agenda of the post-war liberal democracy.

The most solid accomplishment of the Weimar Republic in educational policy was the adoption of the common *Grundschule* in place of the great variety—and unequal level of expectations—of public elementary schools throughout the nineteenth century. One historian has called this "an almost unparalleled series of measures for educational equality";[79] certainly it is comparable to the adoption of the comprehensive secondary school in England in the 1960s. In other respects, however, hopes for educational reform were frustrated by the political paralysis, which characterized the period, and by the lingering "cultural pessimism" among educated Germans, many of whom were shaped by the *Wandervogel* movement of the pre-war years. Having hoped for a renewal of culture on a distinctively German basis, they saw the post-war regime as aping the worst features of liberal democracy, even as an imitation of what was considered American superficiality.

> For large segments of the educated classes, the Weimar Republic was discredited in advance, morally bankrupt before it was established. For four years the Germans had battled the West, and many of them elevated that struggle too into the metaphysical realm, believing the Germanic and the Western characters were antithetical. When the republic did come, it was almost a parody of their fears. This was the Liberal state as they had dreaded it—divided, defenseless, and defeated, the victim of selfish interests at home and abroad.[80]

One of the unresolvable issues, which undermined the Weimar Republic was a struggle over whether public schools should have a confessional character. Although the Social Democrats—opponents of confessional schooling—were the largest party in the National Assembly elected in 1919, they were forced into compromise with the Catholic Center Party and Protestant conservatives who would not vote for either a new constitution or the Treaty of Versailles absent a promise to protect confessional public schools.[81] The compromise was to leave the decision about whether schools would be organized on a confessional basis up to "those entitled to determine the education of the children," though with a provision that the "Christian interdenominational school [*christlichen Gemeinschaftsschule*]" would be the norm unless parents requested otherwise. In one significant change, clergy supervision of schools—which had become more a burden than a source of real authority for most pastors—was abolished.

While in most of Germany this compromise protected the existing confessional schools (even as it proclaimed the nonconfessional common school as the norm), in areas where confessional schools did not exist, it failed to respond to the demand of the Catholic Center Party that they be created if parents so demanded.

> In the southwestern states of Baden and Hesse "simultaneous" or "common" schools (*Simultanschulen*) prevailed. These schools combined all denominations into one

local school, encouraged secular instruction, and sanctioned a "mixed" faculty. Religious instruction was provided in separate classes for the various confessions, but religion was taught more as a literary or cultural subject than as an object of faith or catechistical tutelage. The common schools in Baden had been established in a flush of progressive enthusiasm by a liberal-dominated legislature in the 1860s. Despite a Catholic majority, Baden long had been considered the most liberal of the German states. Grand Duke Frederick displayed an ardent liberal partisanship, whereas the National Liberal party, numerically strong and in favor with the government, disclosed a confident outlook bordering on arrogance. The National Liberals maintained a stranglehold on state politics and systematically blocked Catholic demands for more equitable treatment and better representation in the legislature.[82]

Over the next several years, efforts at the national level by the Center Party to open the way for confessional schools in such areas would lead to a political crisis, which severely weakened the alliance of moderate parties on which the Weimar Republic depended.

Article 120 of the Weimar Constitution provided that "the education of their children for physical, intellectual and social efficiency is the highest duty and natural right of parents, whose activities shall be supervised by the political community," while Article 144 stated that "the entire educational system stands under the oversight of the State, which can share this with the [local] communities." As Helmreich observes, this careful balance "was directed against the extreme Socialist demand for 'community upbringing' (Gemein-schaftserziehung), but it was also aimed at the Catholic theory that parents' rights over their children's education were outside the sphere of the state."[83]

Another article of the constitution "prohibited the federal states from changing the existing organization of their school systems until the enactment of the Reich school law," and, in fact, "the stalemate produced by the failure of repeated attempts to pass school legislation in the Reichstag enabled confessional schools to thrive."[84]

Nonconfessional schools prevailed in the states of Baden, Hesse, Saxony, and Thuringia and in the city-states of Bremen and Hamburg, but only about 4 percent of the schools in Prussia were nonconfessional by 1931, and 92 percent of Catholic schoolchildren and 95 percent of Protestant schoolchildren in Prussia were attending schools of their own confessions.

There were, in fact, four authorized alternatives: the "common" Christian interdenominational public school; the confessional public school (considered an alternative to the first, but, in fact, much the dominant variation); the "worldview" school; and the "free secular [weltliche] school."[85] Schools based on a worldview were those whose distinctiveness was not religious but based on some form of humanistic pedagogy. In addition, nongovernment elementary schools could be established if "there is in the municipality no public elementary school of their religious type or of their worldview, or if the [public] educational administration recognizes a special pedagogical interest."

As a result of this process of compromise, Article 146 of the constitution provided that "the public educational system is to be structured organically," by which was meant the vertical integration urged by Suevern and others: in principle all children would attend the same common primary school (*Grundschule*) before going on to one or another form of intermediate and secondary education. Since the 1890s, there had been proposals to institute such common schools (*Einheitsschule*), "a single institution of primary and secondary schooling with a diversified curriculum in the upper grades . . . Despite determined resistance from conservatives and unfortunate entanglements in confessional conflicts, presecondary and private primary schools were gradually abolished during the 1920s. All pupils were henceforth to receive four years of common elementary schooling in the . . . *Grundschule*."[86]

The article further specified that

> for the admission of a child to a particular school, his gifts and interests, not the economic and social position or the religious confession of his parents, is decisive. In each community, therefore, elementary schools will be established based upon the confessional or worldview demand of those responsible for education [i.e., parents or guardians], provided that a well-organized school system is not affected thereby. The desires of those responsible for education are to be respected so far as possible.[87]

This compromise left room for each group to press for its preferred type of school at the local level. Socialists could seek "secular" schools; Liberals could insist that interconfessional schools were the norm unless parents asked for an alternative, and Catholics and Protestants could count on most parents to request continuation of the existing arrangements. Indeed, rivalry over the religious character of public schools "lasted for the entire Weimar Republic and exceeded in intensity and scope all other educational policy conflicts."[88] These came to a head in 1927, when a bill was finally filed to implement the educational provisions of the Weimar Constitution. This bill, prepared largely by the Center Party (which had agreed to join a coalition government) would have established the complete equality of common and confessional schools, as had the Dutch Constitution adopted a decade before. "Furthermore, the school bill implicitly favored confessional schools, since it required a petition by a given number of parents to establish a new type of school, and the great majority of existing schools in Germany were confessional. Moreover, confessional schools were to be permitted in formerly exclusive common school areas such as Baden."[89]

There was an immediate uproar, with Liberal charges that this violated the constitutional preference for the nonconfessional school. A government education official who had been ousted by the devoutly Protestant new interior minister charged that the school bill signified "an assassination of the spirit of a democratic community," a "deadly sin against the . . . young republic," and a "blow against ideological tolerance, which the . . . republic [desperately] needs." The Baden Teachers Association predicted that the education bill would lead to conflicts within communities and would undermine respect for the constitution. Most ominously, Adolf Hitler joined in the attack with a speech in which he attacked the government's education bill as "a malicious example of drowning the nation in a flood of particularism," and urged "the bourgeoisie to examine and support the Nazi vision of a classless, united Germany."[90]

The school bill failed, but the struggle and passions which it aroused— like the *Kulturkampf* to which Catholics likened it—had dire effects for the fragile German democracy.

> The worsened Catholic-Liberal relations contributed to a split in the bourgeois middle, making political cooperation more difficult and hindering a moderate evolution of the Weimar state. Moreover, the bitterness and anger felt by both Catholics and Liberals as a result of the school fight unintentionally aided a growing bourgeois demoralization and sense of despair. With continuing bourgeois fragmentation, menacing new splinter parties such as the Nazis were offered a fertile ground for manipulation and exploitation. *Kulturpolitik* itself further split the Center, intensifying internal conflicts and standing as a block to active and fruitful cooperation with Liberals.[91]

Amid this political turmoil, the great majority of public elementary schools continued to be either Protestant or Catholic in Prussia and Bavaria until after the National Socialists came to power in 1933. Even the nominally interdenominational schools found in some areas were often de facto confessional; the population was so overwhelmingly Protestant in some areas and so overwhelmingly Catholic in others that provision was made only for one form of religious instruction and children of the other confession might attend nongovernment Catholic or Protestant schools, which received a subsidy from public funds. In 1932, just before the Nazi takeover, there were roughly 4,560,000 Protestant elementary schoolchildren in Germany, of whom 3,365,000 (74 percent) attended Protestant public schools; 1,142,000 (25 percent) attended interdenominational public schools; 24,000 attended Catholic public schools; 29,000 attended secular public schools; and 17,000 attended nongovernment schools. Catholic students were even more concentrated in confessional schools with 2,295,000 (85 percent) of 2,702,000 attending Catholic public schools; 337,000 (12 percent) attending interdenominational public schools; 64,000 (2 percent) attending Protestant public schools; 6,000 attending secular public schools; and 17,000 attending nongovernment schools. There were in that year altogether 52,959 publicly supported elementary schools in Germany of which 29,020 (55 percent) were Protestant; 15,256 (29 percent), Catholic; 8,291 (16 percent), interdenominational; 295 (1 percent), secular; and 97, Jewish.[92]

Despite this measure of structural diversity, German education was not marked by a commitment to parental choice. It was the rights of the established Catholic and Protestant churches rather than those of individual parents that accounted for diversity in elementary schooling, and it was selection by schools rather than by parents that marked secondary education.

AUSTRIA

During the period of political agitation around 1848, Austrian Liberal reformers gained power briefly, and sought to bring education under the direct control of the State rather than of the Catholic Church while promoting reforms of university education comparable to those in Germany—"that we honor as models of thorough scholarly education," according to the new minister of public instruction—over the previous forty years.[93] In July 1849, they produced a plan for the reorganization of secondary schools, with an eight-year *Gymnasium*, preparing for universities and a six-year *Realschule* (without Latin), preparing for technical colleges; this remained the norm for more than a century. In a compromise with the Church, they included a preamble, which stated that the goal of all secondary schooling was moral and religious development, though what this meant was left undefined.[94] Later, as we will see, the order of these goals was reversed to "religious and moral"!

One of the effects of the 1848 revolution in Austria was that State officials "now gained a more unified and centralized control over all the crown lands than they had enjoyed at any previous time in the monarchy's history." The reforms of the educational system, which had been carried out during the brief period of Liberal ascendancy strengthened the central authorities in their efforts to achieve the (partial) rationalization of the system. Leo Thun, the minister of religion and instruction from 1849 to 1860 was convinced that the State must take the lead to raise academic standards and transform curricula while continuing to assign to the Catholic Church an important role in supervising and even providing public *Volksschulen*.[95]

The period of reaction in Austria after the 1848 revolution led to a concordat with the Vatican in 1855, confirming an unprecedented degree of Church supervision of the content of Catholic religion courses, which were mandatory for all children baptized as Catholics, whether their parents wanted them to receive such instruction or not, and approval of religion teachers. As political controversies in subsequent decades, even after the abolishment of the monarchy in 1918, would show, the State was unwilling to give up providing Catholic religious instruction in public schools where it could be kept safely under government control. Austrian Liberals

> much preferred the evil that they knew to the imponderables of complete religious freedom, and they agreed to favor some religions with recognition by the state together with paying the salaries of clerics. They made a nod in the direction of freedom of conscience by saying anyone could worship in private as he wished but a religious organization had to be legally recognized to conduct public services or proselytize. Even irreligious liberals did not want Muslims or Baptists disturbing the serenity of Austria or making claims on the state for financial support.[96]

The central government in Vienna, strengthened in the aftermath of the 1848 revolution, "had the authority to establish standards and basic procedures for all levels of public education . . . The same regulations were binding on all institutions that wanted public accreditation even though community and provincial governments had financial and operating responsibilities for the primary schools and many secondary schools."[97]

The Austrian Imperial Primary School Law (*Reichsvolksschulgesetz*), adopted in 1869, "provided for mandatory free primary education under secular state control for boys and girls from six to fourteen," though implementation was very uneven. "The new regulations obliged the local authorities to operate general *Volksschulen* with an eight-year program or, alternatively, five-year *Volksschulen* with separate three-year *Buergerschulen*."[98] This extension of the period of compulsory schooling from six to eight years aroused strong opposition from peasants who saw no reason for depriving them of the labor of their children for such a useless purpose; provision was finally made in 1883 for leaving school after six years. Despite such resistance, "the improvement in education was quickly noticeable. While 57 percent of school age children attended school in 1869, the figure stood at 83 percent in 1883. Army recruits who could read and write their names rose from 45 percent in 1870 to 67 percent in 1883."[99]

By 1908, the Austrian educational system included *Volksschulen*

> with one to eight classes depending on local circumstances. All eight grades might be together in one class in the countryside. The *Buergerschulen* were elementary schools with three classes taught according to subjects with specialization by teachers. Located in the cities, these schools contained only 5 percent of the students in 1913. Teacher training academies were four year schools predominantly run by the church, which trained children from the age of fifteen in pedagogical techniques to be used in elementary schools . . . the *Realschulen* were seven year schools, which stressed science and technology . . . The three kinds of gymnasia, Classical, Real, and Reformreal, all provided preparatory work for entrance into the university . . . [100]

On the eve of World War I, however, academic secondary schools in the Austro-Hungarian Empire enrolled only about 3 percent of youth aged 11 to 18.[101]

The situation of Austria—the German-speaking remnant of the Austro-Hungarian Empire—was even more desperate than was that of Germany in the immediate wake of the war. Despite the economic crisis and the loss of most of the territory, which had previously been ruled from Vienna, "the church-state controversy divided Austria more than any other issue in the crucial years of writing the constitution." In part this was because of an unusual geographic situation: in the shrunken territory of Austria, the city of Vienna represented one-third of the population, and was politically controlled by Socialists, while Catholics had the upper hand in the provinces.

> The constitution of 1920 became a monument to the struggle when it was adopted without articles regulating church–state relations and with an especially prominent gap on the distribution of authority in the schools between the federal government and the provinces, which did little to disguise the fact that the basic conflict was over religious education . . . Indeed, the parties have become so jealous of the issue that . . . any law dealing with primary or secondary schools requires the same two thirds majority needed for a constitutional amendment.[102]

The most important advocate of progressive reform of the Austrian educational system during the period between the wars was socialist leader Otto Gloeckel of Vienna, a "fiery anticlerical" whose "ultimate goal was a secular, unified school of eight grades in which all children regardless of social background would study together during the eight years of compulsory education without being broken up into groups after five grades when the gymnasia skimmed off various social and academic elites." Paradoxically, "while he was one of the best influences on school reform, he was one of the worst influences on polarizing Austrian political life between the laws. He participated as a full contributor to the tragedy of the First Republic, tainted as so many others by the degree of ideological emphasis he brought to the struggle." In 1919, serving briefly as national undersecretary for instruction, Gloeckel issued a decree that no child could be required to attend "religious exercises" at public elementary or secondary schools, except when that was required by provincial law. This Gloeckel Decree "caused an immediate reaction and remained a source of bitter contention for fourteen years,"[103] until the authoritarian Dollfuss regime.

Why such a "conscience clause" should have been so bitterly opposed by the Catholic Church at the time requires some explanation, since it would now be considered completely consistent with Catholic teaching. The issue was that most Austrian children, even those whose parents were indifferent to or even opposed to Catholicism or to religion in general, were baptized as Catholics as a matter of custom. The Church was unwilling to refuse them baptism in view of the belief that unbaptized persons faced eternal peril; on the other hand, having baptized them, the Church considered these children— thus, virtually every child in Austria—its special responsibility, even if parents were failing to raise them as Catholics, and believed it had an obligation to ensure that baptized children received religious instruction and participated in religious exercises.

Austrian Socialists were equally determined to win the battle over the religious character of schooling. "Attacks on the church in the socialist press were frequent." In 1921 Marxist theorist Otto Bauer described "school reform as a revolutionary victory in the class struggle." The high stakes seemed to justify the use of such undemocratic measures as regulatory decrees, which had not been approved by the parliament. As a national education official and then, for much longer, as unchallenged head of schooling in Vienna, Gloeckel "forced change at a pace even his allies conceded was too fast. His methods were at once energetic, effective and dangerously partisan at a time when reform depended not only on the strength of ideas but on the ability to persuade half the population that reforms did not threaten values they held to be important." In his eighteen months as national official, he issued sixty-seven major and many minor decrees and instructions, a pace comparable to that employed several years later by the fascist government in Italy.[104]

Reform included, Gloeckel and others believed, a pedagogical approach with three elements: "instruction (1) should have a basis in the life of the pupil (*Bodenstaendigkeit*), (2) should be integrated on the elementary level (*Gesamtunterricht*), and (3) should involve the pupil actively (*Selbsttaetigkeit*) . . . for example, in using a trip down the Danube to teach history, literature and art." Ironically, these principles would later be invoked by Catholics to justify the practices, which they advocated. For example, when Gloeckel— as head of education in Vienna—disciplined religion teachers for asking children whether they had attended mass on the previous Sunday, Catholics contended that this was simply a good example of *Selbsttaetigkeit*. Taking pupils to local religious shrines was "learning by doing," a good progressive education principle.[105]

By 1925, the archbishop of Vienna had concluded that it was impossible to retain the Catholic character of public schools in the city, and called for establishment of a separate, publicly funded, Catholic system; there was considerable interest, in particular, in the Dutch model. Other bishops, from parts of the country where the public schools had not been secularized, did not support this solution and continued to insist upon Catholic instruction and exercises in the public schools. The Austrian prime minister, himself a Catholic priest, insisted that "the school systems could not be separated without giving up claims to have the state enforce attendance at Catholic schools for all Catholics"; it could open the door to the complete secularization of public schools in a country where, at least officially, 95 percent of the population was Catholic.[106]

Despite these bitter conflicts over the role of religion in schools, Austria made more progress than did Germany during the 1920s in creating a vertically integrated system of schooling allowing the more able pupils to progress through a coherent sequence.[107]

This is perhaps the best place to discuss the changes in Austrian education under the authoritarian regime that seized power in 1933–34 and ruled until Hitler's annexation of Austria in 1938. While some would consider this "fascist" regime together with that of the Nazis in Germany, in fact, its totalitarian ambitions were much more modest and, with respect to education, might best be compared with the Franco government in Spain or the Vichy government in France during World War II.[108] Without making excuses for generally loathsome regimes, it is a fact that in each case they were restrained— as the Nazis were not—in their use of schooling for indoctrination by the political necessity of an alliance with the Catholic Church.

The Austrian government of Chancellor Engelbert Dollfuss and his successor, Kurt von Schuschnigg, counted on schools and youth organizations to promote a strong and romantic sense of Austrian nationality, something which had never developed over the centuries of Austrian leadership of a multinational empire.

> Austrian patriotic education before 1918 had focused on the Habsburg dynasty, which represented the whole of the multinational empire. There was no specifically Austrian consciousness. To the extent that Austrians identified with an ethnic nation, they considered themselves Germans . . . With the collapse of the Habsburg empire, however, the traditional object of Austrian patriotism disappeared. At the same time, political and economic considerations made unification with the new federal German republic attractive.[109]

It was to counter this attraction to merger into a greater Germany—an attraction that would be satisfied with the Anschluss in 1938—that Austrian schools began using elementary readers with titles like *My Fatherland, My Austria, O Thou My Austria, I Am an Austrian,* and *The Austrian Has a Fatherland.*

> Development of the intellect became secondary to appealing to students' emotions. The schools and youth groups were not only supposed to tell students that they owed absolute devotion to the *Volk* and the state; they were also to foster this devotion by organizing all school and youth group activities so as to arouse a desire to participate in the greater national cause. They organized social activity around a patriotic idea and used symbols and rituals to constantly reinforce the young person's sense of belonging to the national community. Belonging to the nation elevated the individual by allowing each person to identify with its greatness. At the same time, the community demanded the subordination of the individual to the larger whole. In this manner, the state hoped to channel and intensify the natural idealism of youth in the service of the state. In some ways, though, the Austrian educational reform differed significantly from the Nazi and fascist programs, since the clericofascists made Catholicism a cornerstone of their ideology. The Catholic Church bolstered the authoritarian state because it taught unquestioning faith and obedience to a great cause. Emphasizing universal Christian principles, however, the clericofascist ideology rejected the social Darwinism and glorification of violence that characterized other "fascist" movements. The clericofascists did introduce militarist elements into public education, but they did not propagate theories of racial superiority or programs of military conquest.[110]

Chapter Six

The Civil Society Alternative

THE NETHERLANDS

A new Dutch Constitution was adopted in 1848, drafted primarily by the Liberal leader J. R. Thorbecke, often considered the greatest Dutch statesman of the nineteenth century, who was concerned to reduce the potential of conflict of the sort which had led to the Belgian secession. At this time, it should be noted, only 6.4 percent of the population was entitled to vote, and so the parliament reflected only very inadequately the state of popular opinion.[1] As early as 1829, Thorbecke had published an anonymous pamphlet calling for educational freedom and suggesting that public schooling should become the exception and schools created by the initiative of citizens the rule. His concern was not to promote faith-based schools but rather to reduce the role of the State.[2] State monopoly of schooling, he had charged, was a relic of the French Revolution and Napoleon. Napoleon had tried to use this monopoly, Thorbecke wrote, to win youth over to his side and enlist them for his military purposes.[3] The new constitution, adopted partly in response to the new political upheavals that year in France and elsewhere,[4] reflected the Liberal desire to reduce the supervision of the state over society, though it began by reiterating the state's ultimate responsibility for education:

> Public education is a matter of continuing concern of the government. The arrangements of public education, with respect for everyone's religious convictions, shall be regulated by law. In all parts of the kingdom public authorities shall provide public elementary education. Providing education is free, under the oversight of the authorities and, in addition, with respect to secondary and elementary

education, subject to investigation of the qualifications and the moral character of the teachers, both of which are to be regulated by law. (Article 194)

The legislators were willing to accept the principle of educational freedom, but conditioned its exercise on a number of conditions. Retention of the language first introduced in 1815 about the "continuing concern of the government" was a signal that public schooling was to be in a preferred position. Attempts were made to add a stipulation that "in every community, without exception, the authorities must offer adequate public education," but this was softened to the form eventually adopted in Article 194.

There were also differing understandings of the meaning to attach to the phrase "providing education is free."

> The Conservatives understood it to mean the freedom to provide private education—freedom for a teacher to establish a private school, but only if local authorities deemed one necessary. Catholics argued that "freedom of education" was an individual right—the freedom of an individual or individuals to establish private schools. The Liberals, like the Conservatives, understood "freedom of education" to mean the freedom of teachers to give education but not the right of parents to determine the kind of education they wished for their children.[5]

Hofstede de Groot, now also chairman of the Dutch Teachers' Fellowship, published a book that criticized the extension of educational freedom in the new constitution, in terms that have been heard more recently in the American debates over "vouchers." He charged that it would permit schools to be opened in which "all sorts of socially disruptive tenets could be imprinted in youth, tenets of riot, assassination, class hatred, deceit, plunder, communism, religious warfare, atheism." Would the State really give up its control over schooling, "by which alone the population can make a good use of their rights and truly form one Nation. How would that make any sense?" Because of the two sharply divided religious camps in The Netherlands, the common schools would in an instant become sectarian schools, and religious warfare would soon follow.[6]

Even before adoption of enabling legislation, some 150 new private schools were established.[7] All difficulties had not been removed, however, despite the new constitutional guarantee. In some cases, village public schools were converted to private status by demand of the local parents, but in other communities—where leadership remained in the hands of a theologically liberal or secular elite—local authorities refused approval of schools that would compete with the public school.[8]

It was not until 1857 that the parliament managed, after repeated failures, to adopt a new law governing elementary education (meanwhile, in Prussia, a similar requirement to adopt such a law was avoided for decades more, demonstrating how difficult it was to reach agreement in this sensitive area), replacing that of 1806. One of the unsuccessful bills had provided that public schools could have a denominational character when local circumstances made that practical—thus prescribing only a "relative neutrality" dependent upon the presence or absence of pupils who might be offended—but this was rejected by those who insisted upon an "absolute neutrality" that took no account of local religious sentiments.[9]

The 1857 law gave more responsibility to local authorities that appointed local school committees to oversee the schools. While there were still government inspectors, these came to have a less direct contact with schools.[10] The law maintained the nonconfessional public school, though in areas with an overwhelmingly Protestant or Catholic population the school inevitably took on the character of its environment.[11] It also made it easier to gain approval for private schools, though an effort to include subsidies from the national government for private schools was eliminated during floor debate; local community or provincial subsidies were possible.[12] The law most notably put in place a number of provisions to improve the quality of instruction and of school facilities. There was a noticeable shift from the idea that schooling was concerned with maintaining the existing social order and perpetuating the class position of pupils to the idea that it could in fact serve social mobility. The 1857 law provided that

> primary education, while teaching applied and useful skills, shall be made service-able to the development of the rational capacities of the children and to their rearing in all Christian and social virtues [a reversal of the order of terms from the 1806 law]. The educator shall refrain from teaching, doing, or permitting anything in conflict with the respect owed to the religious ideas of dissenters. Provision of education in religion shall be left to the churches. For this purpose, classrooms shall be made available to pupils of the school outside school hours.

Dodde notes that "the Christian and social virtues, to which [children] should be educated, had in 1857 more a humanistic than the religious meaning they had had in 1806."[13] After 1857, the public school provided no religious instruction at all, at least officially, though in many cases the Bible continued to be read; sometimes this was in an attempt to head off the establishment of a private confessional school.[14] The fact that this law was enacted by a coalition of Liberals and Catholics would be a source of encouragement to Belgian

Liberals, who hoped to find similar support for the elimination of religious instruction from public schools; "for the first time, in a nation of the Old World, separation of Church and State had been consistently applied in the area of elementary schooling."[15] The Liberals would be disappointed.

Dutch Prime Minister van der Brugghen, though an orthodox Protestant and—until their disagreement over the 1857 law—an ally of Groen van Prinsterer, rejected the latter's goal of re-establishing a "Christian State." "I can look upon Christianity only as a moral life-force," he told Parliament in 1856, "as a leaven mixed into all spheres of life." Earlier he had written to a fellow reformer, "If a Christian consciousness is raised up among the people, there will be Christian schools. It is no use to force them upon those who don't want Christian education." Thus he supported strictly neutral public schools, with full freedom and state support for private schools.[16] Reluctantly, Groen came around to the same position, and urged that the language about "Christian virtues" be removed from the education law, since it created a misleading confidence on the part of many parents.[17] In an 1862 speech in parliament, he said that he had wanted close collaboration of Church and State when it was possible to think of the State as being Christian, but there was nothing to be gained from an understanding with the present State: "Separation is now our desire."[18]

Despite the efforts of Groen and others, the growth of private confessional schooling was initially rather slow, in part because The Netherlands were going through a difficult period economically. Another factor was the informal religious character of many public schools in Catholic and to some extent in Protestant areas. Braster notes that the Catholic legislators from the heavily Catholic south, contented with the local public schools, all voted for the 1857 law, while those from the largely Protestant north all voted against it. In 1858 only thirteen new Christian schools were established, another six in 1859, and eleven in 1860. The proportion of pupils enrolled in public schools dropped only from 79 percent to 75 percent between 1857 and 1876.[19]

While the 1857 law disappointed those who had hoped for funding of private schools, it was also a matter of grave concern to the advocates of religiously neutral schooling to which "all children would go, undivided." Members of the Maatschappij tot Nut van 't Algemeen were concerned that confessional schools—particularly if subsidized—might squeeze out public schools in many communities, especially those with a heavily Catholic population. "Every penny given to the 'school with the Bible,'" a liberal Protestant pastor preached, "contributes to an increase of division among our people."[20] It had been in response to this concern that language was inserted in Article 194 requiring that public elementary education be available everywhere.[21]

The schools that, over the years, had been founded by the Nut as models for nonconfessional schooling of good pedagogical quality were mostly taken over by local authorities as public schools.[22]

In order to help with the costs of schools founded to teach on the basis of an orthodox Protestant worldview, the Association for Christian National Primary Education was established in 1860, based on "the unchangeable truths, whose living power for Church and School was revealed with a richly blessing splendor in this land in the period of the Reformation," with Groen van Prinsterer as its honorary chairman. Funds were raised from wealthy sponsors to support individual schools. In 1868, the groups that had seceded from the Hervormde church started their own Association for *Gereformeerde* Primary Education, and the two groups often cooperated. Finally, in 1969, the various organizations concerned to promote Protestant schools would unite.[23]

Meanwhile, inspired in part by the 1864 papal encyclical *Quanta Cura*, the Catholic bishops began to promote private Catholic schooling, and issued an instruction in 1868 that every Catholic child must receive a Catholic education.[24] The same year, the Nut sent a notice to its 300 local chapters warning of "an ecclesiastical movement aimed against the neutral school,"[25] and calling on them to work to increase support for public schools.

In effect, both orthodox Protestants like Groen van Prinsterer and Catholics had realized at last that the effort to create a public system divided on confessional grounds—as in Prussia and some other German states—was hopeless, and turned to seeking public support for private schools. Even before such support was obtained in Utrecht by 1875, 55 percent of the pupils were in Protestant, 11 percent in Catholic, and 2 percent in nonconfessional private schools, leaving only 32 percent in the public schools.[26]

For seventy years, until the Pacification in 1916–20, one of the dominant issues in Dutch political life was the so-called school struggle (*schoolstrijd*) over, first, the freedom to establish and operate nonstate schools with a confessional basis and, second, the right to public funding for these schools. The freedom was already implicit in the 1806 legislation, but the conflicts which had led to the separation of Belgium made it clear that it should be anchored more firmly in fundamental law.

The Dutch "school struggle" (*schoolstrijd*) had three phases: from 1830 to 1848 it was about challenging the state monopoly in the name of educational freedom; from 1848 to 1857 it was about the character of public schools, whether they would be Christian or not; while from 1857 to 1917 it was about the effort to put private Christian schools on the same footing with public schools.[27]

One of the aspects of the Hervormde church to which the separatists had objected in the 1830s was the reorganization in 1816 (as the new kingdom was being established) that tied the church more closely to the government. This was objectionable to those who held to the arrangements which had been sanctioned by the Synod of Dordt two centuries before.[28] This objection, at least, was removed in 1852, when members of the local community were given the authority to choose their own church leaders and to call their pastors.[29] After many delays in implementation, the first such elections were held in 1867, with considerable success for the more orthodox members of the Hervormde church. In 1870, the church in Amsterdam had its first opportunity to call a pastor under this arrangement, and the orthodox majority chose a young pastor named Abraham Kuyper (1837–1920) of whom the world would hear more. His first battles—before he became involved with the school issue—was over whether the church should be congregational (*vrije kerk*) or a semi-established "people's church" governed by a national synod. "Within the Dutch Hervormde church, as it were, a double struggle ensued: struggle between orthodox and modernists and also struggle between supporters of a free church . . . and supporters of a people's church."[30] The result was a second separatist movement in 1886, this time more "mainstream" than the *Afscheiding*, known as the Doleantie, led by Kuyper and others and resulting in the Gereformeerde Church—really, one should say churches, for there was a succession of further schisms.

Kuyper had already distinguished himself with a book criticizing the Maatschappij tot Nut van 't Algemeen for its campaign against the development of private confessional schooling.

> For the sake of tolerance, the "Nut" seeks to remove every conviction that raises itself above the superficial. It wants unity, but the false kind that is created through killing life . . . A specific, a settled conviction is in its eyes a "prejudice," an "outdated," and "immoderate notion" . . . Tolerance, yes, but tolerance out of indifference, out of superficiality, out of lack of principles . . . It is the undermining of any solid conviction, under the slogan of the struggle against witch-hunts and sectarian conflict and religious hatred . . . I have no hesitation about setting against the Nut's dogma—"tolerance through removal of doctrinal differences"— this other: "respect for the convictions of other based on the solidity of one's own convictions."[31]

In 1871, Groen supported Kuyper and two others—unsuccessfully—for election to parliament, with the primary issue their demand to remove the "wretched clause" in Article 194 of the 1848 constitution that required the government to provide elementary schooling everywhere in the kingdom. This clause, they pointed out, "provided a basis for setting up state schools even in small communities where there were just a few or even no pupils to attend one; parents who sent their children to a Christian school were thereby confronted with doubled costs, since the public school had to be financed even if no one attended it."[32] In 1874, Kuyper was elected, and soon became an effective voice for orthodox Protestant concerns in parliament, including school issues.

In 1872, the *Anti-Schoolwetverbond*, or Antischool Law Association, was founded to oppose the Liberal school legislation, and many preachers and teachers from the separatist *Afgescheidenen* joined with orthodox elements within the Hervormde church (this was still before the Doleantie) to organize a movement of protest. By 1874 it had 144 chapters with more than 10,000 members.[33]

Catholics were equally active. In 1871, for example, the provincial voters association of North Brabant, a heavily Catholic area, resolved that "the voters' association demands from its candidates that they be opponents of modern liberalism, especially in its principles and positions which have been condemned by the highest church authorities, and specifically in what affects education and the relationship of Church and State." All other considerations of social or economic restructuring would take a second place. "For the present-day historian, the question of neutral versus private education, in comparison with other problems, can give the impression of a 'shibboleth' that mesmerized the Roman [Catholic] world. For the Catholics of 1870, it was the main issue in a struggle over their holiest possession: the identity of their belief and their religious community."[34]

The cost of schools in The Netherlands continued to be borne almost entirely by local authorities and by parents until 1878 when a new generation of Liberals, more committed to government intervention and less to freedom, and explicitly hostile to confessional schools,[35] enacted education legislation providing that the state would pay 30 percent of the cost of public schools, and under some circumstances even more. Other provisions of this law increased significantly the costs of all schools, whether government supported or not. The legislation was opposed by supporters of confessional education, since it would make their schools much more expensive to operate. Confessional schools would remain free, Abraham Kuyper noted, "yes, free to hurry on crutches after the neutral [school] train that storms along the rails of the law, drawn by the golden locomotive of the State."[36] If the Liberal school program prevailed, Kuyper urged, the lion—symbol of freedom—should be replaced on the shield of The Netherlands by an eagle with a lamb in its claws!

In Utrecht, for example, the new funding from the national government led to the establishment of additional public schools and a corresponding decline in the proportion of pupils attending private confessional schools. "Nonetheless, Catholics and Orthodox Reformed, firmly convinced of the need for their schools, formed more associations and built more schools. That they were not to be deterred became evident as major changes began to occur on the political level."[37]

In fairness to the Liberals, it had become clear that the system of popular schooling had many deficiencies, and increased expenditures, both by local communities and by the national government were necessary, along with higher requirements for the quality of schools. In addition, however, the Liberal legislation reflected a growing anticlericalism and even antireligious sentiment in some elite circles, which departed significantly from the traditions of Liberalism as expressed by Thorbecke and was informed by a distinctively ideological tendency. "In the eyes of the Liberals, education was pre-eminently a matter of national interest . . . In the demand for confessional education, the Liberals saw only a struggle for churchly tyranny, which would lead to a situation of divisions such as had existed before 1795. The public school was in contrast, for them, a symbol of national unity." They were afraid of the intolerance of the religious groups, "and did not see how, precisely from the perspective of liberal principles, they themselves erred."[38]

Liberal prime minister Kappeyne van de Coppello warned that making concessions to the advocates of public subsidies for confessional schools would have the result that "the men who brought us the reform of the Constitution and the constitutional order would have labored in vain . . . The struggle for liberty would have been useless . . . destroyed through the wrangles of factions. Dominance by priests and churchly intolerance would then be dominant in our country."[39] While to Thorbecke, the role of the State was to provide support for schooling but without becoming involved in the content and goals of education, "by Kappeyne it was nearly the opposite: the State, the State, and again the State; everything must derive from it, in the spirit of 'the modern worldview,' which must penetrate the entire state apparatus, in a principled struggle with churchly authority, which was on its last legs." In an important parliamentary speech in 1874, Kappeyne insisted that "the State cannot leave to chance, to arbitrariness, to the care of any association whatsoever, what belongs to it in the first place: education."[40]

Over against this emphasis of the "Young Liberals" on the supremacy of the State over civil society, Abraham Kuyper articulated what would be his influential concept of "sphere sovereignty" (*souvereiniteit in eigen kring*). The associations and institutions that make up the civil society, Kuyper insisted, should not be considered subordinate divisions of the State, enjoying only those rights and that scope which the State chooses to entrust to them, but possess their own fundamental rights deriving from the purposes for which they exist. This concept was based upon John Calvin's teaching about the "Common Grace" of divine Providence that made possible the lives of all in society, not just those who had received the saving grace of redemption from sin. As Kuyper would put it in a lecture at Princeton, the Calvinist approach to social, political, and cultural activity was informed by the belief "that in the whole world the curse [of sin] is restrained by grace, that the life of the world is to be honored in its independence, and that we must, in every domain, discover the treasures and develop the potencies hidden by God in nature and in human life." Thus there was no possibility of a retreat into private spirituality or church life: "The Calvinist cannot shut himself up in his church and abandon the world to its fate. He feels, rather, his high calling to push the development of this world to an even higher stage, and to do this in constant accordance with God's ordinance, for the sake of God, upholding, in the midst of so much painful corruption, everything that is honorable, lovely, and of good report among men."[41]

The role of the state, in this view, is to mediate among these "spheres," ensuring that justice is done, the rights of individuals are protected, and tasks that can only be undertaken by the whole society are carried out. The state must not, however, seek to take over the functions of the family, to define the canons of art or of science, to prescribe the teachings or practices of religious organizations, to tell business where to invest or how to produce, or to interfere in what occurs between teacher and pupils. Government touches upon all of those spheres of activity, of course, as it carries out its own mission, but it does so as it were from the outside, preventing abuses. The relationship between government and the other spheres of social life is thus of an entirely different nature than the relationship among levels of government.

> Autonomy of parts of a whole and sphere sovereignty of radically distinct societal relationships are principially [i.e., in principle] different matters. In a differentiated society the degree of autonomy depends upon the requirements of the whole of which the autonomous community remains a part. Sphere sovereignty, however, is rooted in the constant, inherent character of the life sphere itself. Because of their intrinsic natures, differentiated spheres like the family, the school, economic enterprise, science, and art can never be part of the state.[42]

The concept of sphere sovereignty thus goes beyond that of decentralization of decision-making or even of subsidiarity. "A truly pluralist social order seems to require recognition of the fundamental and not merely the relative independence of different spheres and institutions in a differentiated society. To achieve this recognition, the ontological status of institutions must be grasped and upheld . . . the subsidiarity-autonomy framework does not do this."[43] Sphere sovereignty insists upon the right of the school—for example—to function by its own rationality and in accordance with its own purposes, not those of government or of any other sphere (including the family or a church).

Contrary to the usual stereotype about religious leaders in politics, Kuyper's concern was not to dominate the society and culture of The Netherlands, but to make room for institutional pluralism.

> He struggled against uniformity, the curse of modern life; he wanted to see movement and contrasting colors in place of gray monotony . . . Thus the "antithesis," that originally [among orthodox Protestants] meant the unrelenting struggle against devilish modernity, with Kuyper imperceptibly [changed] to a teaching about diversity and about the independent, to-be-honored power of differences. All that was not logical . . . but it was successful and contributed to giving Dutch society a very distinctive flavor. The origin of what would later be called "pillarization" (*verzuiling*), the system through which each religious group thanks to government subsidies can create its own social world that includes everything from nursery school to sports club or professional association, lies in Kuyper's conservative love for pluriformity.[44]

Although Kuyper assumed the mantle of Groen van Prinsterer as principal spokesman for the orthodox Protestant position, he did so with a significant variation. For Groen, the school was the instrument of a Christian State or, when that State was no longer Christian, of the Church; for Kuyper, by contrast, it was the instrument of parents.[45] As a result of this shift, Protestant schools in The Netherlands, to this day, are owned by associations; they are not "church schools." Kuyper hesitated over whether Christian schools should seek subsidies from an un-Christian—perhaps even an anti-Christian State—lest that lead to unacceptable state controls.[46]

It was Kuyper who, after Groen's death in 1876, became the leader of the Anti-Revolutionary Party (ARP) and, in 1878, formulated its program demanding decentralization, reform of the voting franchise and the laws governing education, and laws protecting the lower classes. Kuyper's distinctive contribution was, in the name of God's sovereignty over all aspects of life, to give his confessional political party a strong agenda of social policies going well beyond explicitly "religious" concerns; "by associating Calvinism with social reform, Kuyper was able to bring broad, *klein* burger, sectors and even segments of the working class behind the Anti-Revolutionary movement."[47] This was the first party program in Dutch history and, in the very year when the Liberals achieved their goal of enacting legislation to place new burdens on confessional schooling, their opponents achieved the nation-wide organization that enabled them to reverse the Liberal program.[48]

The Liberals had overreached. This threat against the schools that many of them had labored to establish aroused the orthodox common people and created a movement that, in a decade, reversed the political fortunes of the Liberals and brought state support for confessional schools. A massive petition drive collected, in five days, 305,102 signatures from Protestants and 164,000 from Catholics, asking the king to refuse to sign the new legislation. When that failed, a national organization, "The Union 'A School with the Bible' " (the 'Unie') created a permanent mechanism for the mobilization of orthodox Protestants, in close alliance with the Anti-Revolutionary Party. "How our hearts vibrate with holy joy," the Unie's first annual report, in 1879, proclaimed, "whenever we remember the glorious days of the People's Petition, the blessed July days of 1878. What a calm enthusiasm among us Christian people . . . To prevent the enthusiasm from being lost, to maintain the organization, to keep the petitioners united around the 'School with the Bible,' such is the goal of the Unie."[49]

Together with the orthodox Protestant Anti-Revolutionary Party, the Catholic Party gained a majority in parliament by 1888, as a result not only of the mobilization around the schools but also of a revision of the election law the previous year which greatly extended the franchise among the (male) population, thus bringing the religiously conservative common people of the countryside and small towns into political participation for the first time. As an historian of Dutch liberalism has pointed out, the effort to smother the last flickering flame of orthodox religion only succeeded in fanning it into vigorous life, and "no one has done as much harm to liberalism as Kappeyne."[50]

Kossmann suggests that this period in The Netherlands, and also in Belgium, marked an abandonment, by religious conservatives, of the earlier effort to restrain the role of the State, and an emphasis, instead, upon building up the capacity of societal institutions to resist any overreaching by the State, and indeed to arrange for the State to subsidize the costs of these institutions in what the Belgians called "subsidized freedom" and the Dutch Christian Democrats called "social decentralization." Dutch Protestants, he notes, were as a result of several centuries of political dominance, more willing to trust government than were Dutch or Belgian Catholics who had resisted one government or another for an equal period.[51]

The phenomenon of "pillarization" (*verzuiling*) which would shape Dutch and Belgian life over the next hundred years represented an overcoming of the previous division between Liberals and Conservatives and its replacement by a division along religious or worldview lines. Within both the Catholic and Protestant "pillars" a great effort was made to build solidarity not limited by class differences; this is often described as a vertical in contrast with a horizontal integration of social groups.[52] Emancipation of the "little people" for whom their Catholic or orthodox Protestant beliefs were central, their emergence into public life, bringing their convictions with them, required intensive organization. The passions and the habits of cooperation, developed during the long struggle for confessional schooling, then found expression across the whole range of social life in both The Netherlands and Belgium. A Dutch political scientist notes that "*verzuiling* is inexplicable apart from the 'school struggle.'"[53]

The School Law of 1889 provided the same 30 percent state subsidy to confessional schools as to local government schools (the latter, of course, also received local government funding) and began a process that would lead in 1920 to the full financial equality of all schools meeting the quality requirements set by the State. The 1889 law also forbade local authorities from making their schools free, a strategy which many had employed to compete with private confessional schools.[54] It was based upon a recognition that the only solution for the continuing *schoolstrijd* was to maintain the neutrality of the public school, so that it would be accessible for all families which did not want confessional schooling while providing subsidies to private schools for those parents who wanted confessional schooling. The explanation submitted with the bill pointed out, "Now that more than 27 percent of school-attending children attend a private school, the lawmaker who wishes to promote popular schooling must take that into account . . . Established and greatly developed through private initiatives, free [i.e., nongovernment] education deserves the support of the State rather than its opposition."[55]

The enactment of this law was deeply discouraging to many members of the Nut who saw it as a political defeat which was only confirmed by the succession of governments dominated by the confessional (Protestant and Catholic parties) over the next two decades. It seemed sadly ironical that the common people in the countryside, for whom the Nut had labored in so many ways for more than a hundred years, gave their support to political parties which rejected the Nut's program of nonconfessional schooling and other social institutions.[56] Nut members considered themselves the "thinking part of the nation," and were disappointed that the people at large were not ready to follow their leadership.[57] Despite their concerns, however, when the Liberals returned to power they did not seek to reverse the 1889 law.[58]

Political initiatives in favor of public schools were supported more effectively by *Volksonderwijs* (education of the people), a militant pressure group established in 1866 to counter the growing organizations of supporters of confessional schooling, and still in existence today as the Vereniging voor Openbaar Onderwijs. Unlike the Nut, which was formally nonpolitical (though with a membership overwhelmingly opposed to public funding of confessional schools), the new organization sought to mobilize political support for a public school monopoly of popular schooling. In 1908 the Nut overcame its reservations and entered into a "covenant" with *Volksonderwijs* to work together locally to support public schools, though the alliance proved an uneasy one. The Nut's belief in nonconfessional schooling proved to be greater than its commitment to public schools as such, and in some areas the Nut took advantage of the new state subsidies to establish its own private schools. This was especially the case in the Catholic south of the country, where Nut chapters were "centers of anti-Catholicism."[59]

Meanwhile, the Unie continued to press for distinctively orthodox Protestant schooling, and Catholics insisted that Catholic schooling was essential for their children. There was a growing recognition, as expressed by an annual Unie report, that "the State as such is becoming more and more unbelieving; it wants to be neutral, but whoever wants to be neutral must have no belief, and thus be unbelieving. As a nation we can—alas!—no longer call ourselves a Christian nation."[60]

This alienation extended to public schools, which were often accused by the supporters of confessional schooling of promoting socialism and undermining patriotism. It didn't help when an organization of public school teachers gave broad distribution—350,000 copies—to a speech defending the refusal of some teachers to celebrate, with their pupils, the birth of Princess Juliana, heir to the throne, on the grounds that this would violate the neutrality of the school.[61]

A decisive turning point in the *schoolstrijd* came in 1902, when the convention of the Socialist Party in Groningen adopted a resolution calling for public funding of private schools, a position out of line with the position of its sister parties in Germany, Belgium, and France:

The congress of the SDAP calls upon the State to ensure that sufficient general compulsory primary education is universally available free of charge; deems it necessary for this purpose to raise the standard of primary schools and for the State to pay all costs and for the schools to be subject to the expert supervision of the State; acknowledges that a large proportion of the working class in The Netherlands demand religious education for their children and deems it undesirable to thwart that, since social democracy must not interfere with the unity of the working class against believing and nonbelieving capitalists in the social sphere for the sake of theological differences; demands that the private schools meet the same material requirements as the state schools, also with regard to the position of the teachers, whose independence must be guaranteed by the State, just as the parents' freedom of choice is guaranteed; and only subject to the complete fulfillment of these conditions declares itself to be in favour of measures intended to provide for equal treatment of private and state schools.[62]

This much-discussed decision was justified by the party's chairman as a way to preserve the political unity of the working class by preventing the Catholic and Anti-Revolutionary (orthodox Protestant) Parties from using support for confessional schools as a way to attract working-class support.[63] Continuation of the agitation over schools would inevitably push the more important issues of universal manhood suffrage and various forms of social legislation supported by the Socialists into the background.[64] In addition, given the reality of widespread support for these schools, equal public funding for them would be "an opportunity to bring privately run schools under the control and management of the state. In exchange for full funding, the denominational schools would have to accept more state supervision."[65]

Socialist leader Troelstra also hoped—as did many Liberals—that the confessional parties would fall apart as soon as the school issue was resolved.[66] In fact, one of the important results of the Groningen vote was to prevent the sort of alliance on the basis of anticlericalism that brought together Socialists and middle-class "Radicals" in France, and similar alliances in Belgium and elsewhere. The post-war continuation of the SDAP (which was dissolved under the German Occupation), the PdvA or Labor Party, has continued to support public funding of confessional schools. Obviously, this continuity of support helps to explain why the Dutch model of educational pluralism is stable and uncontroversial. Dissidents from the 1902 decisions were among the founders of the Dutch Communist Party a few years later, and this has continued to oppose the funding of private schools, though with little effect.

The combination of a nationwide mobilization of Catholics and orthodox Protestants around education, and the partial subsidies that began to be available for confessional schools, led to strong growth of the private sector in education. In 1870, there were 260 Protestant and 279 Catholic schools; by 1889, the number had grown to 486 and 517. There was a steady decline in the proportion of pupils attending public schools, a decline that would not be reversed—and then only slightly—for more than sixty years.[67]

Abraham Kuyper became prime minister in 1901, and three years later he proposed a new education law which provided that both private and public teachers would be paid directly by the State. There was fierce resistance from Liberals and Socialists who insisted that the public school was the "bulwark of enlightenment against the darkness" and that confessional schools were incapable of forming "real free citizens." Kuyper's bill passed, but it seemed as though the decision through compromise was as impossible as ever because of the principled opposition.[68] Another law in 1907 made private secondary schools eligible for subsidies.[69]

The 1913 elections resulted in a political stalemate in which none of the three political groupings—the Christian parties, the Liberals, and the Socialists—was able to govern. "This crisis was resolved by an arrangement in which each group got what it wanted most: The Liberal Party formed their (last) government, the Social Democrats got universal manhood suffrage, and the Christian parties got full state support for their private religious schools. The last Liberal cabinet of Cort van der Linden did put an end to the political strife that 'had succeeded in driving a wedge into our society and split our people into two peoples.' It appointed the Bos Commission in 1913, which became known as the Pacification Commission. This Commission produced its report on 11 March 1916, which accepted the principle of equal financial treatment of state and private schools."[70]

As The Netherlands sought unity in the face of the threat of the world war just beyond its borders—the commission formulated language for a constitutional provision, enacted the following year, for public subsidizing of private elementary schools that met requirements yet to be specified on the same basis as public schools. In 1920, an elementary education law to apply the new constitution was adopted by an overwhelming majority. By this time there were thirty representatives of the Catholic Party, twenty-three of the Protestant parties, twenty-five socialists, and only eighteen Liberals; in 1878, when they adopted their ill-fated school law, the Liberals had had 60 percent of the members of parliament! This power shift reflected in large part the extension of the voting franchise from 12 percent of men over twenty-three in 1887 to 52 percent of the adult men in 1897 to the universal adult franchise, including women, by 1919.[71]

Supporters of public schools, by contrast, were placed on the defensive and had difficulty defining clearly what the distinctive character of their program should be. Were they to be simply the schools for parents who had no strong preference, or could they have a distinctive educational mission of their own? If so, how was that consistent with avoiding anything that could offend anyone? Or did the "neutrality" of public schools have a strictly negative significance?[72] These questions would be asked with renewed force after World War II, as we will see.

Between the wars, political life in The Netherlands—as in Belgium—was dominated by confessional parties, but these did not use their position to seek to impose a particular worldview or political philosophy, but rather to give the divisions in society a stable organizational and institutional form, recognized in law and supported by public policies. "The chief goal of the Dutch Roman Catholic *Staatspartij* (RKSP) in these years was . . . to protect and to strengthen the Catholic community in its constantly increasing equipment with schools, associations, trade unions, and so much more."[73]

The interwar period saw a rapid shift from public to confessional schooling. Whereas, in 1850, 77 percent of Dutch elementary students attended public schools, by 1920 the proportion had dropped to 55.3 percent. After the Pacification of 1917–20, the proportion attending public elementary schools dropped to 37.7 percent by 1930 and to 26.8 percent by 1960, rising again to 31 percent in 1980, and 32 percent in 1992. Of more than one million students attending nonpublic elementary schools in 1960, 37 percent attended Protestant, and 60.4 percent, Catholic schools; by 1980 these proportions had shifted to 43 percent Protestant; 57 percent Catholic.

BELGIUM

The self-conscious educational agenda of Catholics was strengthened by the papal encyclical *Mirari Vos* (*On Liberalism and Religious Indifference*) in 1832, rejecting the efforts of Lamennais and other Catholic liberals to come to terms with various aspects of modernity. Pope Gregory XVI wrote:

Academies and schools resound with new, monstrous opinions, which openly attack the Catholic faith; this horrible and nefarious war is openly and even publicly waged. Thus, by institutions and by the example of teachers, the minds of the youth are corrupted and a tremendous blow is dealt to religion and the perversion of morals is spread. So the restraints of religion are thrown off, by which alone kingdoms stand. We see the destruction of public order, the fall of principalities, and the overturning of all legitimate power approaching.

This exhortation encouraged the effort to provide a Catholic education to every Catholic child, which in Belgium meant almost every child. Among the concrete steps taken by the bishops was the establishment of a number of Catholic teacher-training institutions; for example, in 1838 a teacher-training department was added to the minor seminary at Roeselare, and others were established the following year. In this way, teachers with the appropriate training would be available to ensure the Catholic character of public schools as well.[74]

Further support for Catholic schooling was provided by the teaching orders which expanded greatly after the removal of the barriers which had existed before 1830. The Brothers of the Christian Schools, already well established in France, were educating 7,132 Belgian pupils by 1842, and other teaching orders were founded.[75] During this period Catholic efforts to provide instruction at all levels flourished,[76] while anticlerical groups failed to match their efforts. As a Liberal would write some years later,

> If Liberals had joined together at this time, if they had, with their contributions, created schools and trained teachers, we would probably have escaped the long and ardent quarrels which have resounded in Belgium for half a century and from the intimidating difficulties which have not yet been resolved. But they made the mistake of relying too exclusively on public authorities.[77]

As the franchise was extended, government power came into the hands of their Catholic adversaries, just as occurred in The Netherlands with the confessional parties.

The moderate liberalism, committed to educational freedom, of Rogier in Belgium was replaced two decades later by a more aggressively anticlerical liberalism that sought to use popular schooling for the uplift of the Belgian people, just as in The Netherlands, the moderate liberalism of Thorbecke was replaced by the radical liberalism of Kappeyne van de Coppello. "From 1870 to 1878 the struggle of the parties developed in an atmosphere of growing irritation and, from political grounds, it tended to pass to religious grounds." Some Catholics seemed to be calling into question the constitution itself, while some anticlericals charged that members of religious orders teaching in "adopted" public schools were teaching "distrust and hatred of constitutional principles." For Liberals, beginning to experience the strains that would lead to the separation of a more radical wing and the eventual establishment of the Socialist Party, the demand that the 1842 law be revised in a way that would exclude clerical influence in public education at all levels came to be the one point on which all could agree.[78]

In 1872, a movement began to collect funds from the public to provide private secular alternatives to public schools which were perceived, by anticlerical groups, as too much permeated with religion. In imitation of Catholic collections to support the Papacy (experiencing financial difficulties because of the Italian government's seizure of Rome in 1870), the School Collection was established, with collection boxes labeled "*Denier des écoles—Schoolpenning*" in various public places, "to establish in the entire country schools which are free [i.e., private] and exclusively secular." The most significant use of the funds collected—which fell far short of the hopes of the sponsors—was to support the "model school" founded in Brussels by the Ligue de l'enseignement. The inspiration for this was the schools established in The Netherlands by the Nut to provide "by their improved programs, their rational instructional methods, the arrangement of their facilities, an example for all the schools of the country." The Brussels school, opened in 1875, offered a model of instruction which included many elements which would characterize progressive and alternative schooling in Europe and the United States. It was guided by the belief that "it is an error to think that one should teach things to children because of their use for adults." To the contrary, "the ideas presented to children should be chosen because of their actual effect" on the children. So far as possible, lessons should be given "in the presence of the things which are their object," which argued for making science—which can more readily be taught in this way—central. A special hallmark of the school was the trips which pupils took to experience the geography and cultures of Belgium.[79]

In other respects, the model school failed to serve as the intended example. For one thing, it was quite expensive and thus served primarily the children of the prosperous and liberal bourgeoisie of Brussels. Since the school was supported in part by the contributions of the general public, including many workers, this seemed inappropriate, and critics were not convinced by the claim that the intention was simply to provide a model for emulation; after all, what assurance was there that this model could in fact be replicated at a lower cost, and that workers and peasants would be as satisfied with the education that their children received in such a school? In addition, the instruction rather neglected reading and language arts in general, since "mere verbalism" did not fit with the pedagogical methods of the school, and history emphasized the immediate experience of the children rather than introducing them to the events and central characters of the past.[80] In many respects, in fact, the criticisms of the model school are those which are still made of schools influenced by progressive educational theory.

The pedagogical approach based upon student interest and immediate experience pioneered at the model school would be given official approval for elementary schools nationwide sixty years later in the government's *Plan d'études* of 1936 but, again, it did not prove a success; only a few schools implemented it, and it was criticized for a lack of emphasis upon results.[81] Arguably, the greatest impact of this school was in Spain where it served as the inspiration for the Institución Libre de Enseñanza, founded in 1876 and destined to shape several generations of anticlerical Liberals and have a significant impact on the educational policies of the Second Republic in the 1930s.

The high point of Liberal efforts to secularize Belgian education came in 1879, a year after the similar effort in The Netherlands. "Just as in the Netherlands, so also in Belgium, the form this took called forth such a rejection that their triumph, in fact, became their defeat." Although Catholics and anticlericals were embattled in many parts of Europe, in France and Italy, Germany and Spain, Kossmann claims that "nowhere was this conflict as hysterical as in the traditionally homogeneously Catholic Belgium." This judgment seems questionable—the conflict took on hysterical qualities in each of the countries—but it is certainly true that Belgian Liberals (like French "Radicals") exhausted themselves in the struggle against the Catholic Church in a way that made it difficult for them to address other social issues effectively. Anticlericalism was, in fact, the only common ground shared by the various factions within the Liberal camp.[82] Later in the century, "the Socialists saw themselves, with some pride, as carrying the Liberal program of anticlericalism further than the weak-willed Liberals had dared. Around the turn of the century, the Socialists virtually took over the Flemish Free Thinkers League . . . which Liberals had created."[83]

The radical wing of the Liberals had been calling for a reorganization of public instruction to be secular and obligatory, and they seemed to have the opportunity to carry out this program when, in the June 1878 elections, Liberals gained a majority in both houses of the parliament. In the formal statement of its policies with which it opened the legislative session, the new government stated that "public instruction should depend exclusively upon the civil authorities," which was taken by their opponents as "a declaration of war against Catholicism; one could, from that moment, consider the hostilities as officially begun."[84]

As a first step, a ministry of public education was established, and a minister—Van Humbeéck—appointed who was at the radical end of the Liberal-dominated cabinet. Catholic opponents noted that, fifteen years before, the new minister had given an address as a Masonic event at which he proclaimed that "a corpse . . . bars the way of progress; this corpse of the past, to call it squarely by its name, is Catholicism." The Catholic press began to refer to him as "the grave-digger." The situation was in fact more complicated than the rhetoric suggested. Dominant elements among the Liberals wished to avoid a damaging confrontation with the Catholic Church in order to realize other elements of their program. Many Liberals understood that the great majority of Belgian parents "wanted for their children the same religious education which they themselves had received," and that recent Liberal victories in Flanders, in particular, would be threatened by measures which prevented that. They feared that the clergy would condemn secularized public schools and provoke a general desertion of them, which, in fact, did subsequently happen. The more radical wing of the Liberals, however, insisted upon concrete anticlerical measures, and their support in parliament was essential.[85]

In January 1879, Van Humbeéck introduced a bill to modify the elementary education law of 1842, including the abolition of religious instruction as a regular part of the school program. Article 5 required that teachers "lose no opportunity to inculcate in their pupils the precepts of morality, to inspire in them the sense of duty, love for country, respect of national institutions, attachment to constitutional freedoms." At the same time, they should "abstain, in teaching, from any attack against the religious convictions of the families whose children are entrusted" to them. This language requiring respect for philosophical convictions, De Groof notes, remained in the succeeding education laws of 1884, 1895, and 1914.[86]

Each commune would be required, under the proposed law, to maintain at least one public school—not an "adopted" Catholic school—and the government would prescribe how many. Elementary schoolteachers would be required to possess a diploma from a state institution, which "tended to institute a sort of monopoly of the State with respect to the training of elementary school staff." The goal, Catholics thought, was to turn them into state functionaries, to remove local control or influence in strongly Catholic areas: "there is always more intelligence and less tyranny in a central administration than in local administrations," one Liberal wrote. The changes sought were very much parallel in their effect to those that would be instituted several years later by Jules Ferry in France, though in its focus upon securing public schools, the legislation failed to address the two most important issues from the perspective of the Liberals' social program: making schooling both free and obligatory, as would occur under Ferry's reforms.[87]

The Catholic charge that Liberals were seeking to extend state authority was not unjustified:

> The creation of the Ministry of Public Instruction, the institution of school committees which, except in [larger cities] were nothing but emanations of the central authority, the transformation of [school] inspection into a powerful state structure . . . the requirement for communal teachers to have a diploma from a state normal school, the restrictions placed upon communal prerogatives with

respect to nominating and supervising teachers or the adoption of private schools: so many dispositions which testify to a clear intention of centralization and even, in the case of teacher training, a tendency to the establishment of a virtual state monopoly. Justified by the need to defend constitutional liberties in the field of public education, and by the theory that the diffusion of elementary instruction was a matter of the general interest and therefore the communes must in this area be subjected to state tutelage, this policy went too much against the current of the independent traditions of our regions not to arouse a violent reaction. The Catholics profited from that, by posing as the great defenders of communal liberties.[88]

This excessive (for the time) expansion of the role of the State seems, Lory notes, paradoxical for a party which placed the highest value on individual independence. "Faced with a Church disposing of an enormous power of mobilization," Liberals were forced to use the State as a weapon. By limiting the autonomy of local communities, they believed, they would be liberating individuals.

This system of freedom through constraint, the distant heir of enlightened despotism, would culminate in the measures that were employed, during the period 1879–1884, to oppose the "legal resistance" of local authorities controlled by Catholics. It would contribute greatly to give liberalism an arbitrary and oppress-ive appearance, which would turn away a whole electoral clientele more attached to fundamental freedoms themselves than to a party whose practical position did not seem to correspond to its ideals.[89]

The Liberals took encouragement from the support that Dutch Catholics had given to the 1857 legislation in The Netherlands. Émile de Laveleye, an influential journalist, had published a book in 1858 describing the Dutch com-promises in glowing terms, and his was still an influential voice because of his 1872 book *L'instruction du peuple* and his continuing advocacy of an extension of the state role in education.[90] What the Liberals failed to notice was how the position of Dutch Catholics had changed during the intervening decades, partly under the influence of the 1864 encyclical *Quanta Cura* and the promotion by the bishops of private schooling.

In fact, Belgian Catholics saw in the Van Humbeéck legislation the threat of a state monopoly through militantly secular schools, and the bishops sent a letter addressed to Catholic parents, accusing the proposed legislation of being antireligious and charging that "to submit the child to the regime of a school without God is to wish to destroy in his heart the Christian life from the very start." They ordered that at every Sunday mass a prayer be added, "From schools without God and teachers without faith, deliver us, Lord!" Protest meetings were held both in cities and in the countryside, with an intensity unmatched since the movement leading to independence in 1830. A petition with 317,000 signatures was submitted to parliament, and the extensive Catholic press carried out an early example of a coordinated media campaign.[91]

Heated debate in the parliament went on for more than a month. The government's position was that "secular instruction and religious instruction must be separated. . . . We believe that in uniting them, one condemns the country, sooner or later, to disorders, to religious hatreds." One of the Catholic opposition, in criticizing the proposed marginalization of religious instruction, argued that

> in Belgium, the State, the commune, the civil authorities teach, to put it simply, as delegates of the parents . . . We do not make the absurd claim to want instruction to be a continual catechism course, but we want the teacher of our children, each time that he has the opportunity to imprint better moral and religious ideas in their minds, in relation to history, to literature, or to other matters, that he seize it . . . We don't want the minds of our children to become accustomed to the idea of a divorce, of an absolute separation between religion and the other aspects of life. To confine religion entirely to certain moments in the day is to distort, we believe, the mind of the child. It is to give him the prejudice that, when he grows up, when he is in the world, apart from the moments consecrated to religious obligations—the Sunday mass and the Easter communion—he doesn't have to bother his mind with religion.[92]

Another Catholic leader rebuked his Liberal fellow-legislators, charging that

> according to you, it's up to the State to fashion future generations, to form the public spirit, the character, the moeurs of the nation, to reflect its ideas there rather than to be itself the reflection of the ideas of citizens; to mold childhood in its image, instead of fashioning itself in the image of the country. This pretension is what distinguishes despotic governments from all free governments; it is the common principle of countries which are unfree.

Yet another called for adopting the English system of education, under which (since the 1870 education legislation) government subsidized freedom, intervening only when nongovernment schools did not meet the needs, and thus "fertilizing that individual initiative which is the true strength, the distinctive character of nations which are free and which wish to remain free."[93]

Catholic eloquence was answered by Liberal eloquence, with one legislator asking,

> Gentlemen, do you know what the danger is? It is the spirit of fanaticism and of intolerance which sows discord in families, in the community, and in the State, which would seek, under the pretext of religion, to separate children in school in order subsequently to separate citizens . . . It is this spirit of intolerance and of fanaticism which, if it is not stopped and contained, will lead us to civil war after having made us pass through religious war. . . . Do you know what the danger is? It is the stubborn and fanatical resistance of the Church to the most glorious conquests of the French Revolution.[94]

Another urged that "to organize elementary instruction is to fashion the Belgium of the future, it is to prepare the future generations who will hold in their hands the destinies of the patrie. The State must take on this task."[95]

Liberal leader Frère-Orban (who had been the principal speaker at the founding Liberal Congress in 1846) sought to enlist Pope Leo XIII as an ally, claiming that the Belgian bishops were, in fact, more radically opposed to the state role in education than was the Vatican, but the pope

> retaliated by saying that while the Belgian constitution was, from the Church's point of view, not an ideal constitution (being man-made) it was one in which the Catholics enjoyed real freedom and liberty of expression and they owed it as a duty not to attack the constitution but to defend it whenever the very real liberty of the individual was in danger . . . Thus, overnight almost, Belgian Catholics found themselves . . . standing as staunch and very real defenders of the Belgian constitution.

They charged that "the very people who were posing as apostles of enlightenment were seeking nothing more than the enslavement of the rest of the population"[96]—what one described, with some exaggeration, as the 98 percent of the population who were not entitled to vote.[97] The rhetoric escalated on both sides.

After this intense debate, both in the legislature and in the press, the law was adopted in June 1879 by the Liberal parliamentary majority, providing that

(1) municipalities were required to establish their own elementary schools, and could not simply adopt a private (in almost all cases, a Catholic) school;

(2) religious instruction was no longer a required subject, though a classroom would be made available before or after school so that the local priest could provide it to those children whose parents wished it;

(3) all schoolbooks must be approved by the government;
(4) teachers would be appointed by the local council, with preference given to graduates of state (rather than Catholic) normal schools; and
(5) oversight over schools would be exercised only by local and higher levels of government, and thus not at all by the clergy.[98]

There is considerable evidence that the secularization of public schools was not as drastic as the rhetoric on both sides suggested. The government allowed schools to keep crucifixes and other religious symbols in classrooms where this was the custom, and prayers continued to be said in many public schools.[99] This was in large part a deliberate attempt—in vain—by the government to convince the public that "nothing has changed," and thus to counter widespread resistance to the new law.[100]

The Catholic reaction was rapid and successful. The Catholic Church forbade clergy to cooperate with public schools by providing the optional religious instruction in schools.[101] Of a total of 7,550 elementary school teachers, 2,253 (1,200 men and 1,053 women) left the public schools which had been made neutral, often at considerable sacrifice. Already in December 1879—at least according to the calculations of the Catholic Party—the free Catholic schools enrolled 379,000 pupils; the public schools, 240,000. The proportion of enrollment in Catholic elementary schools rose from 13 percent in 1878 to 61 percent (more than 75 percent in Dutch-speaking Flanders) in 1880; by 1882 there were 622,000 pupils in Catholic elementary schools. There were 168 public schools without any pupils at all.[102]

The issue became cast by Catholic leaders as one of personal liberty against the arrogance of an elite with charges that "the very people who were posing as apostles of enlightenment were seeking nothing less than the enslavement of the rest of the population."[103] There were many stories about government retaliation against teachers and teacher-trainees who followed their conscience and left the public schools.[104]

Nor were Liberals in a mood to back down; the government called upon Pope Leo XIII to restrain the opposition which it was experiencing from the Belgian clergy and, when he did not, broke diplomatic relations with the Vatican. It has been said that "the Dreyfus case in France and the Ulster issue in England perhaps cut more deeply and polarized opinion more sharply. But both were shorter lived, and neither involved so many people's daily lives for so long a period as did the church–school issue in Belgium."[105]

The struggle over schooling had the secondary effect, as in The Netherlands, of mobilizing Catholics to create a wide range of institutions and forms of social and political expression in an "astonishing expansion of the 'Catholic movement.' By the press, fliers, meetings, and petitions, in a few months it gained all of Belgium."[106] Great efforts were expended to establish new private Catholic schools, or to expand those already in existence; funds were collected both locally and nationally through a *Denier des écoles catholiques* which was much more successful than that organized a few years earlier by the Ligue de l'enseignement on behalf of secular private schools.[107]

The elections in June 1884 were a victory for the Catholic party, which maintained a parliamentary majority for the next thirty years; the Liberals were out of government until 1918.[108] Most observers attributed this change— previously the Liberals had controlled the government for thirteen years— to the school issue. Parliament was called into a special session in July to consider replacing the "misfortune law" (*ongelukswet*) of 1879. Despite Liberal resistance, a new law was adopted in September, giving autonomy back to local authorities and ensuring educational freedom. Elementary schooling would no longer be a concern of the State. Municipalities could again designate private "free schools" to meet their obligation to provide education, and had complete freedom to appoint teachers, without the requirement of a state diploma.[109] Religious instruction was again made a part of the curriculum, with a new variation: alongside Catholic instruction, Protestant or Jewish instruction could be offered if justified by the number of pupils.[110]

This decentralization of control of popular schooling under municipal auspices for public schools or in private schools, some of which were subsidized, limited the role of the central government to defining a minimum curriculum and offering a model program that local authorities could choose to adopt or to reject.[111] The effect of this abdication by the State of any guiding role for schooling was generally negative in the smaller or more backward communities, many of which sought to reduce their expenses for schooling below the level required previously by the government. Within a year, the salaries of 3,316 teachers were reduced and 880 lost their jobs. Hundreds of communal schools were closed, and 1,473 private elementary schools were "adopted" to meet the obligation to provide instruction. In 1905, it was estimated that 14 percent of the children were not in school at all.[112]

Over the next few years, there was an increasing pressure for public funding of free schools, as the priority of Catholics shifted away from seeking to maintain the denominational character of public schools.[113] A Catholic leader in Parliament argued, in 1894, that "in many localities, public education is submitted to rather than accepted willingly; the moment a free school is opened, pupils crowd into it."[114] Liberals strongly opposed any subsidies. "They claim that this will ensure educational peace," one of them told his fellow legislators, "the contrary will be true: it will be educational warfare! . . .

Immediately public schools will be attacked so that the pupils of these schools will go to private schools . . . Let private schools be created, let them multiply or disappear, that's the work of society, but is no concern of the State."[115]

The following year, debate began over a bill to provide such subsidies. In filing it, the responsible minister argued that it "takes into account a fact that has been confirmed by experience for several years: that, in our country, the great majority of parents want the education of their children to include religion." The proposed legislation would ensure that "free schools be put on the same basis as communal schools, from the point of view of state subsidies." Another Catholic legislator added that "We Christian parents feel an irresistible repugnance about confiding our children to teachers without faith who . . . will infuse into them the poison of atheism."[116]

A Socialist opponent countered that

> the Church represents the most complete form of the principle of authority in morality, while the dynamic tendency [of modern times] is toward moral self-government . . . The Church cannot achieve universality. Efforts are in vain: they encounter the resistance accumulated over centuries . . . A moral community, as vast as humanity, is more and more necessary and is only possible outside of all cults . . . Socialism is the projection toward the future of the ideal of justice; it is the idealization of humanity pursued by itself. It attaches itself to the moral and intellectual community transmitted by previous centuries; it has received them from the hands of the 18th century itself.[117]

Increasingly, in fact, Socialists articulated almost an alternative religion, based upon "a deep commitment to education, secularism, progress, and moral uplift," which put them in fundamental opposition to the educational and social institutions through which Catholics were competing with them for the loyalties of the working class. "Progress in history, the Socialists believed, was a long battle against ignorance, poverty, and the 'tyranny of priest and church,' a battle that led finally to 'freedom and equality.' The Socialists challenged the Church as a symbol of oppression with their own anticlerical and messianic 'New Gospel,' a 'struggle against injustice.'" Rivalry with the Church's popular influence led to events like the "festival of youth" in Ghent in 1896, intended to provide an alterative to first communion celebration,[118] rather as the Communist regime in East Germany after World War II provided a *Jugendweihe* ceremony as a substitute for Protestant confirmation. In particular, the Socialist Maison du Peuple in Brussels, established in 1881 on the basis of a bakery cooperative came with increasing elaboration to provide "a restaurant, library, theatre, schools, bands . . . the place where husband, wife and children met to laugh, play, re-create . . . every Sunday. Gradually dramatic groups, choral societies, fanfares, bands, trumpets and accordion societies, etc. were formed." This Belgian innovation served as a model to Socialist parties in other countries.[119]

In 1895, Socialists in Brussels "voted a resolution against religious education classes in state-supported schools, called on local governments to drop the classes, sent parents forms so they could request taking their children out of such classes, and called on all Socialist organizations to get people to sign petitions against religious education."[120] Despite Liberal and Socialist opposition, the new law came into effect and provided that state subsidies would go not only to communal schools and free schools which had been adopted by municipalities, but also directly from the government to other free schools which were considered "adoptable." Religious instruction was again made a required subject in elementary school.[121] The quality of schooling was improved by this law, but the Catholic position was strengthened as well.[122]

The strong anticlericalism of the Socialists had had the effect

> to dilute significantly the Socialist commitment to a class-conscious position and to alienate workers who found strident anticlericalism offensive. Essentially, the Socialists opted for a vision of society in which the support or opposition to the Church that cut across class lines was almost as important as class conflict. At the same time, they dismissed as potential supporters lower-class individuals who were religious.

So strong was this opposition to religion (not just to "clericalism") that "Brussels Socialists . . . virtually dominated the International Free Thought Federation." Their position was "not simply a call for the greater separation of church and state, but a constant attack on Christianity itself."[123]

Eventually, however, this hostility to religion came to seem a diversion from the economic goals of the Socialist movement. Conflict over religion and schooling was reduced greatly as Belgian Socialists, like those in The Netherlands, adopted the Erfurt Doctrine—first elaborated by the German Socialists, which insisted that religion was a private matter and should not be allowed to threaten the unity of the working class in pressing its economic demands. In 1913 the Socialist Party ended its traditional alliance with the "free thinking" associations. During the same period, the Masonic lodges became less politically active.[124] School issues became increasingly the subject of negotiations, rather than winner-take-all votes, and both sides backed away from dealing with them as matters of fundamental principle.

Whether to make elementary schooling obligatory had been debated for decades. Several Belgian Liberal leaders participated in an international conference on social welfare, held in Frankfurt in 1857, which voted unanimously that instruction should be both obligatory and free for those whose parents could not afford to pay tuition. The same proposal had already been made by radicals during the French Revolution, and an unsuccessful attempt had been made to include this in the Belgian 1842 law.[125] In the aftermath of the 1857 conference, a Belgian Mason, J. M. Funck, published an influential brochure on the subject, in which he argued that the parliament should

> make elementary instruction obligatory, give it prestige and independence, pull it away from the influence of religion so it knows no other guides and chiefs than the State and the commune which it serves; shelter the schoolmaster from need so he will be respected; then write in your law the great maxim of Belgian Liberalism: the priest in his church and the teacher in the school, and from that day the countryside as well as the cities will belong to the cause of progress; you will form a complete generation of men who will all reach a certain moral level; you will have intelligent populations to whom you can address yourselves, with whom you can enter into contact, who will know how to understand your writings and will appreciate them. After all, the salvation of Liberalism rests in propaganda; not a hidden propaganda, which addresses the isolated individual, but a broad, public, propaganda, which addresses everyone and is in the interest of all; in a propaganda which consists of spreading floods of light among the people, in order to enlighten them about their real interests, to put them in a position to choose between reaction which goes backwards and progress which advances, between the men of the past and the men of the future.[126]

Other Liberals resisted the proposal to make schooling obligatory. J.-L. Trasenster, an ally of Frère-Orban, wrote that the history of Germany and France demonstrated that it had been an instrument of oppression, with the goal of imposing religious beliefs, and was thus in fundamental conflict with Liberal principles. Among Liberals, this question of obligatory schooling became the dividing line between those—the "Doctrinaires"—whose emphasis was on safeguarding individual freedoms, and the "Young Liberals" or "Radicals" who looked to government to correct social inequalities even at some cost to individual rights.[127]

Catholics tended to agree that obligatory school attendance would violate the rights of parents, and in any case would be unjust unless adequate subsidies made it possible for all Catholic children to attend Catholic schools. Early in the twentieth century, however, a split developed among Catholic political activists, as it had some years earlier among the Liberals, between those who wished to limit the activity of government and those who argued that government action was needed to promote social justice and the general welfare. The Christian Democrats called for compulsory schooling, arguing that, while children did not belong to the State but to their parents, there were nonetheless obligations upon parents that the State could enforce in the case of neglect. In 1911, the Catholic education minister filed a bill to make schooling obligatory until age 14. Liberals and Socialists were placed in a dilemma, since the law also provided for public funding of the schools which children would be obligated to attend. Catholics proposed that parents be provided with a voucher (*schoolbon/bon scolaire*) for each child of mandatory school age, to be used in the school of their choice.[128] The bill was unsuccessful, but in 1913, with a strengthened Catholic majority, a new bill was filed, abandoning the voucher but providing an increased state subsidy. During the debate, a Catholic leader pointed out that so long as educational freedom was protected through appropriate subsidies compulsory attendance would not violate the rights of parents:

> But I hasten to add that there is no such thing as neutral education and, if there were, it wouldn't be worth anything. What, after all, is the purpose of the school? It is to complete the work of the family, to continue it, to assist it, to make the child into a man. What does that require? It is necessary to develop him physically, intellectually, morally, religiously; it is necessary to tell this child where he comes from, and where he is going, what should be the rule of life applied to his conduct. If you don't tell him that, I declare to you that all education falls short, because the instruction lacks a base and a guide.

Liberals and Socialists objected strongly to this way of understanding educational freedom; one of them charged that "your bill, if it is adopted, will bear bitter fruit. It will aggravate antagonisms which are already so deep; . . . antagonism of belief, in giving half of Belgians an education which tends to make them believe that the other half consists of the impious, or heretics, of people without faith or law."[129]

Once again, however, the Catholic majority triumphed over such objections, and the new law was adopted in May 1914, just a few months before the invasion of Belgium by the Germans put an end to education reforms. All children were obligated to attend school for eight years, and state subsidies were increased so that free (private) schools as well as communal schools could provide education without tuition charges. Meanwhile,

> the map of Belgium, especially in Flanders, was black with Catholic nuclei. Schools, convents, guilds, insurance societies, recreational, trade, and voter associations,

religious, parochial, and philanthropic associations, associations for women, girls, soldiers, students and pupils, banks, credit institutions, museums, farmer unions, some united with one another and overlapping, some hierarchically dependent on the bishops or on the State, all led through priests who often besides their organizational work had hardly any time for their pastoral duties—all this formed the impenetrable, unimaginably ingenious complex of Catholic power. It was to a considerable extent maintained by the State,

including the salaries of some 6,000 priests. Liberals found that, as with the Revolution of 1830, the constitutional revision of 1893 had the effect of strengthening the Catholic position.[130]

When universal male suffrage took effect . . . the percentage of Catholic voters increased. The urban lower middle class, rural and small-town artisans, and farmers, at least initially, voted more Catholic than the upper class. One of the great battlegrounds between the Socialists and Catholics would be vying for the support of these groups.[131]

With few exceptions, the anticlerical and secular groups were much less successful in creating institutions to support their worldview, especially as the more radical elements of the Liberals became Socialists and turned to economic and social issues. There were occasional mobilizations and petitions around particular issues—as occurred in opposition to the 1895 education law—but not the sort of sustained organizational life that translated into effective influence on national education policy. The situation was different in those industrial regions where trade unions were able to influence local authorities.[132] Nevertheless, the school issue continued to be useful as a common ground on the Left, as it was a permanent mobilizing issue for Catholics; a Catholic historian wrote in 1905 that "still today, even though the class struggle absorbs a part of the activity of nonbelievers, anticlericalism is the only ground on which the most reactionary Doctrinaires [business-oriented Liberals] manage to come to an understanding with the most violent Socialists," and he warned his coreligionists that "if, by an unexpected change, our adversaries could ever return to power, the struggle would begin again, and it would be more terrible, you may be sure, than it was twenty-five years ago . . . We must therefore keep ourselves always ready to fight the good fight."[133]

Although the effort, in 1911, to institute vouchers to pay for schooling failed,[134] in 1914 the Loi Poullet made public and approved private elementary schooling completely tuition free on an equal basis, subject to employment of qualified teachers and to following the general curriculum guidelines of the Ministry of Education.

Over the next years, the "Sacred Union" of political parties, initially directed against the German invasion which occupied almost all of Belgium, "could not survive without freezing problems as delicate as the *question scolaire.*" In this spirit, Liberals and Socialists approved almost unanimously in 1919 new subsidies for private schools, and two years later a secular course on morality was introduced in public schools, though for all pupils rather than as an alternative to the required religious instruction. This spirit of compromise— what has been called the *trève scolaire et religieuse* (school and religious truce) remained necessary because the post-war governments were coalitions, "philosophically heterogeneous," and divisions existed on both sides of the issue over schooling: the anticlerical camp included both Socialists and Liberals, who differed strongly on the economic issues which were coming to be more important to both than pressing for secular schooling, while the Catholic camp similarly included both bourgeois and working-class elements. The former oppositions, based upon religious loyalties and worldviews, came to seem a barrier to solving the difficult problems of rebuilding after the destruction caused by being a primary battlefield of the war, and then the consequences of the worldwide Depression.[135]

Chapter Seven

Totalitarian Schooling

NATIONAL SOCIALIST EDUCATION AND INDOCTRINATION

The use that Hitler and his associates intended to make of education was no secret years before they took power. In *Mein Kampf,* Hitler had written that the educational efforts of the State that he sought to establish would find their crowning achievement in burning race consciousness and race feeling into the hearts and minds of youth. Once in power, he insisted that "no boy and no girl must leave school without having been brought to an advanced understanding of the necessity and the nature of purity of blood."[1] Nazi educational policy insisted that "physical culture is a matter for the state, whose duty it is to see that the principles of hygiene, more particularly racial hygiene [sic!], are taught throughout the nation, not only in ordinary schools but in state-controlled activities outside the school program. The dangers of contaminating German blood with elements from other races are to be emphasized."[2]

In 1933, his first year in power, he boasted that "your child belongs to us already today. Who are you? You will pass away, but your descendants already stand in a new situation. In a short time they will not know anything else."[3] From exile in 1938 Erika Mann wrote sadly that "the German child today is already a Nazi-child and nothing further. The school that it attends is a Nazi-school, the youth organization that it belongs to is a Nazi-organization, the films that it is allowed to see are Nazi-films, and its life belongs without reservations to the Nazi-State."[4] A contemporary American observer noted that "National Socialism is in itself a gigantic educational enterprise . . . intensely anxious, almost frantically so, to root its principles in the hearts and minds of the German people in a manner to insure their permanent popularity and acceptance."[5]

An historian has written that what Hitler intended was not only the creation of a new form of political order, but also a new form of German life; all spheres of German life must be redirected or newly created in accordance with the principles of the uniquely permitted ideology, as he announced in a speech in September 1933. This was a challenging program, which Hitler himself said would be a thousand times more difficult than the winning of political control.[6] In contrast with the more modest determination of an authoritarian regime that its orders be obeyed, it is characteristic of a totalitarian regime to seek to mobilize its subjects to believe wholeheartedly in its goals. Nazi propaganda chief Josef Goebbels proclaimed in November 1933 that "the revolution that we have made is a total one. It has seized all spheres of public life and restructured them fundamentally. It has entirely changed and re-formed the relationships of people with one another, the relationship of people with the State and to the questions of Life itself [Dasein]."[7]

In an echo (whether intended or not is unclear) of Fichte's Addresses to the German Nation (1807), Hitler proclaimed in a widely noted speech in 1938 that, under his regime, "youth learns nothing else but to think German, act German." By entering the *Jungvolk* at ten, then the Hitler Youth at fourteen, then one or another Nazi organization for a few years more, German children "will never more be free for their entire lives."[8] The same year, a leading Nazi educational theorist wrote that "a people does not endure because new children are born," but only when those children "imbibe the eternal spiritual content" of the race.[9] It should be noted that no special role is attributed to the school in this process; indeed the basic educational strategy of the Nazis was to weaken the influence of schools as well as of families, and to strengthen that of youth organizations and camps, where the full emphasis could be put on indoctrination without distraction by the need to convey skills and knowledge. Nazi leaders were fond of references to the Spartans and Romans in their descriptions of how camps and boarding schools would shape youth who were free from the errors and the softness imposed by families and by schools.[10]

In the first months of Nazi rule, any educators suspected of potential disloyalty to the new regime—including activists in either the Catholic political party or the Social Democrats—and Jewish teachers were systematically fired from schools, universities, and the education bureaucracy.[11] One third of Prussia's provincial school superintendents and 22 percent of its local superintendents were fired in 1933, as were about three thousand teachers nationwide.[12] Few protests were heard from their colleagues, and indeed it appears that educators (and university students) were among the most enthusiastic supporters of the Nazi regime. Many had resisted the requirement of the Weimar Constitution that they educate their pupils for democracy, and most of the schoolbooks in use before 1933 had little good to say about it; indeed, the Nazi regime continued to use these books for its own purposes. There is much evidence, also, that anti-Semitism was common in German classrooms. The pressure to conform to the new political order after 1933 was thus matched, among much of the teaching force, by a readiness to do so.[13] Fritz Stern argues that "a thousand teachers in republican Germany who in their youth had read and worshiped Lagarde or Langbehn were just as important to the triumph of National Socialism as all the putative millions of marks that Hitler collected from German tycoons."[14] Over time, however,

> even dedicated Nazi teachers, many of whom had belonged to the National Socialist Teachers' League—the NSLB—since its inception in 1929, found it difficult to cope with rebellious [Hitler Youth] members. They . . . were reluctant to discard the notion that it was the function of the school to impart knowledge and to foster intellectual training. Hence, they frequently clashed with politicized students who welcomed the excitement of revolution, but who were repelled by the work and occasional drudgery involved in real learning.[15]

Professors of education were particularly susceptible to supporting the new Nazi regime enthusiastically. Keim suggests that this may in part be attributable to their loss of status under Weimar. Some among them, of course, opposed the Nazis and went into exile, but it is notable that educators were more likely than other public employees to join the Nazi Party.[16] This may reflect the fact that, at least since the 1850s, educators had allowed their political positions to be determined largely by professional interests, and many hoped—correctly—that the Nazis would abolish the confessional character of schools and also—incorrectly—that they would strengthen the professional position of teachers.[17]

Historian Harald Scholtz distinguishes three periods of Nazi control of German education. In the first, the existing structures were left unchanged, but there was a massive effort to mobilize teachers and pupils into organizations dominated by the Nazi Party. Within a year, 230,000 teachers had joined the Nazi teachers' organization, and they represented one-fourth of the members of the Nazi Party itself. By the end of 1935, 45 percent of all youth between the ages of ten and eighteen were members of Nazi youth organizations. Camps, excursions, uniforms, and a general sense of emerging from the political and economic stagnation of the Weimar period produced general enthusiasm for the new order.

In the second period beginning in 1936 the government intervened more directly to impose its ideological monopoly, for example, by abolishing the confessional character of most *Volksschule*, by eliminating religious instruction from secondary schools, and by forbidding the Catholic and other non-Nazi teacher organizations. During this period, in 1938, a law governing education nationwide—one of the tasks which the Weimar regime was never able to achieve—was adopted, and "for the first and only time, Germany was given a nationally centralized system of educational administration."[18]

The third period begins with the war in 1940 and is marked by the strongly anti-Christian initiatives of Martin Bormann and a growing emphasis on boarding schools to create an elite of whole-hearted Nazis for leadership roles.[19]

While schools were required to join whole-heartedly in these efforts to remake the German people through its youth, in fact their influence and effectiveness was considerably reduced by "something of a youth rebellion conducted largely by Nazi students enrolled in the Hitler Youth and directed against the educational structures and authorities of Germany. Moreover, that rebellion transcended the mere alteration of the Weimar system and continued without abatement even against Nazi controlled schools until 1945."[20]

Selection (*Auslese*) was at the heart of the Nazi education system, both the negative selection of those considered 'unworthy of life' and thus of schooling,[21] and the positive selection of a future leadership class. To identify those eligible for the latter group, special *Ausleselager* offered promising youth the opportunity for a vacation in camp with a strong emphasis upon assessment of their ideological and character traits.[22] Those selected at age twelve were sent to one of a number of boarding schools: *Napola* (*Nationalpolitische Erziehungsanstalte*) and Adolf Hitler schools, and then to one of the higher institutions for Nazi leadership, the *Ordensburgen*, which were intended to be a German equivalent of Harvard or of Cambridge University. "What we builders of the future leadership want," said an SS leader, "is a modern State along the lines of the Greek city states. Five to nine percent of the population, those chosen as best, should rule, the rest should work and obey."[23] Paul de Lagarde, one of the intellectual forefathers of the Nazi ideology, had called in the 1870s for such elite state boarding schools in the countryside to train leaders whom the people would trust and follow,[24] and Lietz's *Landerziehungsheim*, established in 1898 and soon emulated by others, provided a model of intensive community in isolation from family and society. Like the country boarding schools, these Nazi schools stressed the assessment of character rather than academic achievement, outdoor rather than classroom activities, and community spirit through singing.[25]

As intended, these institutions served only a very small proportion of German youth, altogether 17,000 or so, and were in full operation for no more than three or four years, but the post-war reflections by students who were selected to participate suggest that they were quite effective at developing blind loyalty to the regime and a habit of command. "Graduates of the *Napolas* should feel obligated to no moral principle except exclusively the will of the Führer."[26] "My pedagogy is hard," Hitler said in one of his recorded conversations. "In my *Ordensburgen* youth will grow up who will terrify the world. A strong, dominating, unshockable, gruesome youth is what I want . . . I want no intellectual education. Knowledge spoils youth for me. I'd like them to learn only that which their instinct for play inclines them to."[27] In fact, Hitler frequently expressed contempt for formal schooling and "denigrated the teaching profession as fit only for incompetents and women. He therefore insisted throughout his life that youth learns best on its own in the hard school of life."[28]

The Nazi understanding of education had definite affinities as well as clear disagreements with the *Reformpaedagogik* ,which had, for the previous four decades, called for a less intellectual education with more focus on development of the heart than of the head.[29] The Nazi polemic against overintellectual education was consistent with the alternative schooling, which many enthusiasts for child-centered education had called for and in some cases implemented, though with a very different final intention. Reform pedagogy was concerned with development of the unique person on the basis of his or her natural gifts and inclinations, while the Nazi educators wanted to create loyal followers and future leaders; what they had in common was that both minimized what could be learned from tradition and human experience, and sought to create a new humanity through education.

They also shared a rejection of the effects of the social and cultural forces associated with modernity: individualism, diversity of worldviews, mobility. Pedagogical reformer Hermann Lietz, for example, "believed that rampant ideas of progress, prosperity and free competition had all but destroyed the social and spiritual content of European life."[30] Alfred Andreesen, Lietz's successor at the head of his country boarding schools, was an enthusiastic Nazi and edited the writing of his predecessor to stress his nationalistic proclivities. "As Lietz once anticipated that the citizens of his schools would be in the forefront of the struggle for a new Germany," Andreesen wrote, "so today do the schools feel even more obligated to belong to the vanguard in the struggle for a people's community and a new Germany based on power and dignity."[31]

Some Nazi educators were intrigued by the Waldorf schools of Rudolf Steiner, and cooperated with Peter Petersen, developer of the Jena Plan curriculum; the language which they employed, about seeking not the transmission of knowledge and specialized abilities but the harmonious development of the entire person, sounded very much like progressive education.[32]

The commonality between the progressive education of the late Empire and Weimar periods and the Nazi education goals are to be found in their rejection of many aspects of modernity, "enlightenment," and liberal individualism, and interest in reaching back to older forms of community.[33] The cultural pessimism and rejection of the Liberal state that characterized much of the pedagogical experimentation before and after the war, its fascination with the virtues which it imagined to reside in the German *Volk*, found a resonance in the Nazi program. A deliberately anti-intellectual education, valuing experience over reflection, the irrational (as in Steiner's *Anthroposophism*) over reason, served Nazi purposes very well indeed, and such reform pedagogical ideas as spending a year working on the land and stressing emotional community over formal relationships became part of the new regime's program to remake German youth.[34]

Ellen Key, who had proclaimed the "century of the child," was also a supporter of eugenics and euthanasia. The *Napolas*—Nazi boarding schools located in rural areas—had much in common with the Weimar-era *Landerziehungsheimbewegung* of Lietz, Wyneken, and others; both provided educational experiences without report cards or tests and with a strong emphasis upon character education through practical experience.[35] Indeed, Alfred Andreesen, headmaster of the Hermann Lietz Schools, "devoted himself to coordinating the Lietz schools with the Nazi movement. He organized pro-Nazi rallies at his schools, which culminated in a massive festival for the Hitler Youth from all of the Lietz schools."[36]

Of the alternative schools in existence in 1933, some greeted the Nazi era enthusiastically, others managed to get along with the new regime, yet others were closed for various reasons, and some were converted into Nazi schools. One of the best known of the alternative educators, Kurt Hahn of Salem on Lake Constance, was forced into exile as a Jew and because of his earlier opposition to the Nazis,[37] and went on to found the famous Gordonstoun school in Scotland as well as Outward Bound. Minna Specht's decidedly left-wing Walkemuehle was closed immediately by the Nazis, and she went into exile to Denmark and then to Britain. On the other hand, Paul Geheeb, founder of the Odenwaldschule in Hessen, sought to get along with Nazi directives for a time, but then took refuge in Switzerland where he was able eventually to start a new school serving primarily refugee children from many countries. The Odenwaldschule continued, however, under other leadership and with Nazi teachers and policies; "we want to work in harmony with parents and national youth organizations [the Hitler Youth] to prepare the young people in our trust so that they will dedicate themselves with their entire bodies and souls to serve their *Volk*," the new director assured prospective parents in 1939, "Leading and following is the premise of our community,"[38].

What these Nazi institutions were not successful in achieving was a good quality of academic outcomes. There was also a decline in the quality of the schools which the great majority of German pupils attended. The strong emphasis placed by the regime on political mobilization had the effect of devaluing academic effort. We get a glimpse of the effects in the report of a meeting of the parent association of a secondary school in Bamberg in 1937. The school's director warned that student work had deteriorated to such an extent that 31 percent had received report cards marked "in danger" or "grave danger." The parents complained that the Hitler Youth on "an almost daily basis take the children away in the afternoon or evening and returns them home as late as 10:30 p.m.," and that those who became Hitler Youth leaders were expected to attend many additional meetings at all hours. They complained also about "the sneering and threatening tone of the lower leaders and their habit of belittling adults." The director called for "a clear-cut division of competence for both educational factors, the school and the Hitler Youth," but it proved impossible to maintain academic standards in the face of the political power of the Hitler Youth and its adolescent leaders.[39]

While a Germany preparing for war required a well-educated workforce, in fact by every indication the quality of schooling declined. Baldur von Schirach, Hitler's official charged with the Nazification of youth, wrote in 1938 that "we understand the national socialist revolution as a revolt of the German soul against the arbitrariness of the cold intellect." This was consistent with Hitler's own statement in *Mein Kampf* that education should concentrate on the essentials, to ensure the adequate development of the body, of character, of the will, and of decisiveness. The content of schooling should build national pride, leading to a willingness for self-sacrifice; after the development of the body and of willpower, schools should stress "German studies", German language, history, geography, drawing, singing, which lent themselves to transmitting an ideological viewpoint.[40] In history, for example, teachers were advised that the purpose of the subject was not scientific (*wissenschaftlich*) but rather practical, and that the crowning achievement of all history instruction "is nothing but educating pupils to follow the Fuehrer."[41]

Although this abandonment of traditional academic standards seemed contrary to what was widely assumed to be the special emphasis of German education, it was suggested at the time that "the disastrous number of unemployed university graduates after the [First] World War caused people to turn away from intellectual attainment as a measure of success. Largely in answer to this situation, National Socialism sponsored more or less a reversal of leadership values, proposing the soldierly type of man devoted body and soul to Germany's natural resurgence as the model to be followed." A law was enacted requiring that homework be assigned for only four out of six schooldays, to ensure that youth would have enough time for the Nazi youth organizations.[42] "Even before the outbreak of World War II accelerated the process of educational deterioration, Germany was confronted by a grave decline in academic levels of achievement, undisciplined and foundering schools. A dissatisfied, overburdened and superannuated teacher corps whose ranks were dwindling rapidly faced an organization of politicized, activist youngsters which looked on with equanimity mingled with joy as the educational structure of the Third Reich crumbled all around."[43]

Because of the devaluing of academic work, it was natural to reduce secondary schooling by a year in 1937, and by 1943—under the pressures of the war—it effectively ended for many at age fifteen. The famous German universities found that their students were not prepared and that "they now had to devote the first few semesters to remedial work, that science professors could not teach their unprepared students and that language departments could no longer assign readings in foreign languages."[44]

The German tradition of autonomous and denominational youth movements was also abandoned and youth associations were gradually dissolved and their members incorporated by compulsion into one national organization, the *Hitlerjugend*, and its female counterpart, the League of German Girls (BDM). The HJ was founded in 1926 (the BDM in 1930) and had 108,000 members at the time of the Nazi takeover; by 1934 it had 3.6 million members, and in 1936 it became an official state organization. Organizations for boys and for girls aged ten through fourteen were also established, and mandatory events were scheduled several times each week, including on Sunday mornings to prevent church attendance.[45]

At the end of 1932, before the Nazis came to power, there were about 100,000 members in the Hitler Youth, but the numbers grew to 2.3 million a year later and 3.5 million a year after that. Parents were under strong pressure to enroll their children at age ten in the *Jungvolk* and then to continue them in the Hitler Youth or the League of German Girls (*Bund Deutscher Mädel* or BDM) at fourteen.[46]

In July 1933, the new regime had negotiated a concordat with the Vatican in which, in exchange for international recognition of its legitimacy, it had guaranteed that the Catholic Church and its members would enjoy various protections, including the right to choose freely between Nazi and Catholic youth organizations.[47] The Nazi leadership decreed that same summer, however, that membership in the Hitler Youth would be denied to those who also belonged to a Catholic organization; this represented significant pressure, given the educational and other opportunities which depended upon membership in the Nazi organization. Without even the slight external protection provided to Catholics by the interest of the Nazis in maintaining a relationship with the Vatican, the Protestant youth organization had been merged into the Hitler Youth in December 1933, though groups associated with the anti-Nazi "Confessing Church" network chose to dissolve instead.[48] Pressures were brought on Catholics as well; for example, in April 1934 the police in Munich forbade the wearing in public of uniforms or insignia of Catholic youth and young adult organizations.[49]

As a contemporary observer wrote, "some work is still being done by church Sunday schools, but the activities of the Hitler *Jugend* fill the weekends in such a way as to conflict seriously with this type of instruction . . . What is obvious is that the religion of National Socialism . . . must ever remain the supreme faith."[50] No competing faith would be permitted; the law of December 1, 1936 made membership in the Nazi youth organizations compulsory for all youth between the ages of ten and eighteen. This law pointed out that, since the entire German youth must be prepared for its future duties, they must become members of Hitler Youth; membership would no longer be "voluntary":[51] "The unification of all youth under one standard has meant the formation of a 'new type' of German youth, to be processed in turn to a 'new type' of manhood."[52]

Education under the new political order must be "guided and controlled by the state and not by loyalties to religious sects, the family, or other social groups. Education must be the interpreter and defender of state will." The traditional control of education by the *Laender* was ended in 1934, "so that virtually every school, formal or informal, is now subject to centralized jurisdiction."[53] In 1935 Hitler's interior minister insisted that "we National Socialists demand the secularization [*Entkonfessionalisierung*] of all of public life . . . Catholic youth organizations don't fit any more in our current times. These organizations are often involved in spheres which the National Socialist State must take charge of for itself alone in order to fulfill its responsibilities. All such things are designed to disturb the German national community."[54] This concept of "national community" through nonconfessional schools had long been a fundamental article of faith of Germany's Liberals, who most recently after World War I had called for all segments of society to cooperate in rebuilding the German nation. "The state," they asserted, "must be filled with *Volksgeist* [spirit of the people]; the *Volk* must be filled with *Staatsgeist* [state idea]."[55] There was no place in this program for the role of "mediating structures" between the individual and the State, for the "little platoons" and the local loyalties through which most individuals experience freedom and responsibility; ironically, the effort to free individuals from all external constraints helped to prepare the way for totalitarian subjection of individuals to the State.

Youth organizations had become an important aspect of German life since the late nineteenth century, offering an opportunity to escape from the constraints of middle-class life and enjoy hiking or biking trips, evening gatherings, and a variety of projects, all characterized by "youth leading youth." While the churches sought to continue direct work with youth under the Nazi regime, this was limited to religious instruction in church on no more than two afternoons a week and two Sundays a month.[56] Increasingly the Nazi organizations filled every free moment of a boy's or girl's life, and cut into schooling; the usual Saturday morning classes were waived for youth who took part in Nazi youth organizations, while those who did not were given political education in their schools. Youth organizations, which had originally developed as an alternative form of subculture and sphere for experiencing freedom became, as in the contemporary Soviet Union, simply another instrument of mobilization of the population by the Party/State.

Every effort was made to arouse the enthusiasm of youth through a variety of exciting activities, including trips—by 1939 there were 1,700 youth hostels—and playing at being soldiers or sailors with real guns. On the other hand, it was made illegal for youth to go on a trip with more than three persons unless under the sponsorship of a Nazi organization. The Nazi youth camp in the countryside and the Nazi youth center in cities came to replace schools as the primary focus of education. Schoolteachers "could only resign themselves to this outside-of-school absolutizing of youth, since they could not offer a model for political indoctrination which was capable of competing with it." As a Nazi educator wrote in 1934, "National Socialist camp education is the symbol of the national community which is coming into being."[57]

The principle behind the education provided through these Nazi organizations was to create situations through which youth would "experience National Socialism" rather than being told about it. This "learning by doing" was based upon an assumption of the racist worldview which underlay the regime that "Nordic" peoples are primarily emotional and oriented toward action, rather than rational, and should be educated primarily through experience.[58] Young men left the Adolf Hitler schools, some reported later, with no higher ambition than to die an heroic death for the Fuehrer.[59] It seems likely that the willingness of a generation of German youth—with some noble exceptions—to be swept into a profoundly irrational movement reflects the confusion and disillusionment which their parents manifested in response to the defeat in 1918 and the Weimar years. In the Nazi movement youth felt themselves led by their peers toward a hope-filled future rather than by the ineffective older generation.[60]

It soon became clear that the belief system promoted by this intensive effort to mobilize youth—as well as adults—not only to work for but also to believe wholeheartedly in the Nazi program would bring the government into conflict with the churches. In *Mein Kampf* Hitler had written that both Protestant and Catholic confessions provided a useful support for the German people, though he warned that the confessional division benefitted the international Jewish conspiracy. In his private conversations after taking power, however, he expressed the conviction that Christianity had no future and must be rooted out in Germany; it was of crucial importance for the future whether the German people "have the Jewish Christian religion and its feeble morality of pity or a strong heroic belief in God in Nature, in God in their own people, in God in their own destiny, in their own blood . . . You are either a Christian or a German; you cannot be both."[61] Several days after Pearl Harbor brought the United States into the war, Hitler reassured his intimates that "the war is going to be over. The last great task of our age will be to solve the church problem. It is only then that the nation will be wholly secure." Referring to the churches as "organized mendacity," he said that they must be destroyed by making sure "that the state is absolute master . . . The point that must be reached is to have the pulpits filled with none but boobs, and the congregations with none but little old women. The healthy young people are with us."[62] In fact, as Erika Mann wrote in 1938, the Nazis knew that they must destroy both the family and the churches in order to achieve unlimited power.[63]

The National Socialists' position, before they came to power, had been that confessional schools should be replaced by community schools (*Gemeinschafts-schule*),[64] but Hitler's initial statement of his government's policy in 1933 promised that "the national Government will allow and confirm to the Christian denominations the enjoyment of their due influence in schools and education." The Nazis took steps, however, to eliminate this source of alternative loyalty as soon as they were securely in power. The extension of direct and exclusive State control in education was an important element of the Nazi program of radical centralization and imposed uniformity, in which everything possible was done to eliminate competing sources of opinion and independent thinking. "The influence of uncontrollable or, from a National Socialist perspective, opposed educational forces (such as Family, Church, private schools, residential homes, and alternative pedagogies) was eliminated to the greatest extent possible. In this connection the closing of almost all experimental and private schools was considered a decisive measure of educational policy."[65]

In 1936, for example, the private (mostly Catholic) elementary schools were ordered closed because they "contradict the spirit of the National Socialist *Volksgemeinschaft*,"[66] and only those private schools serving pupils with special needs were allowed to continue, "under the careful supervision of the state, for in its very essence National Socialism does not and cannot acknowledge any right to attend or support autonomous private schools instead of public schools."[67] As a leading Nazi educational theorist wrote, "What the German Empire did not wholeheartedly wish to achieve (since monarchy was allied with Protestantism), and what the republic could not achieve (since liberalism and socialism needed the support of the Roman Catholic Church), this, National Socialism has undertaken to bring to an end."[68]

A primary instrument of the Nazi program was to turn the confessional public schools into "German community schools" (*Deutsche Gemeinschafts-schule*). Of course, the Weimar Constitution had already given preference to these "common schools," but with protection for the confessional schools, which enrolled the great majority of pupils. The Nazis set out to implement the unfulfilled intentions of the Liberals under Weimar and indeed under the empire. Indeed, it has been suggested that the entrenched education bureaucrats who continued to serve after as before the Nazi takeover took advantage of their new masters' lack of program for the organization of the schooling system to achieve what they had sought in vain under Weimar and indeed before, the uniformity of all popular education in a standard nonconfessional elementary school.[69]

In 1937 Hitler insisted that "this Reich will hand over its youth to no one, but will take its education and its formation upon itself."[70] In the boarding schools intended to create a Nazi elite no religious instruction or services were offered; in 1942, of 6,093 young men enrolled in those schools, only one in four still believed in God.[71] Nazi leader Martin Bormann issued a directive in 1939 that

> The creation of an ideologically objective school system is one of the most important tasks of the Party and the State . . . Not for nothing have the political Catholics, above all, realized the importance of teaching the young and controlling their spiritual growth and character building . . . [Thus]

> (a) the State ought to be the basic organizer and controller of the school system. In many cases, the private schools and institutions can be simply transferred from the [Catholic teaching] orders to the State . . .

(b) in many cases, particularly where public schools are available, private schools can only be regarded as superfluous, especially those which cannot be regarded as ideologically objective. The pupils should be put in the public school system, and the private schools closed.[72]

And, in a second directive two months later, he ordered that "[b]y the end of the year, no educational institutions should exist which are under denominational influence."

To implement these directives, all government subsidies for nongovernment school salaries were canceled, and many religious schools were closed or taken into the state service. Religious instruction in public schools was greatly reduced, and teachers were urged to replace Christian teaching with a "Germanified" religion that omitted the [Jewish] Old Testament and inculcated loyalty to the regime. Nazi ideologue Alfred Rosenberg boasted that "the curriculum of all categories in our schools has already been so far reformed in an anti-Christian and anti-Jewish spirit that the generation which is growing up will be protected from the black [i.e., clerical] swindle." As a young girl wrote in her confirmation class, "In our religious knowledge period [in school] we have to speak about our Führer and must learn poems about him. We do not need any poems or sayings about Paul or John."[73] Similarly, a prescribed dictation for primary school stated that "as Jesus freed people from sin and hell, so Hitler rescued the German people from ruin . . . Jesus built for heaven, Hitler for the German earth."[74] Catholic religion teachers were ordered to begin their lessons with "Heil Hitler!"[75]; in a religious context, the word *Heil* commonly means grace or salvation as in the phrase describing Jesus Christ as "das Heil der Welt." The verse that German children had learned for generations in their first year of school,

> Ich bin klein, mein Herz sei rein (I am little, let my heart be pure), soll niemand drin wohnen als Jesus allein (no one shall live there but Jesus alone).

was changed to

> soll niemand drin wohnen als der Fuehrer allein (no one shall live there but the Fuehrer alone)

COMMUNIST AND POST-COMMUNIST EDUCATION

The Communist regime in power in East Germany—the German Democratic Republic or DDR—for forty years was particularly insistent upon ideological orthodoxy, as the very name of its dominant party (Socialist Unity Party of Germany or SED) suggests. "Of all the East European Communist parties," one observer concluded, "it seems that the SED takes ideological issues most seriously."[76] In contrast with West Germany, in the east, the authorities decided to maintain ideological control of schools which had been brought under direct state control and emptied of confessional character by the Nazis and use them "to re-educate the population on the basis of new values, new norms of behavior and a new image of society." They assumed a subordination of the interests of the individual to those of the State, requiring that schools adapt the former to the latter.[77]

Not facing the entrenched resistance which would prevent such radical changes under democratic conditions in the Federal Republic (BRD), the Soviet occupation authority and then the government of the DDR in rapid order created an eight-year elementary school, eliminated religious instruction from schools, forbade private schools, required co-education, laid down detailed instructions for curriculum and instruction, and gave the whole educational system a strongly ideological character.[78] Schools were charged with "the all-round development of the socialist personality" of every child.

In 1948 the guest speaker at the DDR's Pedagogical Congress was the President of the Soviet Academy of Pedagogical Sciences; the teachers present were urged to study Marxism in order to ensure that the ideological character of the educational system would be secured. Many Soviet works on how to teach were translated and distributed widely.[79]

The character of East German schooling was marked until the end of the regime in 1989–1990 by the experience of the 1950s, when its mission was less one of education than of re-education of an entire society, starting with the teachers themselves. By 1949 two-thirds of the teachers had been replaced by others—often with no training or experience for the task—considered more politically reliable. To this end, a high official of the regime insisted in November 1948 that every teacher, every trainer of teachers, every school administrator, and every professor of education have a solid grounding in and commitment to Marxist educational theory as it had been developed in the Soviet Union, and that this be the basis of all instruction.[80] Special stress was placed upon creating, in each school, a Communist Party cell for staff and a Communist organization for pupils, and upon orchestrating ceremonies and events of all kinds to ritualize and reinforce commitment to the new order.[81]

Although presented as the only means to undo the legacy of National Socialism, this Communist program in fact was in essential continuity with Nazi education policies. The first East German school law, enacted in May 1946, insisted flatly that "the education of youth in schools is exclusively an affair of the State,"[82] and its successors under the Communist regime were marked to an increasing degree by the monopoly of all decision-making power by the central State/Party bureaucracy.

The campaign to "build Socialism," beginning in the mid-1950s, was less concerned with changing the economy through abolishing free markets and private ownership of enterprises—this was already largely accomplished—than with political mobilization to "create a new consciousness among the masses." It was thus to a large extent an educational campaign, in the broadest sense, and placed heavy responsibilities on schools and their teachers to "convey a fundamental knowledge of Marxism/Leninism," as the 1965 education statute put it, so that their pupils could "grasp the Meaning of Life in our times and think, feel and act in a Socialist manner." "Pedagogical guidance," wrote an official journal, "is political guidance toward laying the foundations in pupils for the worldview and morality of the working class."[83]

As had been the case under the Nazi regime, the efforts were not limited to what took place in schools but relied heavily upon youth organizations. In March 1946, with most of Berlin still in ruins, the organization 'Free German Youth' (FDJ) was created, claiming, like the Hitler Youth before it, to be an umbrella group to bring together existing religious and other youth organizations; by 1947 it was taking on characteristics of a mass organization and making claims to a monopoly in the interest of unity and progress. At no point over the next forty years was it able to function autonomously of State and Party, however, "or to represent the expectations of youth authentically. Youth protests and youth conflicts found the FDJ constantly on the side of the State." More successful in eliciting enthusiasm were the Young Pioneers (six to nine years old) and the Thaelmann Pioneers (ages ten to fourteen, named after a Communist hero), which played a dominating role in the organization of recreation and youth activities.[84]

A policy statement issued in 1969 by the Ministry for Education of the People (*Volksbildung*) and the Central Committee of the FDJ began by emphasizing the "necessity of further strengthening the political-ideological education of school youth," as a means to further "the revolutionary process of creating the advanced social system of Socialism and the sharpening of the class confrontation between Socialism and Imperialism, especially in the ideological sphere." To this end, "the Marxist-Leninist ideology must penetrate to a growing degree all spheres of life in society." Since "West German Imperialism" was seeking influence over youth through popular media, there must be a concerted effort of "ideological work with youth" to enhance their "socialist consciousness." Citizenship education for youth must be concentrated exclusively on ensuring that "all girls and boys develop a solid class consciousness, that they commit their entire personalities, their knowledge and abilities, their thinking, feeling, desiring, and acting for Socialism, for the strengthening of the German Democratic Republic in every way, and lead a socialist life filled with optimism, joy, and happiness." They must develop "the conviction that Socialism is the future of all mankind, that we in the DDR belong to the victors of history, and that Socialism will also be victorious in West Germany," as well as a belief in the "decisive role of the celebrated Soviet Union and of the socialist community of nations."[85]

The Communist Party thus undertook an "ideological occupation of the school" and of the world of youth in general that was intended to be a cornerstone of its power; as one of its leaders told an American reporter, "We cannot expect the older ones to change their ways, but the youth, they must be convinced of the superiority of Communism."[86] This became all the more important as East German youth came increasingly under the influence of the music, clothing, and lifestyle of Western youth culture, which the party saw as a deliberate offensive on the part of the enemies of Socialism.

Braemer has suggested that, despite its eventual ineffectiveness, the insistent political socialization throughout the East German school program served an important function of legitimizing, in the minds of the ruling elite, their own monopoly of power. Upper-status youth made a distinction between learning to parrot the slogans of Marxism-Leninism and acquiring the technocratic skills necessary to their future careers within the system. Youth of the working-class majority, by contrast, paid little attention to the ideological content of their schooling; they associated politics with a lot of talk. Thus neither group took political education seriously. "The socialist propaganda became so crude," Hahn notes, "the scientific indoctrination so one-sided, that it is hardly surprising that many young people opted for privacy, for fantasy lifestyles, Western rock music and blue jeans, rather than pursue the unrelenting struggle for a better world in which every human activity was subordinated to collective progress."[87]

On the other hand, according to Braemer, political education was functional for the Communist system independently of its actual results. The Communist Party's monopoly of power was justified by its alleged creation of an entirely new historical reality of social justice, peace and prosperity. Was there widespread political skepticism among the masses toward the regime and party, "as a result of its stain of collaboration with the unloved and exploitative occupying power [i.e., the Soviet Union], of the establishment of a new hierarchy of privilege, of the intolerable patronizing and propagandistic stupefying of the individual by bureaucracy and the media, and more besides"? All the more reason to take as a principal task of political leadership making a change in the consciousness of the masses, in order to "substitute for their concrete social experience a fictional image of Socialism." The leading role of the party was essential precisely because the masses had not yet shaken off the vestiges of bourgeois mentality, and the heavy stress upon political socialization in schools and elsewhere in society was evidence that the party was doing its job, whatever the actual effect on the attitudes of pupils.[88]

The primary characteristic of the Communist educational system in the DDR was thus its authoritarian character, and its primary concern was enhancing loyalty to the regime, in direct continuity with the Prussian and Nazi tradition. From this perspective, the ubiquity of ideological content in East German schooling was a means of justifying the lack of the democracy, which was constantly proclaimed as its goal.[89] In rejecting private schools, for example, an influential educator wrote in 1947 that "they are a refuge for minorities, either those with special property interests . . . or to satisfy the interests of particular religious or worldview communities, and in every case would break down that which seems to us the most important thing in the organization of the system of schooling: the inner unity and organic bringing together of our whole school system."[90]

Unity and uniformity were constant themes of public discourse in the DDR, and whatever threatened to disturb them was considered the enemy of the regime. For individuals or families to pursue goals different from those of the State and Party was a form of sabotage. Thus a commentary on family law stressed that one characteristic of a Socialist society was that society, schools, and families had the same educational goal: the total development of the Socialist personality of children. That some families might not share this goal could only be an aberration; there was very little room, in a Socialist society, for a distinction between public and private, between home and school, between outer and inner conviction.[91]

Although religious belief was formally tolerated, pupils from believing families experienced many difficulties in the schools and might be singled out in class for mockery by their teachers. Many learned what could be said in school, and what could only be said at home. Their parents might be excluded from participating in parent activities because they were perceived as unable to be fully loyal to the goals of the school. In 1954 the Protestant churches of the DDR protested the "increasing politicization of schools, "which are increasingly becoming compulsory confessional schools of the materialistic worldview." The fact that "teacher education and practice in schools [were] confined to 'dialectical and historical materialism as the only theoretical basis' necessarily turned these schools into atheistic worldview schools." The churches expressed their opposition to requiring all children, including those from

Christian families, to attend schools which insisted upon a worldview so completely opposed to the Christian faith. They protested, also, against the denial of access to advanced secondary education for youth whose families did not accept the required belief in the materialistic worldview. The government should require teachers to respect freedom of belief or, if unwilling to do so, should allow alternative Christian schools.[92]

Many parents, unhappy with the constant and insistent influences on their children, and with how they were disadvantaged in obtaining educational opportunities by their class background or their religious convictions, were driven to leave for the BRD until the Wall prevented that.[93] After the fall of the Communist regime, its long-time minister of education, Margot Honecker, was confronted with testimony that many Christian parents were furious that their children, despite superior academic achievement, had been denied admission to higher secondary education and thus barred from preparing for the *Abitur* and university studies.[94]

There was great pressure upon pupils to participate in Young Pioneers and in the ceremony of *Jugendweihe*, a school-organized substitute for the churches' sacrament of Confirmation, in which adolescents were inducted into the adult community by vowing "their commitment to their socialist homeland," or lose the opportunity for further study. In the early years of Communist rule, the strong opposition of evangelical and Roman Catholic leaders to the *Jugendweihe* led to low participation, but over time the pressure was too great for all but the firmest Christians to resist, and the opposition of the Protestant churches became muted as a concession to reality; they agreed, for pastoral reasons, to confirm children who had already participated in the Communist ceremony.[95] Similarly, in the first years of the regime there was considerable resistance on the part of a Protestant youth movement (*Junge Gemeinde*) but, with Soviet support, the regime was able to break this and other expressions of protest.[96]

Annual ceremonies in which youth pledged their loyalty to the "great and noble cause of Socialism" were a public expression of daily political indoctrination in the classroom and recreational groups. Through Soviet influence, East German educators adopted Pavlov's theory that conviction developed through repeated verbal expression; by requiring pupils to repeat Socialist slogans over and over, according to this theory, they would come to internalize a Socialist worldview, would acquire "political-ideological convictions about the truth and beauty of the revolutionary struggle of the working class for socialism/communism."[97]

Not that this effort was particularly successful in creating the "Socialist personality" so constantly discussed in East German pedagogical materials, the personality which united knowledge with enthusiastic conviction in Socialist partisanship (*Parteilichkeit*).[98] Sociological studies found that manual workers (in whose name and for whose benefit the system claimed to operate) were far more concerned with their pay and what they could buy with it than they were with building Socialism. East German youth were no less concerned with various forms of diversion, no more politically mobilized, than were those in West Germany.[99]

A 1974 review of empirical studies of East German youth found that the regime "had not yet succeeded in 'integrating' the overwhelming majority of youth to the point that they identified themselves without reservations with the norms and values of the system." A later study noted that those secondary-school pupils who were active supporters of the Communist youth organization tended to be mistrusted by their classmates and accused of seeking to improve their grades and chances for further study by a show of fealty to the regime. One of the "fundamental rights" demanded by a group of East German youth in 1985, in fact, was that their access to higher education not be affected by religious faith or worldview.[100] A study in the mid-1980s found that only 27 percent of youth identified at all with the political goals of the FDJ.[101]

The traditional German dominance by the State of the educational system was, in the DDR, taken to its logical extreme of "an unlimited and centrally operating state educational monopoly." The preamble to the 1965 law, which gave schooling in the DDR its definitive shape, referred to the "leading cultural and educational function of the State." The goal was the creation of a "unitary Socialist educational system,"[102] which would provide a continuous sequence of instruction from kindergarten through university for those with sufficient ability, without limitation by social class.

The stress upon unity extended to an insistence, in the law, upon unitary goals, unitary courses of study, and unitary providers of education; no room was left for diversity, with the exception of the kindergartens which in some cases were under church sponsorship. No possibility of conflict could occur, it was assumed, between the views of (good) parents and those of the State with respect to the best interests of children.[103] The Family Law adopted in December 1965 stipulated, in Section 42, that "through conscientious fulfillment of their educational responsibilities, through their own example, and through a corresponding behavior toward their children, parents educate their children to a socialist attitude toward learning and work, to respect for working people, to keeping the rules of socialist society, to solidarity, to socialist patriotism and internationalism." Thus, Anweiler and colleagues note, "parents are guaranteed no 'natural,' that is, autonomous, right to educate their children (parent rights as a constitutional right), but only a right to raise them in the context of the socialist, that is, communist, order of values, whose norms should be valid for all citizens."[104]

Nor was this unitary political education confined to children; the 1968 East German Constitution stipulated that "the unitary Socialist educational system guarantees each citizen a continuity of instruction, education, and adult education," and defined the function of cultural life as "the full development of the socialist personality." The Communist regime sought in a sense to make society as a whole into an educational system from which there would be no escape.[105]

As late as June 1989, Margot Honecker (wife of the chief of party and state) insisted that there would be no fundamental reforms of the system; she was then—but would not be much longer—the longest-serving minister of education in the world. "Our opponents," she insisted defiantly, "will not succeed in 'blockading' Communism, in marginalizing Socialism." The educational system must continue "to raise socialist consciousness ever higher, to build up in an active way the Marxist-Leninist morality and to overcome manifestations of bourgeois ideology wherever they are to be found and seek to expand."[106]

This program was carried out with German thoroughness so that as a study published in 1987 put it,

> the educational system of the GDR [German Democratic Republic] reveals a logic, consistency, and homogeneity that cannot be matched in any Western state. Indeed, in this respect the GDR surpasses its eastern neighbors. Poland and Czechoslovakia, whose communism is reluctantly embraced, as well as the Soviet Union, whose immensity and diversity makes homogeneity a virtually unachievable goal. East Germany is a small cohesive state firmly committed to its Marxist-Leninist ideology.[107]

One of the earliest measures of the Soviet occupation, in 1945, was to forbid private schools.[108] In order to extend the power of the State and Party to all forms of organized schooling, the few nongovernment alternative schools offering various forms of *Reformpaedagogik*, such as those implementing the pedagogical theories of Steiner, Petersen or Montessori, were suppressed. Their crime was to place a stress upon individualism and creativity that was directly contrary to the educational goals of the regime; they were condemned as providing a form of "late-bourgeois pedagogy" inconsistent with the Soviet models that schools should follow. A single Catholic school, for girls in grades nine through twelve, was allowed to survive in East Berlin.[109]

As an East German educational authority wrote, in an article on "the optimal development of the personality of each pupil," "it is not being multi-talented or possessing originality that are worthwhile in the expression of individuality, but how this is connected with social orientation, activity and responsibility, with making the potential of the individual useful for society, for the collective." The goals of political education were summarized in the sequence of stages by which it was expected to proceed: "Knowledge—Consciousness—Understanding—Conviction—Action."[110]

The effort to impose the Soviet model of schooling, while not entirely successful, was far more so than the contemporaneous effort by American Occupation authorities to persuade West German educators to adopt the comprehensive secondary school. The East German regime obediently informed its subjects that Soviet education was the most "progressive" in the world, and the first priority in school reform, according to the Central Committee of the Communist Party, was to spread the "progressive scientific knowledge of Marxism/Leninism and of Soviet pedagogy" among teachers.[111]

The underlying premise of the Communist educational program was the availability of human beings to serve the purposes of the State rather than to pursue their own purposes. This implied that the school would have to exert an influence of unprecedented intensity, and would not need to adapt itself to the ways in which children differ. The comprehensive, unitary school could be implemented with no concessions to the interests, aptitudes or needs of its pupils, "leveling them down to the lowest common denominator, producing formalistic learning and estrangement from reality."[112]

There was an important exception to this insistence upon the unitary school: children who gave evidence of special talent for sports or for science were identified in the third grade for assignment to specialized schools that promoted these aptitudes intensively at the cost of a well-rounded education.[113] Such exceptions aside, the educational system did not in theory allow for accommodation of individual interests or values. As time went by, however, "the original egalitarian program later faded more and more, and in the eighties the continuing or newly arisen social differentiation, including the differing gifts and dispositions to achievement arising from it, was valued as an important 'impulse to scientific and technical progress.'" Despite the fundamental difference in legal provisions, there were in fact clear parallels between the efforts to promote the academically gifted in the DDR and the continuing academic selection in the BRD. The "expanded secondary school [Erweiterte Oberschule]" in the DDR was a highly selective provision for gifted students, intended to help meet international economic competition.[114]

Quite apart from political indoctrination, many came to feel that the insistence of Communist school authorities upon uniformity placed serious barriers in the way of meeting the needs of pupils. If East Germany suffered from the effects of a "command economy," its schools suffered also from a "command pedagogy" that sought to make uniform "individual gifts, accomplishments, and interests, that demanded too much of the weaker and reined in those capable of greater achievement," that was centrally controlled and prescribed ("led by the nose") by detailed plans.[115]

Chapter Eight

The State and Schooling in Germany and Austria since World War II

GERMANY

The post-war governments in East and West Germany took very different approaches to countering the results of Nazi education policies. "In hardly any other sphere is the division of Germany and the development of two states so clearly expressed as in the functions assigned to political formation and instruction in the educational system."[1] In both, there was an initial determination to engage in what the Western Occupying Powers (Britain, France, and the United States) called the "re-education" of the German people, and the Soviet authorities called "antifascist education." Such a program had been agreed to between Stalin, Truman, and Attlee at the Potsdam Conference in August 1945: "the German educational system shall be supervised in such a way that Nazi and militaristic teachers are completely rooted out and the successful development of democratic ideas is made possible."[2]

In the American occupation zone of what would become West Germany, the military authorities ordered in July 1945 that Nazism and militarism be rooted out of the schools and democratic principles be taught. Schoolbooks and teachers not furthering these goals must be removed, as should any curriculum that supported discrimination on the basis of race, nationality, religion, or political beliefs. Whether churches should once again be given some oversight responsibility for schools, and whether religious instruction should be provided, was left up to the German authorities.[3] It was, after all, awkward to seek to impose "democratic education" by undemocratic means.

After an initial phase of removal of the more notoriously Nazi principals and teachers, the decision was made to exclude from school all efforts on the part of the State to shape the values and the character of children, and to make it possible, once again, for independent schools to provide a competing approach to education. The *Laender* were able to reclaim their traditional authority over schooling, and in fact this control became stronger than before the Nazi period. At the end of the occupation, the goal of political education in the new German Federal Republic (BRD) was to shape a "mature citizen" capable of "understanding political processes and decisions and of acting according to democratic norms and individual interests in his sphere of responsibility and life."[4]

In contrast with East Germany, the confessional character of schooling was re-established in much of West Germany on the basis of the protections for educational freedom and parental choice in the Weimar Constitution, though not without political conflict and attenuation as a result of the mixing-up of the population through post-war conditions with millions of Germans driven out of territories now part of Poland and out of Czechoslovakia. In the general post-war and post-Nazi collapse, the churches emerged strengthened as virtually the only institutions in German life enjoying even a modicum of respect because of their—though often timid and largely ineffective—resistance to the Nazis, and as the only institutions with a mass membership, which had remained at least formally independent.[5] Catholics and Protestants had also learned to cooperate under the pressures of persecution and war, and formed what became the leading political party in West Germany: the Christian Democratic Union.

The reaction of Protestant leadership to the excesses of the Nazi regime was one of repentance "in a solidarity of guilt" with the German people. "We condemn ourselves because we did not believe more courageously, did not pray more devotedly, did not believe more joyously, and did not love more deeply," they proclaimed in 1945. In this spirit, they were ready to call into question their churches' traditional understanding of themselves as allies of the State, and thus the extensive cooperation upon which state-supported and-managed confessional schooling rested. From this perspective, and in line with general trends of post-war Protestant thinking in Europe, the secular or nonconfessional school could be seen as representing progress away from "churchiness" toward an effective engagement with the world. Plebiscites in 1946 and 1947 showed strong support for confessional schools among Catholics and for nonconfessional schools by Protestants, except, significantly, for those living in Catholic areas. Protestant leaders came out in formal support of nonconfessional schools in 1958, and over the next decades many schools gave up their Protestant identity.[6]

Among Catholic leadership, by contrast, the lesson of the Nazi period was precisely the importance of maintaining their Church's independence in providing education. Until about 1960, there was considerable self-congratulation on the part of the Catholic Church about its record of resisting the Nazis, citing the struggle to maintain confessional schools as a primary evidence for this resistance. The bishops saw no need to apologize for efforts to protect their flocks from the threats of atheism and Marxism in the post-war world. As political leaders worked to draw up West Germany's Constitution, in 1948, Catholic leaders pressed for a recognition of the right of parents to demand confessional schooling for their children.[7]

Initially, the Western Occupying Powers—Britain, France, and the United States—were no more inclined than was the Soviet Union to support restoration of the system that had prevailed under the Weimar Republic. In its only official policy statement on the issue, however, the coordinating body of the four military governments stated on December 5, 1945, that

> [i]n matters concerning denominational schools drawing on public funds, religious instruction in German schools, and schools which are maintained and directed by various religious organizations, the appropriate allied authority should establish in each zone a provisional regulation adapted to the local traditions, taking into account the wishes of the German population in so far as these wishes can be determined . . . In any case, no school drawing on public funds should refuse to children the possibility of receiving religious instruction, and no school drawing on public funds should make it compulsory for a child to attend classes for religious instruction.[8]

While in the Soviet Zone nongovernment schools were banned and religious instruction in public schools was greatly restricted though not forbidden, the American, British, and French authorities, though inclined to take the same position, backed down in the face of strong opposition from the Catholic Church and permitted confessional schools in areas where referenda showed that they were desired. The success of demands to restore confessional schooling was furthered by the fact that the churches "were tacitly recognized as the sole institutions above direct military control . . . and as exempt from 'reorientation' into directions determined in Washington, London, or Paris."[9]

In the Frankfurt-am-Main area (Hesse), with the strongest Liberal and nonconfessional tradition of education in Germany, the American "common school" model was followed most closely. This arrangement had two aspects: on the one hand, continuation of the interdenominational character of elementary education, with a gradually diminishing religious content, and, on the other, the comprehensive, nonselective model of secondary education, or *Gesamtschule*.[10]

The sometimes heavy-handed efforts of American educators working in the Occupation Government to impose American forms of schooling aroused strong resistance on the part of many who had also opposed Nazi measures to achieve uniformity. Future Chancellor Konrad Adenauer, a Catholic, pointed out in a 1946 speech that

> the resolution of the issue of elementary education led in the past to bitter conflict among the political parties, until [the compromises reached under the Weimar Republic] . . . The confessional schools based on these compromises were abolished by the National Socialist Government in 1939 through illegal implementation of the so-called German Common School. What should happen now? In every other sphere the illegalities of the National Socialist Government are being abolished. The earlier legal situation is being re-established. We want that for elementary schools as well. It is unacceptable to validate precisely that illegality of the Nazis experienced as painful by the broadest sections of the population. Therefore we call for the restoration of the confessionally organized elementary schools.[11]

The American model of a common public school, dependent exclusively on state and local government and ignoring confessional differences, seemed to some Germans uncomfortably close to the Nazis' German Community School.

In reaction against Nazi education policy and its equation of "ideological objectivity" or neutrality with a totalitarian State pedagogy, the West German Constitution adopted in 1949 assigned no authority for education to the national government, while centralizing authority for schools in the state governments more than had been the case under Weimar or before.

In Bremen, similar to Hesse in its Liberal school policies, the draft state constitution stated that the "public schools are community (nonconfessional) schools where an undenominational instruction in Bible history is given." Pressure from Protestant and Catholic leaders, however, led to constitutional guarantees of the rights of confessional schools and of the explicitly Christian character of religious instruction in public schools.[12]

Schools may be confessionally neutral, but they have a responsibility to develop in their pupils those dispositions considered necessary for the maintenance of the society and the political order. How to define these, and how to implement value-laden programs without conflicting with individual freedoms, is an on-going problem in post-war Germany, as in other countries; it was an especially sensitive problem in the wake of a dozen years of Nazi indoctrination. The 1953 Constitution of Baden-Wuerttemberg, for example, stipulated as the goals of education that youth would manifest reverence for God, the spirit of Christian neighborly love, brotherliness toward all mankind and love for peace, love for people and homeland, moral and political responsibility, occupational and social competence, and a commitment to freedom and democracy. That of North Rhine-Westphalia (1950), more modestly, specified reverence for God, respect for human dignity, and preparation for acting in society. More recent constitutions, such as those of the *Laender* of the former DDR which joined the Federal Republic in 1990, stress social virtues such as Saxony's "respect for all life, love of neighbor, peace, and protection of the environment, love of homeland, a sense of moral and political responsibility, vocational ability, activity in society, and a free, democratic attitude."[13]

In Bavaria, the land with the most conservative and Catholic influence, an initial effort was made with American support to implement interdenominational *Simultanschulen* in place of restoring confessional schools, but this encountered such determined opposition that the attempt was abandoned and the Bavarian Constitution guaranteed a right to confessional education. In 1988 the Bavarian Constitutional Court concluded that the specification of the 1946 state constitution, that "reverence for God" was among the highest objectives of Bavarian schools, was consistent with other provisions protecting individual rights.[14] However, this reverence must not be understood in the sense of establishing a state religion with a particular way of understanding the divine.[15]

Public confessional schools became the norm once again for a time in three predominantly Catholic *Laender*—North Rhine-Westphalia, Rhineland-Palatinate, and Bavaria—though their days were essentially numbered. Baden and the predominantly Protestant *Laender* (including Berlin) opted for nonconfessional public schools, while making provision for public funding of private confessional schools.

The Protestant churches made much less use than did the Catholic Church of the opportunity provided in most West German communities to insist upon confessional schools. By 1965 only 17 percent of public elementary schools were Protestant compared with 40 percent that were Catholic, and 43 percent nonconfessional or other (figures exclude Hamburg, Bremen and Berlin). This contrasts with 1911 when 71 percent of the elementary schools in Germany were Protestant, or with 1932 when 55 percent were Protestant, though it should be noted that the heavily Protestant provinces of imperial Germany were in what became East Germany.[16]

This accommodation of religious convictions began to weaken during the 1960s, not least because the convictions themselves weakened through growing secularization. The resettlement of some six million German refugees from the east in the aftermath of World War II had confused the centuries-old pattern of religiously homogeneous communities, as had the growing movement from rural areas to cities. These events—together with the creation of larger schools in the interest of efficiency and a modern curriculum—had the effect of making confessional schools less practical and less in demand.

Protestant leaders came out in formal support of nonconfessional schools in 1958, and through the next decade many schools gave up their Protestant identity. The Catholic bishops fought a rear-guard action, but with declining support from parents. Thus confessional public schools have faded in significance over the past half-century. A referendum in 1968, for example, over-whelmingly approved an amendment to the Bavarian Constitution that made all public elementary schools "Christian" or interconfessional, with some instruction on a confessional basis. Nongovernment confessional schools were assured of full public funding.[17] Articles 6 and 7 of the constitution affirm parent rights and provide that religious instruction would be an integral part of public schooling, though with a right of excusal. Despite efforts by the Catholic Church, however, the decision of whether to organize schools on a confessional basis was left up to state governments, thus making it likely that only nonconfessional schools would be provided in predominantly Protestant areas.[18]

Apart from taking advantage of these vestiges of an earlier system, parents in the post-war Federal Republic (West Germany) were not able to exercise much influence over the education of their children. The choice of a publicly supported Catholic school, for example, may not offer real pedagogical differences, given the substantial government regulation and pressure for uniformity.

Although educational freedom is explicitly guaranteed by the German Constitution, its actual exercise has been hedged about with restrictions to such an extent that there is not the rich diversity of educational offerings that might be expected in a country with a strong tradition of alternative pedagogies. One legal specialist charges that German educational policy continues to be "marked by a statist understanding" of the role of the school which continues to be rooted in a "Prussian absolutist tradition of the State's comprehensive authority to determine the shape [Gestalt] of the education which occurs in schools." This is in fundamental conflict, he argues, with the present nature of society, which is marked by a pluralistic understanding of values.[19]

While the role of state-sponsored confessional schooling has faded in post-war West Germany, that of nongovernment independent secondary schools, while still numerically insignificant, has grown at a rate which some find alarming. In 1960, 3.2 percent of all pupils in the BRD were in "free" (independent) schools, and this proportion increased to 4.4 percent in 1975, 6 percent in 1985, and 6.1 percent in 1998. The *Laender* of the former DDR naturally had very few if any pupils in nongovernment schools before re-unification, but the number and proportion has grown somewhat, from 0.5 percent in 1992 to 2.6 percent, or 63,000 pupils, in 1998. The proportion of pupils attending "free" schools that year was highest—8.5 percent—in Bavaria,[20] but still very low by comparison with most Western democracies. Government figures indicate that the enrolment in nongovernment schools rose from 570,000 in 1992 to 740,000 in 2000, including 11.6 percent of students in *Gymnasien*. It was reported in 2006 that the number of pupils attending private elementary schools had risen 61 percent in the previous decade.[21]

According to Herbst, "German public schools and their administrators are perceived by many parents as part of a sterile state government, limited in their ability to act autonomously, to respond flexibly to local conditions, or to explore cooperative arrangements with youth clubs, parental groups, and service organizations." The decline of public confessional schooling has encouraged the growth of Catholic and Protestant private schooling. "Based on their understanding of Christian schooling as furthering a balanced education of the whole child, these schools seek to soften society's influence on the growing child, the early exposure to commercialism, and the early introduction to educational specialization."[22]

Article 7 of the post-war constitution guarantees the rights of nongovernment education in language that is close to that of the Weimar Constitution. The first section, in the German tradition, states that "the entire educational system shall be under the supervision of the state." The next section asserts a limited right of parents "to decide whether [the child] shall receive religious instruction," which is offered in most schools, as provided under the third section.

This is as far as the constitution goes in asserting a right of parents to make decisions about the schooling of their children. Nevertheless, some argue that to the extent that the State's own educational system does not provide the variety of forms of schooling—whether religious or pedagogical or structural, whether extended day or bilingual—desired by parents, the State is under a constitutional obligation to provide support to independent schools to meet that demand.[23]

Controversy arose over the extent to which public funds should subsidize the right of parents to make such choices for the education of their children. As early as 1955 the argument was made that a right guaranteed by the constitution should be secured by public funding—especially if independent schools were to be required to be equivalent to state-funded schools.[24]

Initially, the *Laender* education officials agreed among themselves that the language of Section 7 of the constitution guaranteeing the right to nongovernment schooling did not create an obligation to provide public funding to nongovernment schools. A Federal Administrative Court ruling in 1966 found, however, that the stringent conditions for approval of nongovernment substitute schools would be impossible to meet without subsidies.[25]

The provision of subsidies did not put the issue to rest, however, since the ruling left it up to the *Laender* to determine how best to meet their obligation to make it possible for nongovernment schooling to survive. The actual practices varied. In some *Laender*, nongovernment schools were reimbursed for their expenditures in certain categories within limits set by the expenditures of public schools; this "involves considerable administrative work and allows the relevant state authorities a great deal of scope for exercising control and influence." In other *Laender*, the amount of public subsidy provided is based upon "the staff costs for a comparable state school pupil based on the average state school class size . . . the school retains complete freedom as regards the utilization of the aid."[26]

The variation among *Laender* has led to repeated litigation. In 1987 the Federal Constitutional Court issued a ruling based upon the constitutional guarantee that "everyone shall have the right to the free development of his personality" (Article 2.1) that went further than ever before in asserting a right to publicly funded nongovernment education.

The case was brought by several state-approved nongovernment schools in Hamburg that had been receiving a public subsidy at 25 percent of the costs of comparable public schools. The nongovernment schools pointed out that they were having difficulty surviving with this level of support, and that confessional schools in Hamburg were receiving a 77 percent subsidy. The government responded that "the function of nongovernment schools consists of the widening and enrichment of the public school system through alternative offerings." Experience had shown that the greatest demand for such alternatives was for confessional schools on the one hand and for "reform-pedagogical" schools on the other.

The higher support for schools with a distinctive worldview rests in the final analysis on their reliance [upon this support], developed through many years of constant demand. Confessional schools have always played a special role in the German educational system. For this reason, but also as a matter of duty, in order to make up for the closing [by the Nazi government] of the confessional schools in 1939, Hamburg gave them a high level of support in the years after the war.[27]

The Federal Constitutional Court concluded that Hamburg could not treat the support of nongovernment schools as a matter of its absolute discretion, so as to make them prosper or decline as seemed best to public officials. The constitution recognized a right to found nongovernment schools. The basis for this right was the concern of the constitution for human dignity, for the unfolding of personality in freedom and self-direction, for freedom of religion and conscience, for the neutrality of the government in relation to religion and worldview, and for respect of the natural rights of parents.

It was not enough, the court found, for the government simply to allow nongovernment schools to exist; it must give them the possibility to develop according to their own distinctive character. Without public support, such self-determination would not be possible. Nongovernment schools could not, at present cost levels, meet the requirements for government approval out of their own resources. To expect them to do so, the court ruled, would inevitably force them to become exclusive schools for the upper classes (*Standes- oder Plutokratenschulen*). But this was precisely what the constitution, and the Weimar Constitution before it, was concerned to avoid by the requirement that nongovernment schools must not lead to economic segregation. Nongovernment schools must remain accessible for all, not in the sense that they must accept every qualified student, but in the sense that economic circumstances are not a barrier to attendance.[28]

> Only when [nongovernment schooling] is fundamentally available to all citizens without regard to their personal financial situations can the [constitutionally] protected educational freedom actually be realized and claimed on an equal basis by all parents and students . . . This constitutional norm must thus be considered as a mandate to lawmakers to protect and promote private schools.[29]

The constitutional right to the free development of personality requires, according to Jach, that the State abstain from defining a single model of maturity which all schools should strive to develop in their pupils. In particular, it should recognize that the goal of individualization does not necessarily point toward the Liberal model of the free-standing individual, but may rather require meaningful participation in a community. Simply to proclaim "toleration" as the fundamental principle of public schools does not satisfy the developmental need of children to form secure identities in relationship to such communities. The State is thus obligated to make it possible for young citizens to have a variety of types of schooling, based upon different concepts of the meaning of "development of personality," and to support independent schools to the extent that public schooling does not include the necessary diversity.[30]

Where public confessional schools continue to exist (as in North Rhine-Westphalia, the largest *Land*), they are operated by local school authorities and are subject to essentially the same controls as nonconfessional public schools. Public confessional schools may represent an alternative for unchurched parents who object for some reason, including the presence of Turkish and other minority children, to the local nonconfessional school. The confessional character of the Catholic, and even more of the remaining Protestant public schools, may be limited to their periods of religious instruction. Clerical influence, in particular, is strictly limited. Despite the continuing existence of denominational public schools, then, they have tended to become "Christian community schools (*christliche Gemeinschaftsschule*) that differ little, if at all, from [nondenominational] community schools."[31]

Independent schools of all kinds—not including Catholic or other confessional public schools—served only 6.2 percent of the pupils in West Germany of compulsory school age in general education in 1989. Of these, 59 percent attended nongovernment Catholic schools; 17 percent, nongovernment Lutheran schools; 12 percent, nonconfessional independent schools; and 11.2 percent, Waldorf schools.

In a continuation of the strategy adopted in the mid-nineteenth century, government continues to offer denominational religious instruction in public schools as a way of reducing the demand for private confessional schools. Such instruction enjoys a constitutional guarantee, and "must remain as a free-standing subject in the public school."[32] Public schools must therefore provide space, materials, and teachers, as well as any additional costs for religious instruction, and the grades that pupils receive in this subject can count in the same way as grades in other subjects, even for promotion.[33] In addition to such external guarantees, it must be said, there have been notable efforts to make religious instruction "more correct, believable, methodologically modern, and humanly helpful."[34]

AUSTRIA

Repetition of the continuing political crisis over schooling in the 1920s has been, at least in part, avoided in post-war Austria, though the uneasy balance between Vienna-based Socialists and elsewhere-based Catholics has continued. The constitution adopted in 1948 gave the provinces supervisory authority over the elementary and middle schools, thus removing an ambiguity in the earlier arrangements, and the following year parents were given the right to withdraw their children from religious instruction.[35] A 1962 law made explicit the goal of education in elementary schools:

> The Volksschule has the task to educate children morally and religiously, to develop their intellectual activities, to provide them with the necessary knowledge and skills for further training for life, and to lay the foundation for the education of able persons and members of the community.[36]

In addition to the national Ministry of Education, there are regional education boards which are the official employers of all teachers at public compulsory schools and issue decrees and general regulations on the structure, organization, setting up and maintenance as well as on the closing down of schools providing general education.

The first area to be regulated in 1962 was the competency of federal and provincial authorities in the field of education, thus affording a basis for school laws the same year. The constitution defines the term *statutory school-maintaining authority*, which may be a federal or provincial agency. Schools established and maintained by the statutory school-maintaining authority are public schools; they are universally accessible. Schools, which are not public schools, are private schools; they are accredited under the provisions of the Private Schools Act.

Austrian politics after the war continued to be characterized by a balance of power and mutual mistrust between Catholic and Socialist Parties, and a variety of arrangements to allow the interests of both to be protected. This led, in a "school compromise" of 1962, to an unusual arrangement to prevent either party, in a momentary ascendancy, from imposing its will on the educational system.[37] Thus, "school legislation at the federal level (save [for] universities) may only be amended by a two-thirds majority of the Federal Council with at least half of the members present. Laws and decrees regulating school life and school education are drawn up in cooperation with the social partners."[38]

In additional to the national Ministry of Education, there are regional education boards which are the official employers of all teachers at public compulsory schools, and issue decrees and general regulations on the structure, organization, setting up and maintenance as well as on the closing down of schools providing general education.

Since 1993, a greater degree of decision-making authority has been given to individual schools in such matters as defining how instruction will be organized, how discretionary funds will be spent, and what educational specialties to develop. In some provinces there is also flexibility about the amount of time to allot to each subject. These decisions are made in consultation with a school council representing parents, teachers, and older pupils.[39]

In 1999–2000, there were 5,679 public schools and 528 publicly recognized private schools (with *Oeffentlichkeitsrecht*) in Austria, and about ten private schools without that recognition. The federal government pays the salaries of teachers at public schools and for teachers at independent schools which have been accorded official recognition. The Private School Act of 1962 provides that independent schools may obtain recognition as having a public status with recognition of the competencies which they certify if their teachers meet the same qualifications as public school teachers and if the organization including equipment, curriculum and instruction provided

> correspond[s] in the essential parts with the respective curricula of public schools. The head teacher and teaching staff must be in possession of the teaching qualification required for the type of school concerned. Private schools with alternative curricula or deviating forms of organization will be recognized if their curricula and organization are approved by the Ministry of Education. In order to get recognition, they must prove that teaching meets the requirements of the responsibilities of the Austrian school system.[40]

Under the Austrian Private School Act, only those schools operated by the legally recognized religious communities (which means, above all, Catholic, but also some Protestant and Jewish schools) are entitled to public funding covering all of their personnel costs. Schools maintained by statutorily recognized churches and religious communities have a legal entitlement to the provision of teaching posts necessary to fulfill the curriculum. The subsidies normally take the form of the allocation of teachers under contract of employment (under public or private law) with the federation or (for private compulsory schools) with a *Land*; these are known as "live subsidies." It is up to the discretion of the minister of education whether to award subsidies to nonconfessional independent schools which offer a distinctive pedagogy. Only "live subsidies" are permitted, although no legal entitlement for the allocation of such subsidies exists. In practice the public support has covered only a small part of their costs. This unequal treatment of nondenominational schools has been appealed, unsuccessfully, to the European Commission on Human Rights.[41]

The School Education Act [*Schulunterrichtsgesetz*] of 1974 regulates the internal organization of schools and provides for the right of teachers, parents and pupils to participate in decision-making processes in schools. Furthermore, it contains provisions on admission to schools, on entrance exams and aptitude tests, on teaching and assessment matters, on the transfer to and repetition of a grade, on the maximum length and completion of school attendance, on final exams, on school regulations, on the functions of teachers, on teacher meetings, on the relationships of schools and pupils, schools and parents, and schools and teachers, on the extended school community and on other matters.

DIE WENDE: GERMAN REUNIFICATION

The overthrow of Communist rule in late 1989 has been called "the first successful revolution in the thousand years of German history."[42] This led to a widespread hope, especially among intellectuals, that it would be possible to create distinctive new ways of organizing education and society in general, not simply to take over models prevalent in West Germany, "no matter how democratic and efficient they may be judged to be."[43]

More than simply a political upheaval, these events had the potential, they hoped, to lead to "a renewal of [East German] society 'from below',"

> beginning as an emancipation from the embrace of ideology, as a shaking-off of political tutelage by a [single] party and its state instruments of control, as a process of deep-reaching spiritual renewal . . . This emancipation from repression and restriction, from tutelage and dependency, from illusion and errors, from indoctrination and opportunism we had to carry out ourselves—we could not import it with German unification.[44]

Detachment from and even resistance to the Communist system began to grow in East Germany in the late seventies; in its place developed (among the population, though of course not the leadership) a new respect for pluralism. As one New Forum leader would put it in 1989, "we've simply had enough of running after colorful banners. Our parents did that, and we've gone along with it for forty years . . . Now we don't want to make the mistake of waving [new] banners ourselves and seeking to lead others when in fact we know that we don't have the solutions or can offer only fake solutions."[45]

This resistance to political manipulation directed itself with particular force against the regime's efforts to employ schooling and youth organizations to shape whole-heartedly loyal participants More than a dozen reform groups, in particular those with roots in church circles, began to propose new forms and models of schooling. Youth began to create informal autonomous groups in preference to participation in the party-controlled organizations.[46]

In October 1989, when hundreds of thousands of protesters took part in the Monday candlelit marches through the old center of Leipzig, one of the demands that appeared on their placards was for educational freedom, for the right to organize independent schools. Two of the many associations that formed to press for democratic reform were the Initiative Freie Paedagogik (Initiative for Pedagogical Freedom) and the Arbeitsgemeinschaft Freie Paedagogische Einrichtungen (Working Group for Free Pedagogical Institutions).[47]

The educational system was a particular target for reform demands, in part, because it had been—together with the State Security (Stasi), military and police systems—carefully protected from public criticism. The effect of school reform debates in the Soviet Union created strong pressures to engage in a similar debate when the DDR Ministry of Popular Education held its Ninth Pedagogical Congress in June 1989. Many teachers and others sent letters to the ministry before the congress, containing suggestions for reforms. What did the authors of these letters call for? Many urged fundamental reforms, with an emphasis upon limiting the influence of the State in education in favor of that of the family and of teachers. The free development of the personality of each pupil should be respected, rather than treating pupils as the objects of educational manipulation. Ethical and moral norms should be taught on the basis of universal values rather than of one-sided ideology.[48]

A paper containing proposals for school reforms was also submitted by the theological study group of the League of Evangelical Churches. "Christian parents, communities and churches in the GDR," they wrote, "consider themselves a part of society, even with the separation of State and Church." In order to be a part of the process of shaping questions about education, they had held discussions at all levels. Certain areas of broad agreement had emerged. Their concern that Christian children and youth be treated with respect in the schools was an aspect of a fundamental issue about education, which should be characterized by candor, anxiety-free expression of opinion and dialogue about differing ways of understanding life, values, and the world. Although the unitary nature of the system's comprehensive schools was a protection against inappropriate tracking of pupils on the basis of their social class, there was also a need to respond to differing interests and capabilities through more optional offerings. The contribution of religion and the churches in the past and present should be presented fairly.[49]

Recommendations for such changes to a pedagogical congress controlled by the Communist authorities were in vain. After the removal of Margot Honecker as minister in November 1989, researchers found several hundred of these letters, marked "No response" followed by initials indicating that copies had been sent to the Stasi. Honecker made it clear that she regarded the contemporary discussion of reforms in the Soviet Union a serious mistake, and she called for the recognition and stabilization of the leading role of the party with education based firmly on Marxist ideology and an increase in centralization of decision-making to ensure that no schools deviated from this position.[50]

With the sudden collapse of the government of Erich Honecker, the Communist position accommodated itself somewhat to the demands for change, though continuing to call for "renewal of the Socialist school." As late as November 1989, the Action Program of the East German Communist Party (the SED) called for a new educational law that would contribute to producing youth committed to development of "a modern Socialism in their homeland," while Communist Party leader and chief of state Hans Modrow urged that "the renewal of Socialism requires a reform of the educational system." The party did not want pupils to continue to be insincere yes-sayers, he insisted, and schools should become equally hospitable to all religious and philosophical views that contributed to responsible participation in a Socialist society;[51] statements to this effect were published in *Neues Deutschland* on 11–12 November, and 18–19 November, 1989.

For some who were not supporters of Communist rule, the remedy for the stagnation of both school and society was nevertheless a renewal of Socialism "with a human face." This would mean, for example, more dialogue and free expression within the state school, but not a diversity of schools. Reformers called for decentralization of control, for education centered on learning rather than on teaching, for content more directly related to the lives of pupils, and for an emphasis on criticizing existing social arrangements—in brief, for the sorts of changes that progressive teachers often demand in the West, freedom within the present structures to use schools to promote a different agenda. By the late eighties, a democratic, humane school, free from political indoctrination, was among the leading demands of the opposition. Such a school, many believed, would be a place for free formation of opinions and of tolerance.[52]

For others, however, the structure of education itself was part of the problem; they thought it essential that the State relinquish its monopoly on the formation of worldview rather than simply give that a more humanistic form. With the intense grass-roots efforts that developed in the late eighties, groups of teachers and parents began to seek scope to create a distinctive profile for their schools.[53]

The League of Evangelical Churches became a major source of criticism of the regime during the 1980s in quite a different way than had the Roman Catholic Church in Poland.

The Polish church was a refuge for the Poles' faith and a bastion of the resistance to Communist ideology. The Protestant churches in the GDR rediscovered their Reformation calling. They taught the East Germans, by no means all of whom had a religious faith, to assert their individual freedom and their free judgment in the face of the state; they gave them the courage not to be afraid of either the authorities or their prohibitions.[54]

By December 1989, the Christian Democrats were including in their official position a call for a diversity of youth organizations, a constitutional guarantee that the role of parents in education is primary, and the freedom for parents or organizations to establish independent schools, which should receive public funding equivalent to that provided to state schools. Parents should be able to choose among the schools in an area, and the schools allowed to set admission criteria. Provision for publicly funded independent schools was also included in the party's electoral platform of March 1990.[55]

More surprisingly, the Social Democrats, while asserting the primacy of the state school, left room for the establishment and even the public subsidizing of independent schools. Other parties confined themselves to calling for purging state schools of ideological indoctrination and encouraging free inquiry without supporting the formation of independent schools. The ceremony of *Jugendweihe* and other Communist-flavored school ceremonies came under frequent attack by critics who insisted that parents should be allowed to decide whether and how nonpartisan ceremonies might have a role within the life of the school.[56] The required course on citizenship from a Marxist-Leninist perspective was abolished in January 1990, as was the required post-graduate ideological training for teachers.[57] In the policy debates, there was a growing consensus that new forms of schooling would emerge now that the State monopoly was broken, though it was not clear to what extent the resulting competition for pupils would serve educational reform. Would there be a clearer "profiling" of schools as their staff sought to attract pupils through becoming clear about their educational mission, or would schools lower their requirements in order to serve as many pupils as possible?[58]

Despite these pressures for change, many were startled when the education minister of the last Communist-dominated government called for "a renewed educational system" with an emphasis upon allowing each individual to pursue individual interests as well as abilities. Such a system would, H. H. Emons wrote in his March 1990 *Theses for Educational Reform*, include both State-sponsored and independent public educational institutions.[59]

After the elections of March 14, 1990, and the assumption of power by a coalition government of non-Communist parties in April 1990, all talk of a renewal of Socialist education was abandoned. Chief of State Lothar de Maizière spoke, in his declaration of policy direction, of setting aside the "bureaucratic centralized system of state leadership" and developing a new relationship of government accountability and initiatives from society. The unitary system must be replaced, he said, with a differentiated and flexible educational system "that does not exclude alternative models." Minister of Education Meyer stressed that the education system must be totally restructured both in form and in content, and should include support for independent schools.[60]

That month, the Initiative Freie Paedagogik held several large meetings at Leipzig University and gathered 5,000 signatures to a declaration that parents had a right to a free choice of schools and that the State had a responsibility to ensure that there was a diversity of publicly funded schools available, each declaring its educational vision (*ihr Konzept*) publicly, so that parents could make a well-informed choice.

The opportunity to operate independent schools became available under a statutory amendment adopted by the DDR Parliament in July 1990, bringing their status in line with the requirements of Section 7 of the BRD Constitution. This law, which remained in effect under the subsequent reunification treaty, provides for the approval of independent schools if their educational goals, organization and staff qualifications were equivalent to those of state schools.[61]

Subsequently, in the preparations for reunification, education came under the control of the five newly established *Laender* rather than that of the central government. Each state was therefore free to develop its own education statutes and regulations; but these measures were modeled closely upon those already in effect in the BRD. The education statute developed for Saxony, to take one example, provided a right of parents to an education for their children that is concerned with their dignity and personal development, "on the basis of the European traditions of Christianity, Humanism and the ideas of the liberal, democratic and social [note, not 'socialist'] freedom movements." Religious studies were to be a regular subject in the seventh and eighth grade of all state schools, and religious or ethical instruction (by parent and student choice) were to be provided starting in the ninth grade; the latter was to be taught by individuals licensed to do so by the religious denominations. Schools must "respect the philosophical and religious principles upon which parents wish their children to be educated," and avoid political partisanship.[62]

Provisions for independent schools, like other aspects of the new requirements, were subject to constitutional limitations and to the agreements reached over the years among the states of the BRD to ensure the general comparability of their systems. In October 1990, reunification became official and the (formerly West German) Constitution, including its education provisions, came into force in the five new *Laender* of the reunited country.[63]

The organizations of independent schools insisted, during the period of preparation for reunification, that they were pressing for the application of the right to nongovernment schooling not only in their own interest but also in order to create an overall educational system in which all schools—state and independent—would be free within a framework of public accountability to determine their own methods and content of instruction and handle their own personnel affairs.[64]

In a mark of respect for the role of independent schooling in reforming the educational system, the Saxon *Kultusministerin* (minister of religion and education) spoke at the dedication of a new independent Protestant elementary/secondary school in Leipzig in December 1991. The new school law, she told those who had gathered to celebrate many months of effort to organize the new school, would make possible "a differentiated education for all pupils" in order to give them the opportunity of a solid formation and also the "free development of personality" guaranteed by the constitution:

> Pupils have very different interests and gifts [and] their parents very different conceptions of what schooling should look like and where its emphasis should be placed. The educational landscape of Saxony will therefore be so arranged that for each different interest there will be a corresponding offering available. Alongside the varied offerings that the state educational system provides, the independent schools are for this reason especially important. With the distinctive characteristics and varied emphases that mark these schools, they contribute significantly to establishing diversity in the supply of schooling. In no sense are these schools to be seen as competition for but rather as a welcome and necessary expansion of the state educational system.[65]

Chapter Nine

Civil Society and Schooling in the Low Countries since World War II

BELGIUM

The secular forces, less united than their Catholic opponents, were slow to develop a new momentum on the school question after their defeats in the 1880s and 1890s. By the 1930s, however, they placed their emphasis upon the expansion of the state system of schooling in heavily Catholic areas where it was not well represented[1] while continuing somewhat routinely to call for abolishment of subsidies to confessional schools and the complete secularization of public schools.[2] In fact, there were compromises in 1937 and again in 1948 which in each case, recognized an expanded role for the State in the provision of schooling while at the same time increasing subsidies for private schools. The 1948 law also introduced a choice, in state secondary schools, between religious instruction (Catholic in the great majority of cases, but also Protestant or Jewish if demand justified it) and a secular ethics course, though, a few years later, 85 percent of the pupils in public secondary schools still opted for the religious instruction.[3]

Elementary schooling was, as we have seen, primarily the responsibility of the local communes, either through providing schools directly or through "adopting" Catholic schools. As might be expected, in some regions this resulted in schooling of an almost exclusively Catholic character, and Liberals and Socialists came increasingly to believe that direct state intervention was needed to ensure that secular schools were available. In December 1950, the Socialist Congress defended public schools as "the only form of national schooling." This was in conflict with a long tradition of local and regional autonomy, and Catholics would point this out frequently and to good effect. Moderate Socialists, however, expressed support for continued subsidies of Catholic schools, provided that they were subject to more effective state supervision.[4]

The situation began to change in the late 1930s and then with renewed force after World War II, as a rapidly increasing number of pupils continued on to secondary schooling in response to changes in the economy and job market. This created pressure to increase the number of public secondary schools, while requiring expansion of the large Catholic secondary and technical school sector. This "second education revolution" (the first being the achievement of near-universal elementary schooling) made the traditional mechanisms of school finance inadequate. Catholic schools could no longer depend entirely upon tuition, gifts, endowments, and low-paid members of religious orders, while massive investment was needed to create a network of public secondary and technical schools. Between 1945 and 1950, sixty-five new state secondary schools were opened, a 20 percent increase; by 1951, there were 51,000 pupils in public secondary schools against 67,000 in Catholic schools. The fact that state schools charged a lower tuition than the unsubsidized Catholic schools could afford was regarded by the latter as unfair competition, and public funding for private secondary schools became a pressing issue. Thus, "the problem of competition between the [public and private] networks shifted slowly but surely from elementary to secondary education."[5] After World War II, the secondary education question would be "at the heart of the Left-Right confrontation."[6]

Other issues that became politically significant after World War II included the right of public schools to hire only teachers with state diplomas (thus excluding applicants trained in state-subsidized Catholic institutions, of which there were 101, compared with 51 state institutions after World War II), and extension of the alternative of secular ethics classes for religious instruction to elementary schools. There was also a debate about school quality, with the Left charging that Catholic schools were inferior, while Catholic educators pointed out that their graduates did just as well in university as those from public schools, despite the lower costs in Catholic schools; the same arguments had been heard sixty years before.[7] The basis for the positions of the two sides underwent an interesting convergence: both agreed that the basic issue was the right of parents to select a school for their children, rather than the primacy of the State, on the one hand, or of the Church in education, on the other. Indeed, the Christian People's Party (PSC-CVP), founded in 1945, was explicitly independent of the Catholic hierarchy and based its support for Catholic schools on the right of conscience of parents.[8] The disagreement was now limited to whether it was more important to extend the availability of public (thus secular) schools to parents who did not want confessional education, or to ensure that Catholic schools were not too expensive to be a realistic choice and that their teachers were paid adequately; thus, there was a basis for the eventual compromise that sought to do both, through agreeing to increase government expenditures on schooling dramatically.[9]

The final stage (at least to date) in this conflict over the place of private or "free" schools in the Belgian educational system occurred in the 1950s, when the "second school war" broke out and was eventually resolved by a compromise among the three major political parties. This return engagement was, for reasons noted, rather different from the first. The PSC-CVP was not a strictly confessional party subordinated to the Catholic Church, and claimed to speak for the interests of parents, while the Socialists, though committed to secular schooling, did not call into question the existence of confessional schools nor their right to public funding.[10]

Strengthened by election gains which made it unnecessary to maintain a governing coalition with the Liberals, Catholics appointed the first Catholic education minister since 1919 and enacted public subsidies for private secondary schools and a corresponding budget. Supporters of public education charged that this amounted to "sabotage," and an abandonment of the tradition of "Belgian compromise" on school issues in recent decades.[11] That December, a new law was enacted which provided special arrangements for the salaries of members of teaching congregations and other clergy who were working in schools without teaching credentials.

In the budget debate of 1953 a supporter of public schools derided the government's claim that "school peace" could be achieved through putting public and private schools on an equal footing. "There can be no talk of equality," he charged,

> so long as Catholic education or Catholic schools make up the great majority of schools. There can be no talk of equality of education so long as new modern and luxurious Catholic schools arise in every neighborhood, while the building of new and desperately necessary public schools is sabotaged for years and many existing public schools are maintained in a shabby condition. Finally, there can be no talk of equality of education so long as Catholic normal schools remain real diploma factories and the school staff who are formed and trained in these schools take not only all the places in Catholic education but in addition a large share of the appointments in public education.[12]

The calculation of subsidies to schools on the basis of enrollment was seen, by opponents, as encouraging a "hunt for pupils" and pressure, in some communities, upon families to put their children in Catholic schools.[13]

The elections of 1954 were a success for the Socialists, and they formed a coalition government with the Liberals; although education had not been a major issue in the election campaign, the common anticlericalism of the two parties was, again, one of the few areas where they could make common cause.[14] The new government adopted a policy of strengthening and extending public education so that parents who did not want Catholic schooling would have a convenient alternative while placing stricter controls on private schools. While the coalition partners denied that they wanted to limit the freedom of parents, they objected to "subsidizing confessional schooling, at the service of a militant Church and a political party."[15]

The most bitter controversy arose over a measure taken by the new Socialist education minister, firing eighty-two teachers in public schools who had diplomas from Catholic institutions. This was denounced as "the first ideological purge that we have known in this country," as an act of intimidation intended to dissuade future teachers from Catholic teacher education. Wasn't it illegal to discriminate among Belgian citizens on the basis of religion? The minister replied that if Catholics insisted upon the right to train their own teachers in order to protect the distinctiveness of their schools, surely the State had the same right to protect its "spiritual integrity," and that 7,647 of the 16,803 teachers in communal schools had Catholic diplomas.[16]

In response to this and other "secular aggressions," Catholics established a National Committee for Freedom and Democracy which engaged in a variety of protest activities including a petition drive that collected more than two million signatures and very large rallies and demonstrations which could not be matched by the other side, divided as it was on economic issues and with a reduced appetite for defining its agenda in terms of anticlericalism. The government at first tried ineptly to discourage these expressions of popular opinion, for example by canceling trains to Brussels in order to keep down the number of participants in a rally in March 1955, but the movement took many forms, including boycotts of "Liberal" consumer products like Victoria chocolates, Wielemans beer, and Tirlemont sugar! A directive was read in all Catholic churches, reminding parents of their obligation as Christians to send their children to Catholic schools, but otherwise the lead was taken, not by the bishops as in the past, but by associations of parents of pupils in Catholic schools. By contrast, the Ligue de l'enseignement was essentially passive in its support for the government, and "Socialists no longer believed in their ability to mobilize their troops around these questions."[17]

Such expressions of popular support for confessional schooling did not prevent the enactment of a law in 1955 to extend the number of public schools and regulate the subsidies to private schools. For the first time, the State was given the right to establish its own elementary schools directly as a means of inserting public schools into communities where Catholics controlled local government, and municipalities and provinces lost the right to subsidize private schools. In effect, the State was authorized, for the first time, to substitute itself for local government in the provision of elementary schooling when it judged that necessary to ensure the availability of secular schooling. Within three years thirty-eight new state secondary schools were established, and twelve more were planned for the following year; two new state teacher training institutions were also opened. Stricter controls were placed on state subsidies for private, communal, and provincial schools. Parents in all public schools could choose between religious instruction and moral instruction on a humanistic basis.[18]

Catholics made substantial gains in the 1958 elections—the Liberal position that the State should organize and control schooling and the Socialist position that government-sponsored schooling should be expanded to ensure that parents could choose a nonreligious school were not convincing to the voters—with an absolute majority in the Senate but not in the lower house, making it necessary to seek compromises. For a few months, the Christian People's Party formed a government alone, and then in a coalition with the Liberals. There was a general sentiment to bring an end to the conflict over public and private schools in the same way that economic issues had recently been resolved through consultation between the government and its "social partners." A National School Commission representing Catholics, Liberals, and Socialists went to work in August 1958. In November, the agreement was approved by the congresses of the three parties and then signed by the party leaders;[19] it was subsequently—despite some complaints about "rubber stamping"—enacted by Parliament in May 1959, with only two Communists voting against.

The central concern of this *Schoolpact* was to remove all impediments to the further democratization of the educational system by making secondary education broadly available to age eighteen without cost to families. It provided for the expansion of tuition-free education in both public and private schools and measures to increase participation of working-class youth in secondary schools. Government would define curriculum standards while leaving pedagogical methods up to individual schools. In order to ensure that public schools were "neutral," it was required that two-thirds of their staff hold diplomas from public teacher training institutions, and that each public school provide a choice between two hours a week of secular ethical instruction and or of religious instruction. The State would have a right to establish public schools wherever necessary to ensure that parents could find a school corresponding to their choice within a reasonable distance: the standard set was that a state school would be established if sixteen parents wanted it and there was none available within four kilometers. Approved private schools would be fully subsidized, with their teachers paid directly by the state, except for the cost of building facilities and boarding establishments. Local communities could no longer "adopt" private schools to meet their obligation to provide instruction.[20] A commission was established to advise on the implementation of the *Schoolpact*.

To give an idea of the relative strength of the different systems at that point, in 1959 the state schools (*rijksscholen*) enrolled 76,761 elementary pupils; the provincial schools, 1,102; the local community schools, 350,849; and the free or private schools, 460,911. At the intermediate level there were 75,993 pupils in state schools; 17,131 in provincial schools; 51,084 in local schools; and 227,941 in free schools. Note that local communities focused largely on the provision of elementary schooling, and that there was a sharp drop-off in the overall number of pupils at the higher levels of education.[21] Between 1958 and 1965, 376 new state schools were established, while 465 private schools were brought within the subsidy provisions.

Two decades later, however, it was judged necessary to amend the constitution to respond to changing circumstances, most notably to make schooling henceforth be the responsibility of the language-based communities (discussed below), while retaining guarantees of freedom of conscience and equal treatment. The transfer of authority for schooling from national to community level (thus there are no longer "state schools"—they have become "Community schools," which, it should be noted, does not mean schools of the local community) made it no longer necessary to find a political consensus at national level between the Catholic majority of the north of the country (where the rights of non-Catholics needed to be protected) against the non-Catholic majority of the southern part of the country (where the rights of Catholics needed to be protected). Under the specific provisions of the constitution as adopted in 1988 (and a further revision in 1993), the educational system was progressively federalized and each citizen gained recourse to a legal remedy to avoidance of a law or an order by the executive power of a community which is in conflict with the constitution.[22]

Article 24 of the revised constitution (formerly Article 17) is now the legal basis of educational freedom and justice in Belgium. It provides that

(1.1) Education is free; any preventative measure is forbidden; the repression of offenses is only governed by laws or decrees.

(1.2) The Community offers free choice to parents.

(1.3) The Community organizes neutral education. Neutrality implies notably the respect of the philosophical, ideological, or religious conceptions of parents and pupils.

(1.4) The schools organized by the public authorities offer, until the end of mandatory schooling, the choice between the teaching of one of the recognized religions and nondenominational moral teaching . . .

(3.1) Everyone has the right to education with the respect of fundamental rights and freedoms. Access to education is free until the end of mandatory schooling.

(3.2) All pupils of school age have the right to moral or religious education at the Community's expense.

(4) All pupils or students, parents, teaching staff, or institutions are equal before laws or decrees. The laws and decrees take into account objective differences, notably the characteristics of each organizing authority, that justify appropriate treatment.

(5) The organization, the recognition and the subsidizing of education by the Community are regulated by laws or decrees.

The proportion of elementary school enrollment in state schools increased from 8.7 percent in 1958–59 to 16.4 percent in 1972–73, largely at the expense of local public schools; the Catholic proportion remained level, a slight majority of the total. In the upper level of secondary schooling, the private school proportion increased from 61.2 to 63.7 percent.[23] Considered over time, the proportion of pupils attending free (private) elementary schools increased from 49 percent in 1935 to 53.5 percent in 1960 and 56 percent in 1989.[24]

The Belgian system of political and institutional compromise has been described as "subsidized freedom." There was for a time considerable interest in the possibility of developing a "pluralistic school" which would do justice to all of the various currents of belief and worldview in Belgian society. Credit for introducing this idea into political debate is usually attributed to an article in 1960 in a left-wing Catholic monthly, calling for a school

> in which youth of diverse social backgrounds, coming from distinctive political milieus and from backgrounds with differing worldviews, will end up together. The pedagogy of such a school rests more on its attitude than on its contents. This attitude can no longer be a neutral or contradicting one, not [merely] tolerant or passive; it must be actively expressed, based upon respect.[25]

The Belgian Parliament adopted a number of measures, in the early 1970s, to renew and update the compromises reached in the School Pact of 1958.

One of them was the approval of a law authorizing the creation of "pluralistic schools," but this symbolic step seemed to exhaust the reform impulse, since little has been done to implement it. The significance of this measure was limited by the fact that, two years earlier, the legislators had approved financial and organizational measures that strengthened the existing, and firmly separate, public and Catholic systems, and Catholic leaders insisted that a school which sought to represent diverse points of view at the same time was neither pedagogically sound nor consistent with the rights of parents who sought Catholic schooling for their children.[26]

The advocates of this new common school saw it as "socially renewing," as a way of forming a new society; they spoke of it as an engaged school, in the then-fashionable existentialist sense, making no pretense of neutrality with respect to the issues of social, economic, and political life. How it would come into being was less clear, given the constitutional principle of educational freedom. Hope was expressed that several existing schools—public and Catholic—might merge into a single "pluralistic" school. Supporters of Catholic education responded that private schools were an expression of the concerns of a significant group within Belgian society, and that their popularity with parents—whether practicing Catholics or not—was the best evidence that they were meeting a real need. "So long as parents, through 'freedom of choice,' entrusted their children to Catholic schools, the common school, even a pluralistic one, was not acceptable . . . The supporters of pluralistic education, on their part, considered the 'principle of free choice' (for various reasons) as no longer relevant . . . and repeatedly raised questions about the real significance of the choices made by parents."[27] While diversity and democracy might have flourished within the proposed common school, it seems that the actual pluralism of Belgian society was effectively served by a diversity among schools with which the public was quite satisfied.

THE NETHERLANDS

By the 1960s almost no political group in The Netherlands or Belgium wished to reopen the question of equal funding for public and approved nonpublic schools. In the statement of principles of the Dutch Socialist Party in 1959, for example, it was stated that "since philosophy of life and religious convictions are considered of fundamental significance for education and instruction, the party respects the foundations of both public and private schooling. It recognizes that the right of parents to choose schools freely is a demand of democracy. In consequence, it accepts the principle of the education pacification."[28] The Christian Democrats and their predecessor Catholic and Protestant

Parties, naturally, have continued to insist upon "distributed responsibility" in place of centralization of governmental authority over education.[29]

> If the connection with and the influence of social class is a feature that Dutch education has in common with the education systems of all Western industrialized countries, the extent to which differences in worldviews determine the structure and arrangement of the education system in The Netherlands is unique. The right to and the actual possibility of the creation of their own schools by groups with their own worldviews or concepts of society, and the opportunity also to express these viewpoints in that education, is in no other country in the world, except perhaps in Israel, so extensively guaranteed as in The Netherlands.[30]

Ironically, however, there were many who predicted that the victories won by those who had pressed for public funding of confessional schools would be undone by what they expected to be a precipitously declining demand for such schools, as a result of the widespread secularization of Belgian and Dutch society.

There were, on the other hand, institutional structures in place that served to sustain the existing *verzuilde* system in education as well as in some other spheres of society.[31] The structure of Dutch education continues to bear the marks of the conjunction of Protestant "sphere sovereignty" and Catholic "subsidiarity" thinking which made the settlement of the long *schoolstrijd* more than a simple political compromise. These worldviews found a ready reception in The Netherlands because they were consistent with how Dutch society and government had been organized for hundreds of years with highly decentralized authority and reliance upon voluntary associations and semiofficial institutions to carry out many of the functions which in other countries were more likely to be the responsibility of government.[32]

To an increasing extent, in fact, it was possible to speak of an "institutionalization of the pillarization of education" in both countries through the development of a whole range of organizations and institutions—many government subsidized, either directly or indirectly—whose role it is to support the independent but coordinated functioning of schools of the different "philosophical families." Public schools are owned and operated by local government, while independent schools may be owned and operated by an association or a foundation. In 1994 the average government board operated 4.6 schools, while the average Protestant or Catholic board (the former, generally, associations; the latter, foundations) operated two, and other private school boards between one and 1.3 schools; thus governance was, apart from the larger cities, remarkably close to the individual school.[33]

Since the constitution and laws give parents the right to insist upon educa-tion consistent with their own convictions—whether through establishment of a new school if numbers justify that or through transportation to a school at some distance—the issue has arisen whether this right is sometimes asserted for reasons that have less to do with convictions than with avoidance of the local school for whatever reason. Is this in some cases more a consumer free-dom that a freedom of conscience? Jurisprudence has consistently found that government is not capable of judging the sincerity of the request and must take it at face value.[34]

The way the Dutch system functions is that government negotiates with the umbrella organizations (*koepels*) of Catholic, Protestant, neutral, and communal (public) schooling, each of which represents hundreds of boards which in turn, control the schools. Decisions about standards, funding, and the goals of education are made through a process of negotiation which has been described as "the politics of accommodation."[35] In the Scheveningen Consultations (July 1993), for example, the minister of education worked out with representatives of the organizations a series of wide-ranging agreements on decentralization, lump-sum funding of schools, coordination of efforts to address urban underachievement, and other matters.[36] When the government resolved to adopt a broad and coordinated assault on social problems, it would have been un-Dutch to lay out the strategies without an extensive consultative process, including negotiating the ways in which local government and private schooling would collaborate.[37]

The right to operate and to select a nongovernment school has been based upon the concept of *richting*, corresponding to a religious or philosophical worldview, even though it is not necessary that a school be linked to a religious organization or community, much less a "recognized" denomination. Elemen-tary enrollment is divided roughly evenly three ways among Catholic, public, and Protestant schools, with under 10 percent attending an assortment of other independent schools with a pedagogical or religious distinctiveness. Postma lists seventeen religious types represented among publicly funded Dutch schools: "Catholic, Protestant, 4 varieties of more conservative Pro-testant, Anthroposophic (Steiner); Orthodox Jewish, Liberal Jewish, Platonic, Rosicrucian, Orthodox Muslim, Liberal Muslim, Orthodox Hindu, Liberal Hindu, evangelical, and Hernhutter."[38]

This does not count the distinctions among pedagogical types, which may also serve as the basis for parent choice: Montessori, Dalton, Freinet, and so forth. In 1995, there were 250 schools following the pedagogical ideas of Peter Peterson (Jenaplan); 160 Montessori schools; 60 Waldorf (Steiner) schools; 10 Freinet schools; and about 25 schools based on other alternative pedagogies. The demand for such schools increased their number from about 200 in 1975 to about 600 twenty years later.[39]

In 1994, 35 percent of the elementary schools in The Netherlands were public; 29.3 percent, Catholic; 30.3 percent, one variety or another of Protestant; and 5.4 percent of some other "signature." The share of pupils attending Protestant schools has remained remarkably stable, and even increased somewhat, over the past twenty-five years, while Catholic enrolments have declined somewhat, and there has been some increase in the number of pupils attending nonreligious private schools. Although the number of schools overall has declined sharply as declining enrolments (the number of pupils in elementary schools fell from 1.7 million in 1980 to 1.4 million in 1990, before rising again) budget considerations have forced many mergers, these have mostly occurred within the various families of schools.[40] All in all, there is not the sort of massive shift to public schooling which one might expect, given the extensive secularization of Dutch society. The same comment could be made about Belgium.

SECULARIZATION OF SOCIETY

Although the system of differentiated schooling and parent choice of schools had achieved an imposing scope and elaboration in The Netherlands, the 1917–20 Pacification was called into question in the 1980s. There was talk of a new *schoolstrijd*, drawing its sharpness from three developments in Dutch society. The first was a growing secularization, which has proceeded much further than in the United States.

Despite the extensive abandonment of the mainstream churches, however, there continues to be widespread support for institutions with a religious identity; approximately 35 percent of respondents prefer a faith-based school for their own children. The continuing attachment to denominational forms of youth socialization may have less to do, sociologists believe, with an assent to church doctrines than to a sense that religious institutions are effective at transmitting norms and values important for youth.[41] It has also been proposed that the importance attached to denominational institutions and organizations may be greater in spheres of life which are more sensitive to worldview considerations, which would certainly describe schooling and youth work.[42]

Although many social agencies and more than two-thirds of schools continue to claim a religious identity, there is considerable evidence that this has been "hollowed out" by decades of dependence upon the government as well as growing secularization. Since World War II shook up all aspects of Dutch society,

> the nongovernmental organizations that delivered services for the public benefit became more professionalised. The professionals cared less about the identity of the organization than about professional codes . . . This central planning and sub-sidizing had as consequence that nongovernmental organizations who [sic] wanted subsidy made their policies according to the policy of the government. By these trends and by the decentralization, since 1977, many of the private organizations are merged and have loosened (lost) their ties with their constituency. Simultane-ously new organizations are established.[43]

The secularization and "depillarization" (ontzuiling) of many other institutions of Dutch society has raised questions about whether there is still a justification for the verzuiling of the educational system, or whether it would make more sense to recognize parent demand for particular pedagogical approaches as having equal weight as demand for schooling on a religious basis.[44]

LOSS OF DISTINCTIVENESS

The second development, related in a complex fashion to the first, is a certain loss of nerve among those upon whom confessional schooling depends to confirm its purpose, from church hierarchies to teachers. Research by soci-ologist J. A. van Kemenade, who would later serve as minister of education, found that 57 percent of the parents with children in Catholic schools thought that the religious character of a school was important, but only 30 percent of Catholic school teachers agreed![45] In effect, then, there was a sort of betrayal from within resulting from changing conceptions of the nature of professional work, and loss of conviction about the possibility of reconciling religion with professional norms. This has been a matter of deep concern in recent years for leaders in the confessional school sector, and has led to the sensitive question: if schools are no longer distinctively Catholic or Protestant, how does their maintenance with public funds guarantee liberty of conscience?

Some have suggested that the decision of the Catholic bishops, influenced by Vatican II, to replace the catechism with more open-ended religious instruc-tion encouraged confusion about how to approach religious instruction. "Belief is not a question of learning something," they observed in a 1965 Lenten letter, "but primarily of living something." This suggested to many educators that they could legitimately replace traditional beliefs—even the most fundamental—with social concerns.[46]

Further confusion was caused by a proposal, advanced in 1972 by a leading Catholic educator-politician, that public and confessional schools work together in a tertium, or "third way," based upon "a well-considered choice for spiritual pluriformity." This would not only increase efficiency and lower costs, but would be a step forward in Dutch education, away from the *verzuilde* (pillarized) system that he had earlier served as director of the Central Bureau for Catholic Education.[47]

The problem of loss of confessional distinctiveness has been greater in Catholic than in Protestant schools. Asked how they understood Jesus Christ, only 3 percent of the teachers in Catholic elementary schools in a 1993 study replied "the Son of God," compared with 40 percent of those in Protestant Christian (PC) schools. Seventeen percent of the Catholic school teachers said, "a man in whom God appeared," compared with 26 percent of the PC school teachers, while 80 percent of the Catholic school teachers and 34 percent of the PC school teachers said "a great man." In 56 percent of the Catholic schools, it was reported that the "religious instruction" had no connection with the Church's teaching, and only a minority of the teachers surveyed reported that they were committed Catholics. Protestant Christian schools have retained more of their distinctiveness, in part through the efforts of several organizations that work nationwide to this end; for example, most schools require that staff endorse the religious mission of the school. This is even more the case in two groups of orthodox Protestant schools which were organized as the PC schools became less strict.[48]

It seems likely that the greater ability of Protestant schools to maintain their character derives from the urgency which their leaders have felt, for many hundred years, to develop a distinctive approach that would stabilize the identity of Protestant Christian schooling.

PROMOTION OF THE COMMON SCHOOL

The third development in the 1980s was a new and aggressive advocacy of the public school, seen as the means of bridging not only confessional and class differences, but growing ethnic differences within Dutch society as well. Arguably, the moment for such a strategy had already passed. In the years after World War II there had been considerable interest, not only among traditional supporters of public schools but also among some influential Catholics and Protestants, for overcoming the worldview divisions in society through some sort of common school, which would be public but without maintaining the awkward distance from religious matters which had come to characterize the neutral public school.

Under the slogan *Niet apart maar samen* (not apart but together), the Association for Public Education (VOO) called for a new "school struggle" to sweep away what it considered the outmoded and counterproductive relics of *verzuiling* of education. In alliance with the union representing educators employed in public schools, the VOO argued that confessional education was neither demanded by parents nor provided by most Catholic and Protestant schools, and presented an obstacle to the "constructive educational policy" (a slogan of the social democratic Labor Party—PvdA) that government should be free to pursue in the interest of social justice and equality.

Because private (and especially confessional) schooling was established to perpetuate rather than to remove group loyalties, VOO staff contended in a controversial book, it could not contribute to the cultural integration required as The Netherlands became host to an ever-increasing number of families from outside the European Union. "Whenever a private school seeks to contribute to cultural integration, it is faced with a dilemma: give preference to its [own] testimony or to dialogue with those who think otherwise." But such a dialogue would require treating those views as of equal value with one's own, and expressing this equality concretely by the appointment of teachers, parent council and governing board members who hold those views. A private school that refused to make such fundamental changes to its nature could not, by van Schoten and Wansink's definition, be of equal quality with a public school in terms of the new expectations placed upon schools. Thus the authorities would be justified, even required, to withdraw financial support. A private school that did accept such conditions might as well be a public school in any case; having lost its distinctive identity and mission, it would have lost its claim upon support as an educational alternative.[49]

The assault on the rationale for confessional and other private schooling calls into question the value of school distinctiveness in the name of the socializing function of education in a society of growing diversity and need for integration. While this angle of attack has not resulted in changes in the legal status of nonstate schools in either country, nor threatened the right of private schools to full funding equivalent to that received by state schools, it has put many teachers and boards schools on the defensive about any distinctive aspects of their curriculum or school practices that could be perceived as socially divisive, including the assertion that a particular religious tradition possesses essential truth.

Dutch Liberals and Socialists, while continuing to support the system under which public funds allow parents to select schools with a distinctive religious or pedagogical character, do so with a certain reluctance because of a concern that schools should bring together children from different groups—religious, social class, racial—in society. Whether called the "encounter school" (*ontmo-etingsschool*), the "together school" (*gezamenlijkeschool*), the "working-together school" (*samenwerkingsschool*), the "open school," the "ecumenical school," or the "compromise school," or by some more recent label, this remains the ideal for many.[50] In the early seventies there seemed a chance that some variation on this model would become popular, in part because of the need to merge schools to deal with declining enrolments, but the support turned out to be rather shallow;[51] after all, "*verzuiling* was woven more deeply into the structure of education than the propagandists of the *samenwerkingsschool* liked to believe."[52]

Even as Protestant-Catholic differences have grown much less significant in recent years, the presence of a growing Muslim population and, as required by law, public funding for Islamic schools has led to uncertainty whether the present arrangements could cause permanent divisions in society. A Labor Party education official in Amsterdam announced in December 2003 that he wanted to turn private schools into mixed public schools. He argued that the existence of Islamic, Christian, and Jewish schools was promoting segregation and that no new schools should be established on the basis of the beliefs of parents. Only pedagogical methods should be the basis for school distinctiveness.[53]

Braster's careful study of "the identity of the public school" suggests that this identity is, for many, no longer defined in terms of neutrality but rather of pluralism. On the other hand, efforts in the 1970s and 1980s to create "encounter schools" and "working-together schools" as a collaboration of different types of schools were largely stillborn because of lack of organized support and the resistance of the existing systems. Public school advocates, for example, insisted that the public school was already pluralistic and had no need to be coupled with private schools; the latter should simply close.[54]

To a considerable extent, parental preferences seem to be related to perceptions of quality differences among the different types of schooling. Supposedly,

nonconfessional private education is more concerned with the individual development of the child and to attract more children out of "better" circles. Public education is distinguished above all by the equality of individuals, whatever their beliefs or worldviews, political preferences or ethnicity, and the fact that the pupils come from diverse backgrounds. Together with nonconfessional private education, public education distinguishes itself in the eyes of parents in a positive way with respect to attention to creative development, critical thinking, the development of independence and giving freedom to the pupils. The picture of confessional [education] involves above all concern about values and norms, an orderly and disciplined atmosphere, and—especially in Protestant schools—the fact that much is taught about religion.[55]

Efforts to assess the academic effects of the different types of schools, holding constant the social class of pupils and other factors, have shown a consistent advantage for Catholic and often for Protestant schools over public schools, though it is impossible to know to what extent this reflects the motivations of parents who choose confessional schools.[56] The attractiveness of these schools, it seems fair to conclude, is based in part upon a rational decision by parents—whether themselves church members or not—that this will provide better opportunities for their children. The fact that the religious character of many of these schools—especially the Catholic—has grown quite residual, but that they continue to place a strong emphasis upon moral development, makes them desirable to many parents, especially since questions about the meaning of life which have grown no less pressing, are addressed only very awkwardly and defensively in public schools with their commitment to value neutrality.[57]

Another continuing advantage of private schools in general, it has been suggested, is that their boards tend to be much more involved with and supportive of them than are the local government officials who oversee public schools along with many other responsibilities.[58] This has led to much discussion of whether, under the constitution, public schools could be placed under the control of nongovernmental boards, along the lines of American charter schools, in order to give them the benefits of autonomy which are enjoyed by state-funded private schools. "The simplest and most available solution seems to be to remove the control over public schools from the direct influence of the communal council and place it in the hands of an independent management commission."[59] This proposal has been debated for decades— indeed, it was proposed as early as 1938, and again after World War II— with critics warning that it would have the effect of allowing public schools to become distinctive and thus not equally accessible to pupils from families of every religious and nonreligious viewpoint.[60]

Pedagogical arguments for the public support of private schools have been advanced as well. In a world in which youth are exposed to the confused and cynical values presented by the media, it was argued, it was all the more important to provide education rooted in a coherent worldview. The issue was not religious instruction alone, supporters of private schools claimed, but a coherent school climate in which the student's character could be formed through the witness of teachers, through relationships, and through the religious observances of the entire school.[61]

Whatever the continuing vitality of Christianity among the Dutch and Belgian populations—expert opinion differs—there are many indications that most parents and the general public are satisfied with the diverse and decentralized structure of schooling which resulted from the conflicts over the religious character of schools. Indeed, there seems to be if anything an increased interest in school distinctiveness, though focused often now upon pedagogical rather than religious aspects of a school's mission.

As long ago as 1938, a Dutch school inspector and Social Democrat, I. van der Velde, suggested three reasons why the "market share" of public schools had fallen to 31.9 percent.

The private school is by virtue of its fundamentals and its history far more a school of the parents than is the public-authority school. It is understandable that groups of progressive parents develop a wish to have a share in these relationships. What they do not find in publicly run schools, they look for in privately run schools. In many cases the privately run schools show greater unity from an educational perspective. There is stronger leadership, more consultation between teachers, relationships that have a beneficial effect on results . . . What has remained virtually unchanged since 1913 is—let's not mince words—the squabbling between teachers in public-authority schools. Anyone who knew the situation in 1913 and knows it now in 1938, saw and can see the fact of the many organizations quarreling among themselves oh so vehemently on a ship that is in danger. A quarrel that is harmful to reputation and position . . . There is a need to find the unity that for the most part already exists in privately run schools.[62]

As Van der Velde suggested, the solution to the lagging popularity of the public schools was, not to reduce the autonomy and cohesiveness of the private schools with which they competed, but to enable and stimulate public schools to have the same qualities. Seventy years later, that possibility is under active consideration.

Notes

Introduction

1 Glenn and De Groof (2004); updated and expanded edition in preparation for 2011.
2 http://www.vatican.va/holy_father/john_paul_ii/encyclicals/documents/hf_jp-ii_enc_01051991_centesimus-annus_en.html, Section 48.
3 Osborne and Gaebler (1992).
4 Berger and Neuhaus (1996), 164.
5 Wolfe (1989).
6 Thielicke (1969), 259.
7 Humboldt (1993), 92.
8 Tocqueville (1988), 15.
9 Tocqueville (1988), 90.
10 Tocqueville (1988), 515–17.
11 In Fernandez and Jenkner (1995).
12 In Fernandez and Jenkner (1995).
13 http://www.unhchr.ch/tbs/doc.nsf/0/ae1a0b126d068e868025683c003c8b3b?Opendocument.
14 In Fraser and Brickman (1968), 32.
15 In Fraser and Brickman (1968), 76.
16 Cousin (1835), 62.
17 In Fraser and Brickman (1968), 92.
18 In Ulich (1935), 44.
19 Stowe (1836), 75.
20 in Fraser and Brickman (1968), 100, 92.
21 Mann (1844); Barnard (1854).
22 Houston and Prentice (1988), 114.
23 Prentice (2004), 175–76.
24 In Welch (2001), 41.
25 Arnold (1964).
26 In Fraser and Brickman (1968), 188, 248, 268.
27 Gontard (1959), 260–62.

28 Griscom (1823), 2, 161.
29 Cuvier and Noël (1812, 1816).
30 Cousin (1837), 137.
31 Bache (1839), 207.
32 Lannie (1974), 46.
33 Hickson (1840), 23, 34–37; see also *Common School Journal* 3, 6, 94–95.
34 Arnold (1861), 196.
35 Brooks (1837), 12.

Chapter One: Background

1 Robbins (1912), 15–16, 21; Dodde (1991), 30–31, 48–51.
2 Adamson (1967), 207.
3 Dodde (1981), 67–70.
4 Neugebauer (2005), 216.
5 Kaplan (2007), 31.
6 Luther (1962), 348.
7 Luther (1962), 350.
8 Luther (1962), 351–52.
9 Luther (1962), 357.
10 in Cohen (1974), I, 45.
11 In Reble (1999), 86–89.
12 Elias (2002), 90–91.
13 Robbins (1912), 15–16.
14 Melton (2003), 5.
15 Boyd (1966), 191.
16 Wehler (1989a), 284.
17 Reble (2002), 88–90.
18 Furet and Ozouf (1977), 71–72.
19 See discussion in Kaplan (2007), 29–31.
20 Reisner (1930), 30–31.
21 Dodde (1981), 79–87.
22 In Cohen (1974) I, 59–60.
23 de Booy (1977), 26–29.
24 Neugebauer (2005), 221–2.
25 Kaplan (2007), 258.
26 Reble (2002), 122–23; Sparn (2005), 135.
27 Neugebauer (2005), 223.
28 In Fertig (1984), 220.
29 Neugebauer (2005), 223.
30 Wehler (1989a), 284–85.
31 Houston (2002), 39.
32 Herrmann (2005), 101.

33 Text in Reble (1999), 139–47.
34 Melton (2003), 35–36.
35 Melton (2003), 23.
36 Sparn (2005), 140.
37 Deppermann (1961).
38 Melton (2003), 46–47.
39 Wehler (1989a), 287.
40 Fertig (1984), 258–59.
41 Melton (2003), 181.
42 Neugebauer (2005), 235.
43 Dodde (1981), 102–07.
44 Dodde (1981), 112.
45 de Booy (1997), 60–63.
46 Kossmann (2001), 30, 55.
47 Tveit (1991), 57.
48 Sparn (2005), 134.

Chapter Two: The Enlightenment and Romantic Nationalism

1 Melton (2003), 112; see Wehler (1989a), 233–40, 286.
2 Krieger (1970), 84, 95.
3 Neugebauer (2005), 237.
4 Melton (2003), 105.
5 Melton (2003), 200–05; La Chalotais text in Fontainerie (1932).
6 Melton (2003), 210.
7 Melton (2003), 100.
8 Melton (2003), 213; Neugebauer (2005), 239.
9 Neugebauer (2005), 240.
10 Grimm (1991), 235, 239.
11 Komlósi (1991), 265, 286.
12 Čapková (1991), 303–05.
13 Grimm (1991), 235.
14 Reble (2002), 173.
15 Jeismann (1987b), 110.
16 LaVopa (1980), 12.
17 Lundgreen (1980), I, 34–35.
18 Tenorth and Drewek (2000), 178.
19 Lundgreen (1980), I, 52.
20 In LaVopa (1980), 27.
21 Kant (1960), 6.
22 In Herrmann (2005), 97.
23 Ringer (1979), 50.
24 Herrmann (2005), 115.

25 Herrmann (2005), 108.
26 Schleunes (1989), 26, 28.
27 Melton (2003), 167.
28 Reble (2002), 169.
29 Schleunes (1989), 29.
30 Schmale (1991), 733.
31 In Fertig (1984), 228–29.
32 Blankertz (1982), 79; Schmidt (2005), 263.
33 Reble (2002), 161–62.
34 Herrmann (2005), 106.
35 Schmidt (2005), 270–72.
36 Reble (2002), 165.
37 Fertig (1984), 210–11.
38 Blankertz (1982), 80.
39 Fertig (1984), 48–51.
40 Herrmann (2005), 99.
41 Fertig (1984), 264–65.
42 Schleunes (1989), 39–40.
43 Schmale (1991), 636.
44 Reble (2002), 168.
45 Melton (2003), 167.
46 Herbst (2006), 25.
47 In Titze (1973), 38n.
48 In Gay (1969), 37.
49 Lundgren (1980), I, 45, 70.
50 Text in Reble (1999), 423–27; see also Titze (1973), 40.
51 Jeismann (1987b), 110–11.
52 Lamberti (1989), 6.
53 Wehler (1989a), 272.
54 Schleunes (1989), 44.
55 Welch (2001), 38.
56 Herrmann (2005), 119–22.
57 Guimps (1890), viii.
58 Green (1914), 166.
59 Tenorth (2000), 94–95.
60 In Badertscher and Grunder (1998), 145.
61 Compayré (1904), 428.
62 In Downs (1975), 17.
63 Schleunes (1989), 16–17.
64 In Grunz-Stoll (1997), 169–70.
65 In Reble (1999), 354–58.
66 In Reisner (1930), 193.
67 Grunz-Stoll (1997), 170–78.

68   In Fraser and Brickman (1968), 50).
69   Reble (2002), 223.
70   Rousseau (1979), 184.
71   In Downs (1975), 15.
72   Downs (1975), 42–43.
73   In Downs (1975), 55ff.
74   Silber (1960), 140.
75   In Downs (1975), 35.
76   Pestalozzi (1977), 95.
77   Pestalozzi (1977), 116–18, 129–31.
78   Pestalozzi (1977), 134–35.
79   Pestalozzi (1977), 140, 152.
80   Pestalozzi (1977), 174.
81   Pestalozzi (1977), 178–79.
82   Herrmann (2005), 118.
83   Silber (1960), 131.
84   in Reble (1999), 422–23.
85   Tenorth (2000), 157.
86   Downs (1975), 111.
87   Silber (1960), 195.
88   in Downs (1975), 25.
89   Downs (1975), 53, 66.
90   In Fraser and Brickman (1968), 50.
91   Downs (1975), 112.
92   Blankertz (1982), 130, 160.
93   Hamann (1986), 106.
94   Blankertz (1982), 129.
95   Green (1914), 166.
96   Groen van Prinsterer (1976), 17.
97   See Gorski (2003), 39–77.
98   Cliteur (1989), 141.
99   Dodde and Lenders (1991), 140; see also Schama (1977).
100   Mijnhardt (1984), 193.
101   In Groot (1984a), 237; de Booy (1977), 119.
102   Stuurman (1983), 107.
103   Braudel (1984), 196–97.
104   Mijnhardt (1984), 191.
105   Berk (1984), 7; see also Stouten (1984).
106   In Helsloot (1984), 9.
107   In Schelfhout (1979), 160.
108   Vroede (1970), 120.
109   Kalsbeek (1976), 137.
110   Bruggen, Rienen, and Wieringen (1977), 42.

111   Helsloot (1984), 10.
112   Mijnhardt (1984), 194.
113   Helsloot (1984), 10–16.
114   See Berg and Dooren (1978).
115   Groot (1984a), 238, 242.
116   Mijnhardt (1984), 203.
117   Braster (1996), 87–88.
118   Leeb (1973), 263.
119   Schama (1977), 14, 216.
120   Boekholt (1987), 89.
121   Boekholt (1987), 96.
122   In Schama (1970), 609.
123   Bruin (1985), 189.
124   Schama (1977), 533.
125   Vroede (1970), 118ff.
126   Valk (1995), 165.
127   Schama (1977), 533.
128   Vree (1984a), 44.
129   See Glenn (1988), Chapter 2.
130   Vroede (1970), 41.
131   Mallinson (1970), 47.
132   Vroede (1970), 61–65.
133   Kossmann (2001), 30, 55, 59.

Chapter Three: The State Takes Charge

1   Osborn (1934), 156.
2   Spiegel (1968), 249.
3   LaVopa (1980), 37–38.
4   Fichte (1978), 21.
5   Kneller (1941), 91.
6   Fichte (1978), 22ff.
7   Fichte (1978), 28–29.
8   Rousseau (1962), 79.
9   Fichte (1978), 38, 43.
10   Rush (1965), 17.
11   See Meinecke (1977), 44–45.
12   Fichte (1978), 27, 145.
13   Fichte (1978), 148, 150.
14   In Downs (1975), 110.
15   Fichte (1978), 177–78.
16   Fichte (1978), 152–53.
17   Fichte (1978), 180, 183–84.

18 Humboldt (1993), 48–49.
19 Herbst (2006), 27.
20 Jeismann (1987b), 108.
21 Blankertz (1982), 104.
22 Jeismann (1987a), 21.
23 Tenorth (2000), 129.
24 In Fertig (1984), 364.
25 LaVopa (1980), 40.
26 In Reble (1999), 305; see also Blankertz (1982), 120.
27 Reble (1999), 304.
28 Rousseau (1979), 39.
29 Reble (2002), 213.
30 Schmale (1991), 646.
31 Schleiermacher (2000), I, 272ff.
32 Tenorth (2000), 134.
33 Schleiermacher (2000), I, 274, 276.
34 Schleiermacher (2000), I, 285–88.
35 Spiegel (1968), 244.
36 Schleiermacher (2000), II, 12.
37 Winkler (2000).
38 Schleiermacher (2000), II, 13, 127, 133–34.
39 Schleiermacher (2000), II, 282.
40 Jeismann (1987a), 1.
41 Jeismann (1987a), 5–6; Friederich (1987), 123.
42 Jeismann (1987b), 109.
43 Wehler (1989b), 297.
44 Titze (1973), 90–91.
45 Text in Reble (1999), 423–27.
46 Herrlitz, Hopf, and Titze (1986), 45.
47 Jeismann (1987b), 108–09.
48 In Reisner (1930), 233.
49 Titze (1973), 119–21.
50 Lundgreen (1980), 61.
51 In Titze (1973), 139–41.
52 In Herbst (2006), 51.
53 Wehler (1989b), 478.
54 Blankertz (1982), 134.
55 Wehler (1989b), 481.
56 Jeismann (1987a), 9.
57 Tenorth (2000), 155.
58 Lundgren (1980), 77–79.
59 Tenorth and Drewek (2000), 197.
60 Reisner (1922), 149–50.

61 Schmale (1991), 639.
62 Titze (1973), 129.
63 Hamann (1986), 95.
64 Lamberti (1989), 20.
65 Tenorth (2000), 166–67.
66 Blankertz (1982), 165.
67 Lamberti (1989), 19, 6.
68 Reisner (1930), 207–08.
69 Reisner (1930), 217.
70 Reisner (1922), 134.
71 Knight (1930), 135.
72 Knight (1930), 138–40.
73 Knight (1930), 158–61.
74 Knight (1930), 144–45.
75 Knight (1930), 168–71.
76 Knight (1930), 207.
77 Lamberti (1989), 27, 14.
78 Nipperdey (1983), 465.
79 Reisner (1930), 222.
80 Welch (2001), 30–31.
81 Texts in Reble (1999), 466–70.
82 Wehler (1989b), 482.
83 Helmreich (1959), 294.
84 In Lamberti (1989), 16.
85 Helmreich (1959), 43.
86 Helmreich (1959), 40–41.
87 Lamberti (1989), 17.
88 Arnold (1964), 231.
89 Reisner (1922), 132.
90 Titze (1973), 175, 178–79.
91 Reisner (1922), 135.
92 Nipperdey (1983), 463.
93 Kossmann (2001), 89.
94 Schama (1977), 119.
95 Schama (1977), 319.
96 Schama (1977), 375.
97 Dodde (1981), 6ff.
98 In Groot (1960), 59, 84.
99 Vroede (1970), 110.
100 Groot (1960), 82, 84, 89.
101 Valk (1995), 166.
102 Groot (1960), 86.
103 Tyssens (1999), 43.

104 Braster (1996), 90–91.
105 Vroede (1970), 139.
106 Kalsbeek (1976), 146–49.
107 Schama (1977), 430–31, 473.
108 Schama (1977), 494.
109 Bruin (1985), 55–58.
110 Bruggen, Rienen, and Wieringen (1977), 46.
111 In Kalsbeek (1976), 151–55.
112 In Baynes (1985), 41.
113 Schama (1977), 380.
114 Stuurman (1983), 116–17.
115 In Groot (1960), 63.
116 In Groot (1960), 59, 84.
117 Rasker (1981), 36.
118 Boekholt (1987), 99.
119 Braster (1996), 94.
120 Essen (1990), 56–57.
121 Bruin (1985), 193.
122 Boekholt (1987), 103.
123 Boekholt (1987), 97.
124 Schama (1977), 430.
125 Boekholt (1987), 107–09.
126 Dodde (1981), 13.
127 Schama (1977), 539.
128 Vroede (1970), 208.
129 Boekholt (1987), 109.
130 In Bruin (1985), 65.
131 Gerretson (1984), 84.
132 Bruin (1985), 192.
133 Dodde and Lenders (1991), 175.
134 Boekholt (1987), 115–18.
135 Schama (1977), 536.
136 Mijnhardt (1984), 211.
137 Vroede (1970), 133.
138 Valk (1995), 168.
139 Vroede (1970), 75–80.
140 Grootaers (1998b), 268.
141 Vroede (1970), 83, 100.
142 Mallinson (1970), 52.
143 Detailed discussion in Vroede (1970), 144–220.
144 Vroede (1970), 350, 375.
145 Wynants (1998), 20.
146 Dodde and Lenders (1991), 165–67.

147 Helsloot (1984), 34.
148 Kossmann (2001), 111–12.
149 Rawson (1840), 388.
150 Essen (1990), 56.
151 Vroede 1970, 377–79.
152 See Glenn and De Groof (2004), II, 17–81.
153 Billiet (1977a), 50.
154 Depaepe and others (1998), 116.
155 Lamberts (1972), 282.
156 Vroede (1970), 529.
157 Lory (1979), I, 55, 68; Depaepe and others (1998), 172.
158 Vroede (1970), 523.
159 In De Clerck (1975), 19.
160 Lory (1979), I, 15, 145.

Chapter Four: Schooling Becomes Controversial

1 Kossmann (2001), 112–13.
2 Kossmann (2001), 114, 130.
3 Strikwerda (1997), 30.
4 Wynants (1998), 21.
5 Verhaegen (1905), 4.
6 Rawson (1840), 395–96.
7 Vroede (1970), 391, 442–43.
8 Verhaegen (1905), 6.
9 Lamberts (1972), 276.
10 Wynants (1998), 22.
11 De Clerck (1975), 7; Depaepe and others (1998), 116.
12 Rosanvallon (1985), 237.
13 In Lory (1979), I, 274.
14 Lory (1979), I, 134.
15 In De Clerck (1975), 19; Wynants (1998), 24.
16 In De Clerck (1975), 21–22.
17 Lamberts (1972), 372n.
18 In De Clerck (1975), 22.
19 Mallinson (1963), 63; Grootaers (1998b), 270–71.
20 In De Clerck (1975), 26–27; Lamberts (1972), 379–80.
21 Tyssens (1998), 230–31.
22 Lamberts (1972), 381.
23 Lorwin (1966), 153.
24 Strikwerda (1997), 31.
25 Verhaegen (1905), 34.
26 Tyssens and Witte (1996), 12–13, 16.

27 Lory (1979), I, 147ff., 155ff.
28 Tyssens and Witte (1996), 35.
29 For Libre Pensée and the Ligue de l'Enseignement, and the relationship between them, see Lory (1979), I, 305–446.
30 De Clerck (1975), 36.
31 Lory (1979), I, 314.
32 Lory (1979), I, 342–43.
33 Lory (1979), I, 435–45.
34 Lory (1979), I, 445.
35 Lory (1979), I, 168–69.
36 Mallinson (1970), 69.
37 Mallinson (1970), 69.
38 De Clerck (1975), 35.
39 Lory (1979), I, 406.
40 Vroede (1977), 143; Billiet (1977b), 13.
41 Lory (1979), I, 206, 221.
42 Strikwerda (1997), 33.
43 In Kossmann (2001), 167.
44 Lory (1979), I, 234.
45 Strikwerda (1997), 43.
46 Lory (1979), I, 253.
47 Boekholt (1987), 140.
48 Valk (1995), 169.
49 Bruin (1985), 210ff.
50 Heerspink (1898), 61; Vree (1984b), 68.
51 Spijker (1984b), 16.
52 In Oosterhof (1913), 33.
53 Costa (1823), 20.
54 Senden (1845), 379.
55 Schutte (1977), 66–67.
56 Essen (1990), 59.
57 Kalsbeek (1976), 132.
58 Vree (1984a), 32, 46; Mulder (1984a), 58.
59 In Holtrop (1984), 64.
60 Wieringa (1984), 192.
61 Spijker (1984b), 7–8.
62 Jong (1984), 230.
63 Bruin (1985), 221, 228.
64 Bos (1940), 2, 110–20; Gilhuis (1975), 70.
65 Spijker (1984a), 108.
66 Rasker (1981), 44.
67 Gelderen (1984), 118–19.
68 Buddingh' (1976), 49.

69 In Gilhuis (1975), 70, 10.
70 Wieringa (1984), 198; Schutte (1977), 62.
71 Groen (1837), 9–10, 26–27.
72 Langedijk (1947), 18.
73 In Essen (1990), 58.
74 Gelderen (1984), 103; Stokvis (1984).
75 For the developments in the United States, see De Boer and Oppewal, 1997.
76 Wieringa (1984), 206.
77 Knetsch (1984), 73.
78 Hofstede de Groot (1844), 96, 113, 100ff.; italics in original.
79 Wieringa (1984), 198.
80 Gilhuis (1975), 90.
81 Bruin (1985), 241–42.
82 In Gilhuis (1975), 92.
83 Boekholt (1987), 144.
84 Boekholt (1987), 134.
85 Thurlings (1978), 28–29, 89, 96.
86 Groen van Prinsterer (1976), 19, 136.
87 Stuurman (1989), 4ff.
88 Huussen (1989), 22.
89 Mulder (1984b), 101.
90 Bosscher (1989), 103.
91 in Reisner (1922), 159–60.
92 Reisner (1922), 161.
93 Nipperdey (1983), 467–68.
94 Tenorth (1987), 262.
95 Skopp (1982), 356.
96 Welch (2001).
97 Tenorth (1987), 262.

Chapter Five: Consolidation of State Control 1880–1930

1   Mann (1958), 233–34.
2   Melton (2003), 239.
3   Lamberti (1989), 27.
4   Reisner (1922), 161.
5   Skopp (1982), 346.
6   Tenorth (2000), 176.
7   In Reble (1999), 470–71.
8   Wehler (1989b), 489; Tenorth (1987), 263–64.
9   Lamberti (1989), 28–29, 38.
10 Lamberti (1989), 30–31.
11 In Reisner (1922), 161–62; original in Blankertz (1982), 162.

12 Welch (2001), 25.
13 Wehler (1995), 403.
14 Blankertz (1982), 163.
15 Wehler (1995), 397.
16 Text in Reble (1999), 472–75.
17 Text in Reble (1999), 475–80.
18 In Reisner (1922), 168.
19 Blankertz (1982), 165.
20 Wehler (1995), 399–400.
21 Wehler (1995), 402.
22 Welch (2001), 54–55.
23 Wehler (1989b), 491.
24 Lamberti (1989), 13.
25 Wehler (2003), 1195.
26 Lamberti (1989), 38.
27 Welch (2001), 53.
28 Lamberti (1989), 101.
29 Hamann (1986), 113.
30 Herrlitz, Hopf, and Titze (1986), 52.
31 Reisner (1922), 200–202.
32 In Fertig (1984), 240.
33 Kuhlemann (1991), 208.
34 Lamberti (1989), 3, 199.
35 Helmreich (1979), 61.
36 Lamberti (1989), 206–07, 211, 197.
37 Lamberti (1989), 213, 180.
38 Lamberti (1989), 214.
39 McLeod (2000), 77.
40 McLeod (2000), 77–78.
41 Lamberti (1989), 217.
42 Lamberti (1989), 41.
43 In Wehler (1995), 893.
44 Harp (1998), 66.
45 Wehler (1995), 896–97.
46 Reisner (1922), 186.
47 Lamberti (1989), 48.
48 Harp (1998), 16.
49 Harp (1998), 61.
50 Reisner (1922), 189.
51 Lamberti (1989), 55.
52 Lamberti (1989), 12.
53 Lamberti (1989), 10; Fritz (1985).
54 Tenorth (2000), 198.

55   Fritz (1985), 415.
56   Wehler (1995), 898.
57   Lamberti (1989), 63, 216.
58   Lamberti (1989), 14.
59   Lamberti (1989), 84–85.
60   Burrow (2000), 125.
61   Wehler (1995), 1045.
62   Olson (1977), 7.
63   Olson (1977), 13.
64   Blankertz (1982), 233.
65   Fritz (1985), 417–18.
66   Blankertz (1982), 233.
67   In Fertig (1984), 278–79.
68   Wehler (1995), 1200.
69   In Lamberti (1989), 157.
70   Fishman (1976), 2–3.
71   Fishman (1976), 91.
72   Ringer (1979), 72.
73   Ringer (1979), 3.
74   Herrmann (1991), 168.
75   Wehler (1995), 1099–1104.
76   Berg (1991), 132.
77   Stern (1974), 130.
78   Max Planck Institute (1983), 55.
79   Zymek (1989), 178.
80   Stern (1974), xxiv.
81   Tenorth (2000), 255.
82   Fritz (1985), 414.
83   Helmreich (1979), 113; Lundgreen (1981), 15–17.
84   Lamberti (1989), 4.
85   Thiel (2000), 40.
86   Ringer (1979), 42.
87   Herrlitz, Hopf, and Titze (1986), 114.
88   Hamann (1986), 169.
89   Fritz (1985), 421.
90   Fritz (1985), 422, 425.
91   Fritz (1985), 433.
92   Helmreich (1979), 134–37.
93   Cohen (1996), 21.
94   Zeps (1987), 5.
95   Cohen (1996), 23ff.
96   Zeps (1987), 7.
97   Cohen (1996), 30.

98   Cohen (1996), 38.
99   Zeps (1987), 11.
100   Zeps (1987), 23.
101   Cohen (1996), 10.
102   Zeps (1987), 27.
103   Zeps (1987), 29–35.
104   Zeps (1987), 74, 49, 67–68.
105   Zeps (1987), 66, 124.
106   Zeps (1987), 95, 92, 101.
107   Reble (2002), 322.
108   See Giollitto (1991); Navarro Sandalinas (1990).
109   Esden-Tempska (1990), 199.
110   Esden-Tempska (1990), 189.

Chapter Six: The Civil Society Alternative

1   Braster (1996), 99.
2   Kalsbeek (1976), 192.
3   Karsten (2003), 418.
4   Bruin (1985), 246.
5   Valk (1995), 171.
6   Hofstede de Groot (1848), 22–31.
7   Kalsbeek (1976), 196.
8   Langedijk (1935), 61.
9   Braster (1996), 118.
10   Boekholt (1987), 151.
11   Kossmann (2001), 241.
12   Akkermans (1997), 60.
13   Dodde (1981), 31.
14   Braster (1996), 123.
15   Lory (1979), I, 171; Laveleye (1858).
16   See Egmond (1964), 97–98f., 104.
17   Gilhuis (no date, b).
18   In Gilhuis (1975), 115, 146.
19   Braster (1996), 124–25.
20   In Gilhuis (1975), 18.
21   Helsloot (1984), 47.
22   Helsloot (1984), 48.
23   Gilhuis (1975), 200.
24   Gilhuis (1975), 166.
25   Essen (1990), 64ff.
26   Valk (1995), 173.
27   Gilhuis (1975), 87.

28   Schram (1984), 45.
29   Lipschits (1977), 21.
30   Lipschits (1977), 21.
31   Kuyper (1869), 44–45.
32   Essen (1990), 67.
33   Lipschits (1977), 27.
34   Thurlings (1978), 97–98.
35   Langedijk (1935), 140.
36   Gilhuis (1975), 152; Langedijk (1935), 148–49.
37   Valk (1995), 174.
38   Riel (1982), 126.
39   In Doorn (1989), 161.
40   Riel (1982), 111, 225.
41   Kuyper (1931), 31, 73.
42   Dooyeweerd (1991), 289–90.
43   Skillen and McCarthy (1991), 385.
44   Kossmann (2001), 250.
45   Kalsbeek (1976), 186.
46   Kossmann (2001), 406.
47   Hansen (1973), 370.
48   Kossmann (2001), 251.
49   Rijnsdorp (1979), 31.
50   Riel (1982), 108, 111, 128–29.
51   Kossmann (2001), 288–89.
52   Karsten (1997), 35.
53   Kruijt, J. P., and Walter Goddijn (1962), 232; Akkermans (1980), 159.
54   Boekholt (1987), 219.
55   In Gilhuis (1987), 179.
56   Helsloot (1984), 83.
57   Kalsbeek (1976), 232.
58   Tyssens (1999), 50.
59   Helsloot (1984), 86, 118.
60   Rijnsdorp (1979), 37.
61   Braster (1996), 140–43.
62   In Karsten (2003), 425.
63   Bolle (1976), 31.
64   Hansen (1973), 377.
65   Karsten (2003), 425–26.
66   Kossmann (2001), 420.
67   Braster (1996), 137.
68   Gilhuis (1975), 174–77.
69   Tyssens (1999), 50.
70   Karsten (2003), 426.

71 Braster (1996), 135.
72 Braster (1996), 153, 159–60.
73 Kossmann (2002), 67, 70.
74 De Clerck (1975), 13–14; Vroede (1970), 401–16.
75 Vroede (1970), 455.
76 Witte (1977), 443.
77 In Verhaegen (1905), 8.
78 Lory (1979), II, 455–60.
79 Lory (1979), II, 524–25, 549, 553–54, 563.
80 Lory (1979), II, 558–71.
81 Depaepe and others (1998), 166–67.
82 Kossmann (2001), 176, 182, 193, 202.
83 Strikwerda (1997), 127.
84 Verhaegen (1905), 61.
85 Lory (1979), II, 589, 617, 651–52, 626.
86 De Groof (1985a), 51–52.
87 Lory (1979), II, 670, 679–80, 691, 755.
88 Lory (1979), II, 799.
89 Lory (1979), II, 804.
90 Laveleye (1858, 1872); Lory (1979), II, 500–4.
91 Verhaegen (1905), 82, 87, 93, 99.
92 in De Clerck (1975), 52–53.
93 Verhaegen (1905), 120, 128.
94 De Clerck (1975), 54–55.
95 Verhaegen (1905), 102.
96 Verhaegen (1905), 117.
97 Mallinson (1970), 79.
98 De Clerck (1975), 55.
99 Lory (1979), II, 708.
100 Verhaegen (1905), 260.
101 De Groof (1985b), 197.
102 Kossmann (2001), 299; Verhaegen (1905), 136, 178.
103 Mallinson (1963), 97; Billiet (1977a), 52.
104 Verhaegen (1905), 180.
105 Lorwin (1966), 154.
106 Lory (1979), II, 711.
107 Verhaegen (1905), 190, 195.
108 Kossmann (2001), 203.
109 De Clerck (1975), 64.
110 De Groof (1985b), 198.
111 Vroede (1985), 489.
112 Depaepe and others (1998), 138; Kossmann (2001), 303.
113 Tyssens (1999), 65.

114 In De Clerck (1975), 68.
115 In De Clerck (1975), 69.
116 De Clerck (1975), 70–71.
117 De Clerck (1975), 72.
118 Strikwerda (1997), 114, 262.
119 Guereña (2006), 30–31.
120 Strikwerda (1997), 146.
121 De Clerck (1975), 73.
122 Kossmann (2001), 416.
123 Strikwerda (1997), 127, 341.
124 Tyssens (1997), 20ff.
125 Lory (1979), I, 174ff.
126 Lory (1979), I, 183.
127 Lory (1979), I, 191ff.
128 Depaepe and others (1998), 141.
129 De Clerck (1975), 90–95.
130 Kossmann (2001), 399–400.
131 Strikwerda (1997), 33.
132 Tyssens and Witte (1996), 75–76.
133 Verhaegen (1905), xi, xvii.
134 Wynants (1998), 31.
135 Tyssens and Witte (1996), 91.

Chapter Seven: Totalitarian Schooling

1 Knopp (2000), 16, 174.
2 Kneller (1941), 141–42.
3 Knopp (2000), 17.
4 Mann (2001), 21.
5 Kneller (1941), 1.
6 Hofer (1957), 74, 82.
7 Hofer (1957), 89.
8 In Keim (1995), 18.
9 Kneller (1941), 17.
10 Schiedeck and Stahlmann (1991), 186.
11 Keim (1995), 82.
12 Herbst (2006), 97.
13 Keim (1995), 31–32, 73.
14 Stern (1974), 291.
15 Horn (1976), 430.
16 Keim (1995), 158–59, 112.
17 Scholtz (1985), 40–41.

18 Ringer (1979), 44.
19 Scholtz (1985), 47–48.
20 Horn (1976), 425.
21 Peukert (1989), 327.
22 Schiedeck and Stahlmann (1991), 177.
23 In Knopp (2000), 170.
24 Stern (1974), 77.
25 Hahn (1998), 77.
26 Knopp (2000), 180.
27 In Hofer (1957), 88.
28 Horn (1976), 426.
29 Blankertz (1982), 276.
30 Fishman (1976), 53.
31 In Fishman (1976), 87.
32 Scholtz (1985), 111, 134, 137.
33 Langewiesehe and Tenorth (1989), 20.
34 Tenorth (1989), 135–37.
35 Keim (1995), 38; Reble (2002), 313–18.
36 Shirley (1992), 144.
37 Keim (1995), 117, 120.
38 Shirley (1992), 194.
39 Horn (1976), 434.
40 In Scholtz (1985), 122, 129, 60.
41 In Mann (2001), 67.
42 Kneller (1941), 63, 206.
43 Horn (1976), 436.
44 Horn (1976), 439.
45 Wehler (2003), 761–64.
46 Keim (1995), 133.
47 Mann (2001), 138.
48 Keim (1995), 131.
49 Hofer (1957), 149.
50 Kneller (1941), 204.
51 In Hofer (1957), 87–88.
52 Kneller (1941), 157.
53 Kneller (1941), 53, 77.
54 In Hofer (1957), 128.
55 Fritz (1985), 417.
56 Knopp (2000), 86.
57 Scholtz (1985), 65, 103, 93, 118, 74.
58 Schiedeck and Stahlmann (1991), 187, 190.
59 Knopp (2000), 212.

60　Scholtz (1985), 13.
61　In Hofer (1957), 120–21.
62　In Remak (1960), 105.
63　Mann (2001), 30.
64　Zymek (1989), 190.
65　Hamann (1986), 179.
66　In Shirley (1992), 190.
67　Kneller (1941), 211.
68　In Kneller (1941), 185.
69　Wehler (2003) 819.
70　In Conway (1968), 20, 178.
71　Knopp (2000), 220.
72　In Conway (1968), 366–69.
73　In Conway (1968), 182–88.
74　In Hofer (1957), 128.
75　Mann (2001), 101.
76　Tismaneanu (1990), 136.
77　Waterkamp (1986), 237; Mitter (1990b), 600.
78　Reble (2002), 330.
79　Baske (1998a), 168–69.
80　Anweiler, Fuchs, Dorner, and Petermann (1992), 16, 90.
81　Waterkamp (1990), 269–71.
82　*"Aus dem Gesetz zur Demokratisierung der deutschen Schule,"* in Weber (1986), 71.
83　Braemer (1978), 147; *"Aus dem Gesetz ueber das einheitliche sozialistische Bildungssystem,"* in Weber (1986); *Paedagogik* 1978, quoted by Anweiler (1990b), 699.
84　Tenorth (2000), 332–33.
85　In Anweiler, Fuchs, Dorner, and Petermann (1992), 92ff.
86　Gerhart Eisler, quoted by Grothe (1958), 165.
87　Hahn (1998), 140.
88　Braemer (1978), *passim.*
89　Anweiler (1973), 270.
90　In Tenorth (2000), 282.
91　Fishman and Martin (1987), 40; Sontheimer and Bleek (1975), 131.
92　In Anweiler, Fuchs, Dorner, and Petermann (1992), 400ff.
93　Baske (1998b), 174.
94　In Anweiler, Fuchs, Dorner, and Petermann (1992), 461.
95　Buerger (1990), 102–04; Grothe (1958), 223–24; Williamson (1981), 15n; Sontheimer and Bleek (1975), 124.
96　Tenorth (2000), 328.
97　Fishman and Martin (1987), 25.
98　Busch (1978); Fishman and Martin (1987), 157.

99   Volkmer (1979), 117–18.
100 Hans-Peter Schäfer, quoted by Eichberg (1986), 254; Waterkamp (1986), 241; *"Aus einem Protest-Brief DDR-Jugendlicher: Pochen auf die Verwirklichung der Grundrechte,"* in Weber (1986), 400–01.
101 Hornstein and Schefeld (1998), 294.
102 Jenkner (1989), 47.
103 Reuter (1998), 230.
104 Anweiler, Fuchs, Dorner, and Petermann (1992), 409, 12.
105 Ramm (1990), 43.
106 In Anweiler, Fuchs, Dorner, and Petermann (1992), 443.
107 Koenig (1990), 414; Anweiler (1990c), 97; Fishman and Martin (1987), 126.
108 In Anweiler, Fuchs, Dorner, and Petermann (1992), 71.
109 Lost (1990), 50–51; Waterkamp (1990), 263.
110 E. Drefenstedt 1983, quoted by Eichberg (1986), 257.
111 Tent (1982), 314 and *passim*; *"Aus der Entschließung 'Die naechsten Aufgaben der allgemeinbildenden Schule,'"* in Weber (1986), 179.
112 Uhlig (1990), 199.
113 Brandt (1991), 229.
114 Anweiler, Fuchs, Dorner, and Petermann (1992), 13, 26, 125.
115 Kraus and Lange (1991).

Chapter Eight: The State and Schooling in Germany and Austria since World War II

1   Mitter (1990b), 597.
2   In Anweiler, Fuchs, Dorner, and Petermann (1992), 63, 70.
3   In Anweiler, Fuchs, Dorner, and Petermann (1992), 68–69.
4   Giesecke 1983, quoted by Mitter (1990b), 600.
5   Hofer (1957), 126.
6   Spotts (1973), 11, 212.
7   Spotts (1973), 90, 184–86.
8   In Spotts (1973), 58n.
9   Spotts (1973), 55.
10 Tent (1982), 170–72; see also Ertel, Kilz, and Mettke (1980).
11 Herrlitz, Hopf, and Titze (1986), 145–46.
12 Tent (1982), 206–07.
13 Thiel (2000), 45ff.
14 Tent (1982), 112, 127, 139; Spotts (1973), 86; Waterkamp (1990), 262.
15 Thiel (2000), 125–31.
16 Lundgreen (1981), 42.
17 Spotts (1973), 228.
18 Lundgreen (1981), 26.
19 Jach (1991), 7.

20   Vogel (2000), 3–4.
21   Pommereau (2006), 1.
22   Herbst (2006), 134.
23   Jach (1991), 42.
24   Hans Heckel, quoted by Vogel (1972), 38.
25   Weiss and Mattern (1991), 55.
26   Weiss and Mattern (1991), 58.
27   Bundesverfassungsgericht (1987), 12.
28   Bundesverfassungsgericht (1987), 30–32.
29   Bundesverfassungsgericht (1987), 35.
30   Jach (1991), 64–65, 81.
31   Ramm (1990), 48.
32   Avenarius and Heckel (2000), 69.
33   Thiel (2000), 106.
34   Reble (2002), 377.
35   Zeps (1987), 188.
36   In Zeps (1987), 190.
37   Jach (1991), 369.
38   Website of the Ministry of Education, http://www.bmwf.gv.at/.
39   Jach (1991), 371–72.
40   Berka and Geistlinger (1998), 269.
41   Berka and Geistlinger (1998), 270.
42   Hofmann (1991), 139.
43   Koenig (1990), 417.
44   Koenig (1990), 414.
45   Interview with Sebastien Pflugbeil in Rein (1989), 21–22.
46   Hofmann (1991), 8–9.
47   Urban (1991), 233.
48   Gebuerek, Kaack, and Lange (1989).
49   In Gebuerek, Kaack, and Lange (1989), 14–15.
50   Gebuerek, Kaack, and Lange (1989), 2–3.
51   Quoted by Anweiler (1990c), 100.
52   Hofmann (1991), 20–21; Rein (1989).
53   Hofmann (1991), 31.
54   A French commentator, quoted by Brown (1991), 139.
55   Hofmann (1991), 40.
56   Hofmann (1991), 51, 42.
57   Hoerner (1990), 9–10; Gebuerek, Kaack, and Lange (1989), 16; Ruether (1992), 189–207.
58   Kraus and Lange (1991), 16.
59   H. H. Emons, "*Thesen zur Bildungsreform*," quoted by Vogel (1991), 301.
60   Maizière (1990), 344; Meyer quoted by Gebuerek, Kaack, and Lange (1989), 20–21.

61 See Glenn and De Groof (2002), I, 279–83.
62 *"Entwurf..."* (1990).
63 Anweiler, Fuchs, Dorner, and Petermann (1992), 440, 493.
64 Jenkner (1990b), 233.
65 Rehm (1991).

Chapter Nine: Civil Society since World War II

1 Tyssens (1999), 67.
2 De Groof (1995), 464.
3 Tyssens (1997), 12–16, 185, 126; De Groof (1985b), 200.
4 Tyssens (1997), 89–87, 125.
5 Tyssens (1997), 26, 31.
6 Tyssens (1998), 251.
7 Verhaegen (1905), 119.
8 De Groof (1995), 463.
9 Tyssens (1997), 55–56, 74, 85.
10 Wynants (1998), 39.
11 Tyssens (1997), 178.
12 De Clerck (1975), 134–37.
13 Tyssens (1997), 53.
14 Billiet (1977b), 22; Kossmann (2002), II, 271.
15 Billiet (1977b), 26; Witte and Meynen (1982), 223.
16 Tyssens (1997), 105–07, 127.
17 Tyssens (1997), 182, 143–51.
18 De Clerck (1975), 140–44; Tyssens (1997), 157.
19 Witte and Meynen (1982), 227.
20 De Clerck (1975), 150; Tyssens (1997), 170–71.
21 De Clerck (1975), 152.
22 See De Groof (1989).
23 Billiet (1977b), 43ff.
24 Depaepe and others (1998), 116.
25 In De Ceulaer and De Vroede (1980), 88.
26 De Ceulaer and De Vroede (1980), 222.
27 Ceulaer and Vroede (1980), 99, 165–66.
28 In Bolle (1976), 31.
29 Cliteur (1989), 147.
30 Kemenade, Jungbluth, and Ritzen (1987), 220.
31 Hofman (1997a).
32 Doorn (1989), 160.
33 Hofman (1997a), 233.
34 Postma (1995), 121.
35 Lijphart (1968).

36 Hoefnagel (1994).
37 Wouden and others (1994), 117.
38 Postma (1995), 128.
39 Jach (1999), 139.
40 Kessel and van Wieringen (1997), 86–91.
41 Dronkers, Hofman, and Dijkstra (1997a), 25.
42 Karsten (1997), 55.
43 Ploeg (1995), 19.
44 Akkermans (1997), 78–79.
45 Kemenade (1968).
46 Coleman (1978), 137.
47 Schelfhout (1977), 75–80.
48 Vreeburg (1997), 201–13.
49 Schoten and Wansink (1984), 94ff.
50 See Gilhuis (no date, b).
51 Vreeburg (1997), 219.
52 Braster (1996), 173.
53 *NRC Handelsblad*, December 16, 2003.
54 Schoten (1983), 56.
55 Kessel and Wieringen (1997), 101.
56 Dijkstra (1997), 144–81; Marwijk Kooy-von Baumhauer (1984).
57 Dronkers, Hofman, and Dijkstra (1997b), 324–25.
58 Hofman (1997b), 284ff.
59 Ginjaar-Maas (1976), 104.
60 Braster (1996), 162; 165; see essays in Akkermans and Leune (1983).
61 Billiet (1977b), 72–73.
62 In Karsten (2003), 429–30.

References

Adamson, J. W. 1967 [1921]. "Education," in *Mediæval Contributions to Modern Civilisation*. New York: Barnes and Noble.

Akkermans, P. W. C. 1977. "Artikel 208 van de Grondwet, een labyrinth?" in Box, Dronkers, Molenaar, and Mulder.

—1980. *Onderwijs als constitutioneel probleem*. Alphen aan den Rijn: Samson.

—1997. "De juridische vormgeving van de onderwijsverzuiling," in Dronkers, Hofman, and Dijkstra.

Akkermans, P. W. C., and J. M. G. Leune, editors. 1983. *Het bestuur van het openbaar onderwijs*. Den Bosch: Malmberg.

Algra, H. 1965. *Het Wonder van de 19e eeuw: Van Vrije Kerken en Kleine Luyden*. Franeker: Wever.

André, Robert. 1983. *La population de la Wallonie dans la dualité démographique de la Belgique*. Brussels: Fondation Charles Plisnier.

Anweiler, Oskar. 1973. "Gesellschaftliche Mitwirking und Schulverfassung in Bildungssystemen staatssozialistischer Praegung," *Bildung und Erziehung* 26, no. 4 (July/August).

—, editor. 1978. *Erziehungs- und Sozialisations-probleme in der Sowjetunion, der DDR und Polen*. Hannover: Hermann Schroedel Verlag.

—1990a. "Grundzuege der Bildungspolitik und der Entwicklung des Bildungswesens seit 1945," in Anweiler and others.

—1990b. "Ergebnisse und offene Fragen," in Anweiler and others.

—1990c. "Die 'Wende' in der Bildungspolitik der DDR," *Bildung und Erziehung* 43, no. 1 (March).

—1992. *Systemswandel im Bildungs- und Erziehungswesen in Mittel- und Osteuropa*. Berlin: Arno Spitz.

Anweiler, Oskar, et al. editors. 1990. *Vergleich von Bildung und Erziehung in der Bundesrepublik Deutschland und in der Deutschen Demokratischen Republik*. Cologne: Verlag Wissenschaft und Politik.

Anweiler, Oskar, Hans-Juergen Fuchs, Martina Dorner, and Eberhard Petermann. 1992. *Bildungspolitik in Deutschland 1945–1990: Ein historisch-vergleichender Quellenband*. Opladen: Leske and Budrich.

Arnold, Matthew. 1861. *The Popular Education of France, with Notices of That of Holland and Switzerland*. London: Longmans Green.

—1964. *Schools and Universities on the Continent*, edited by R. H. Super. Ann Arbor: University of Michigan Press.

Art, J. 1977. "Het socioculturele leven in Belgie: Kerk en religie 1844–1875," in *Algemene Geschiedenis der Nederlanden* 12. Weesp: Fibula-Van Dishoeck.

Avenarius, Hermann, and Hans Heckel. 2000. *Schulrechtskunde*, 7th edition. Kriftel: Luchterhand.

Bache, Alexander Dallas. 1839. *Report on Education in Europe to the Trustees of the Girard College for Orphans*. Philadelphia: Lydia Bailey.

Badertscher, Hans, and Hans-Ulrich Grunder, editors. 1997. *Geschichte der Erziehung und Schule in der Schweiz im 19. und 20 Jahrhundert*. Bern: Verlag Paul Haupt.

—1998. *Geschichte der Erziehung und Schule in der Schweiz im 19. und 20 Jahrhundert: Quellenband*. Bern: Verlag Paul Haupt.

Baert, G. 1984. "Schoolorganisatie en externe controle in Belgie," 3 HSO (November).

Bakker, W., O. J. de Jong, W. van 't Spijker, and L. J. Wolthuis. 1984. *De Afscheiding van 1834 en haar geschiedenis*. Kampen: J. H. Kok.

Barnard, Henry. 1854. *National Education in Europe*, 2nd edition. New York: Norton.

Baske, Siegfried. 1998a. "Grund- und Rahmenbedingungen," in Führ and Furck.

—1998b. "Allgemeinbildende Schulen," in Führ and Furck.

Baynes, Mary Jo. 1985. *Schooling in Western Europe: A Social History*. Albany: SUNY Press.

Becker, J. W., and R. Vink. 1994. *Secularisatie in Nederland, 1966–1991: De verandering van opvattingen en enkele gedragingen*, Rijswijk. The Netherlands: Sociaal en Cultureel Planbureau.

Beckers, Jacqueline. 1998. "Les politiques scolaires de l'égalité des chances et de l'égalité des acquis dans l'enseignement secondaire (après 1945)," in Grootaers.

Behr, Michael. 1988. *Freie Schulen und Internate: Paedagogische Programme und rechtliche Stellung*. Duesseldorf: ECON Taschenbuch Verlag.

Behrns, J. H. 1857. *Wet tot regeling van het lager onderwijs*. Harlingen: Behrns.

Beks, H., editor. 1976. *Het Onderwijs Gekleurd*. Leiden: L. Stafleu and Zoon.

Beljon, R., and L. de Jonge. 1984. "De vrijheid van onderwijs, beleden en bestreden," in *Onderwijsbeleid in Nederland*, edited by J. D. C. Branger, N. L. Dodde and W. Wielemans. Leuven/Amersfoort: Acco.

Berg, Christa, editor. 1991. *Handbuch der deutschen Bildungsgeschichte, Band IV, 1870–1918: Von der Reichsgruendung bis zum Ende des Ersten Weltkriegs*. Munich: C. H. Beck.

—1991. "Familie, Kindheit, Jugend," in Berg.

Berg, J. van den. 1978. "Die Pluralistische Gestalt des Kirchlichen Lebens in den Niederlanden, 1574–1974," in *Pietismus und Reveil*, edited by Van den Berg and J. P. van Dooren. Leiden: Brill.

Berg, J., and J. P. van Dooren. 1978. *Pietismus und Reveil*. Leiden: Brill.

Berger, Peter L., and Richard John Neuhaus. 1996. "To Empower People" (1977); republished in *To Empower People: From State to Civil Society*, edited by Michael Novak. Washington, DC: American Enterprise Institute.

Berk, Martin. 1984. "Over de Opvoeding der Kinderen: Opvoedkindige Denkbeelden in de Spectatoriale Geschriften, 1730–1780," *Pedagogische Verhandelingen* 7, no. 1.

Berka, Walter, and M. Geistlinger. 1998. "The Legal Status of Pupils: Austrian Report," in Jan De Groof, and Hilde Penneman, editors, *The Legal Status of Pupils in Europe*. The Hague: Kluwer Law International: 243–69.

Biebel, Charles D. 1982. "American efforts for educational reform in occupied Germany, 1945–1955—a reassessment," *History of Education Quarterly* 22, no. 3, special issue: *Educational Policy and Reform in Modern Germany* (Autumn): 277–87.

Billiet, J. 1977a. "Vrijheid van onderwijs en verzuiling in België," in Box, Dronkers, Molenaar, and Mulder.

—1977b. *Secularisering en verzuiling in het onderwijs: Een sociologisch onderzoek naar de vrije schoolkeuze als legitimatieschema en als sociaal proces*. Louvain: University Press.

Blankertz, Herwig. 1982. *Die Geschichte der Paedagogik von der Aufklaerung bis zur Gegenwart*. Wetzlar: Buechse der Pandora.

Boekholt, P. Th. F. M. 1987. "Eenheid en verscheidenheid in het onderwijs, 1795–1860," in Boekholt and De Booy.

Boekholt, P. Th. F. M., and De Booy. 1987. *Geschiedenis van de School in Nederland*. Assen/Maastricht: Van Gorcum.

Bolle, C. M. 1976. "Waar ligt de rode school?" in Beks.

Boogman, J. C., and C. A. Tamse, editors. 1978. *Emancipatie in Nederland: De Ontvoogding van Burgerij en Confessionelen in de Negentiende Eeuw*. The Hague: Nijhoff.

Bos, F. L. 1940. *Archiefstukken betreffende de Afscheiding van 1834*. Kampen: Kok.

Bosscher, D. F. J. 1989. "'Waar is deze strijd om gestreden?' De Nederlandse politieke partijen en de Nieuwe Democratie rond 1945," in Koole.

Bowen, James. 1977. *A History of Western Education, Volume Two: Civilization of Europe Sixth to Sixteenth Century*. London: Methuen.

Box, L., J. Dronkers, M. Molenaar, and J. de Mulder, editors. 1977. *Vrijheid van Onderwijs*. Nijmegen: Link.

Boyd, William. 1966. *The History of Western Education*, 8th edition. New York: Barnes and Noble.

Brabant, Stephane. 1983. Preface to *La Population de la Wallonie dans la dualité démographique de la Belgique*. Brussels: Fondation Charles Plisnier.

Braemer, Rainer. 1978. "Die relative Funktionalitaet der ideologischen Erziehung im allgemeinbildenden Unterricht der DDR-Oberschule," in Anweiler.

Brandt, Horst. 1991. "Innovationsbemühungen Leipziger Schulen," in *Schulvielfalt in Hannover (Theorie und Praxis 37)*. Hannover: Fachbereich Erziehungs-wissenschaften I der Universitaet Hannover.

Braster, J. F. A. 1996. *De identiteit van het openbaar onderwijs*. Groningen, The Netherlands: Wolters-Noordhoff.

Braudel, Fernand. 1984. *The Perspective of the World*, translated by Sian Reynolds. New York: Harper and Row.

Bremmer, R. H. 1984. "Historische aspecten van de Afscheiding," in *Aspecten van de Afscheiding*. Frankener: T. Wever.

Brienen, T., K. Exalto, J. van Genderen, C. Graafland, and W. van 't Spijker. 1986. *De Nadere Reformatie: Beschrijving can haar Voornaamste Vertegenwoordigers*. The Hague: Boekencentrum B.V.

Brooks, Charles. 1837. *Elementary Instruction: An Address Delivered before the Schools and Citizens of the Town of Quincy, July 4, 1837*. Quincy, MA: John A. Green.

Brown, J. F. 1991. *Surge to Freedom: The End of Communist Rule in Eastern Europe*. Durham and London: Duke University Press.

Bruggen, J. van, G. van Riemen, and A. van Wieringen. 1977. "Overheid en onderwijs: een aarzelende verbintenis rond 1800," in Box, Dronkers, Molenaar, and Mulder.

Bruin, A. A. de. 1985. *Het onstaan van de schoolstrijd*. Barneveld: Ton Bolland.

Buddingh', B. 1976. "Christelijk onderwijs: Appèl en uitdaging," in Beks.

Buerger, Klaus. 1990. "Es gibt vieles, über das wir miteinander reden muessen," *Bildung und Erziehung* 43, no. 1 (March).

Bundesverfassungsgericht. 1987. "In den Verfahren zur verfassungsrechtlichen Pruefung der . . . Privatschulgesetzes der Freien und Hansestadt Hamburg" (April 8).

Burrow, J. W. 2000. *The Crisis of Reason: European Thought, 1848–1914*. New Haven, CT: Yale University Press.

Busch, Adelheid. 1978. "Probleme der Erziehung sozialistischer Persoenlichkeiten: Die Diskussion in der DDR seit 1970," in Anweiler.

Bustamante, Hugo, Maurits Van Overbeke, and Albert Verdoodt. 1978. "Bilingual Education in Belgium," in *Case Studies in Bilingual Education*, edited by Bernard Spolsky and Robert L. Cooper. Rowley, MA: Newbury House.

Čapková, Dagmar. 1991. "Der Neubeginn. Die Schule in den tschechischen Gebieten seit 1774. Oesterreichische Reformzeit und Nationale Wiedergeburt der Tschechen," in Schmale and Dodde.

Cliteur, P. B. 1989. "Revolutie en contrarevolutie in de ideologie van de huidige Nederlandse politieke partijen," in Koole.

Cohen, Gary B. 1996. *Education and Middle-Class Society in Imperial Austria 1848–1918.* Purdue, IN: Purdue University Press (October).

Cohen, Sol. 1974. *Education in the United States: A Documentary History* (5 vols). New York: Random House.

Coleman, John A. 1978. *The Evolution of Dutch Catholicism, 1958–1974.* Berkeley: University of California Press.

Compayré, Gabriel. 1904. *The History of Pedagogy,* translated by W. H. Payne. Boston: D. C. Heath.

Conway, J. S. 1968. *The Nazi Persecution of the Churches, 1933–45.* New York: Basic Books.

Coons, John E. 1986. "Educational choice and the courts: U.S. and Germany," *The American Journal of Comparative Law* 34, no. 1 (Winter): 1–43.

Costa, Isaac da. 1823. *Bezwaren tegen den Geest der Eeuw.* Leiden: Herdingh.

Cousin, Victor. 1833. *État de l'instruction primaire dans le Royaume de Prusse à la fin de l'année 1831.* Paris: Levrault.

—1835. *Report on the State of Public Instruction in Prussia,* translated by Sarah Austin. New York: Wiley and Long.

—1837. *De l'instruction publique en Hollande.* Paris: Levrault.

Cuvier, Georges, and François Noël. 1812. "Rapport wegen het Lagere Schoolwezen in Holland," in *Bijdragen ter Bevordering van het Onderwijs en de Opvoeding.* Haarlem: Enschede en Zoonen.

—. 1816. *Première Partie du Rapport sur les établissements d'instruction publique en Hollande.* The Hague.

Debert, Hans, and Christoph Führ. 1998. "Zum Schulwesen in den neuen Laendern," in Führ and Furck.

De Boer, Peter, and Donald Oppewal. 1997. "American Calvinist Day Schools," in *Voices from the Past: Reformed Educators,* edited by Donald Oppewal. Lanham, MD: University Press of America.

de Booy, E. P. 1977. *Weldaet der Scholen.* Utrecht: Stichtse Historische Reeks.

De Ceulaer, Dirk, and Maurits (Maurice) de Vroede. 1980. *De pluralistische school: een requiem?* Wilsele: Helicon.

De Clerck, K. 1975. *Momenten uit de geschiedenis van het Belgisch Onderwijs.* Antwerp: De Sikkel.

De Groof, Jan. 1985a. *Het levensbeschouwelijk karakter van de onderwijsinstellingen.* Bruges: De Keure.

—1985b. *De vrijheid van en het recht op onderwijs.* Brussels.

—1989. *De Grondwetsherziening van 1988 en het onderwijs: De schoolvrede en zijn toepassing.* Brussels: E. Story-Scientia (also published as *La révision constitutionnelle de 1988 et l'enseignement: La paix scolaire et son application,* 1990).

—1990. *Le pacte scolaire: coordination et annotations.* Brussels: E. Story-Scientia.

—1995. "De onderwijspolitiek," in *Tussen staat en maatschappij 1945–1995. Christen-democratie in België,* edited by W. De Wachter, G.H. Dumont, M. Dumoulin, E. Gerard, E. Lamberts, and X. Mabille. Tielt: Lannoo.

Depaepe, Marc, Maurice (Maurits) De Vroede, Luc Minten, and Frank Simon. 1998. "L'enseignement primaire," in Grootaers.

Deppermann, Klaus. 1961. *Der hallesche Pietismus und der preussische Staat unter Friedrich III.* Goettingen: Vanderhoech and Ruprecht.

Derksen, Steven C. 1979. "Kleur bekennen gewenst (het openbaar onderwijs over de christelijke school)," in *In het honderdste jaar: Gedenkboek Stichting Unie 'School en Evangelie' 1879–1979.* Kampen: Kok.

Dienst, Karl. 1998. "Bildungspolitik und Kirchen," in Fuehr and Furck.

Diepenhorst, P. A. 1932. *Groen van Prinsterer.* Kampen: Kok.

Dijkstra, Anne Bert. 1997. "Onderwijskansen en richting van de school," in Dijkstra, Dronkers, and Hofman.

Dijkstra, Anne Bert, Jaap Dronkers, and Roelande Hofman, editors. 1997. *Verzuiling in het onderwijs: Actuele verklaringen en analyse.* Groningen: Wolters-Noordhoff,.

Dodde, Nan L. 1981. *Geschiedenis van het nederlandse schoolwezen.* Purmerend: Muusses.

—1983. *Het nederlandse onderwijs verandert: ontwikkelingen sinds 1800.* Muiderberg: Coutinho.

—1984. "Nederlandse onderwijspolitiek 1945–1983," in *Onderwijsbeleid in Nederland,* edited by J. D. C. Branger, N. L. Dodde, and W. Wielemans. Leuven/Amersfoort: Acco.

—1991. *. . . tot der kinderen selffs proffijt: een geschiedenis van het onderwijs te.* Rotterdam, 's-Gravenhage, (The Netherlands): SDU Uitgeverij.

Dodde, Nan L., and Jan H. G. Lenders. 1991. "Reform, Reorganisation und Stagnation: Der Schulunterricht in den Niederlanden und Belgien 1750–1825," in Schmale and Dodde.

Doorn, J. A. A. van. 1989. "Meer weerstand dan waardering: De Revolutie-ideeën en de Nederlandse politieke traditie," in Koole.

Dooyeweerd, Herman. 1991. *Roots of Western Culture* (1979), excerpted in Skillen and McCarthy.

Downs, Robert B. 1975. *Heinrich Pestalozzi: Father of Modern Pedagogy.* Boston: Twayne Publishers.

Dronkers, J., R. H. Hofman, and A. B. Dijkstra. 1997a. "Waarom blijft de onderwijsverzuiling bestaan?" in Dijkstra, Dronkers, and Hofman.

—1997b. "Verzuiling onder druk? De toekomst van de onderwijsverzuiling," in Dijkstra, Dronkers, and Hofman.

Dumon, Wilfried. 1982. *Het profiel van de vreemdelingen in Belgie.* Leuven: Davidsfonds.

Egmond, Nicholaas van. (1964). *Consequent Christendom: Leven en Werk van Mr. J. J. L. Van der Brugghen.* Wageningen: Veenman.

Eichberg, Ekkehard. 1986. "Gruppenerziehung—Kollektiverziehung—Gemeinschaftserziehung in der Bundesrepublik Deutschland und in der DDR," in *Vergleichende Bildungsforschung: DDR, Osteuropa und interkulturelle*

Perspektiven, edited by Bernhard Dilger, Friedrich Kuebart, and Hans-Peter Schaefer. Berlin: Arno Spitz.

Elias, John L. 2002. *A History of Christian Education*. Malabar, FL: Krieger.

"Entwurf eines Landesschulgesetzes des Landes Sachsen." 1990. Working Paper, November 13.

Ertel, Manfred, Hans Werner Kilz, and Jörg R. Mettke. 1980. *Gesamtschule: Modell oder Reformruine?* Hamburg: Spiegel-Buch.

Esden-Tempska, Carla. 1990. "Civic education in authoritarian Austria, 1934–38," *History of Education Quarterly* 30, no. 2 (Summer): 187–211.

Essen, Jantje Lubbegiena van. 1990. "The Struggle for Freedom of Education in the Netherlands in the Nineteenth Century" and "Groen van Prinsterer's Tactics in His Campaign for Freedom of Education," translated by Herbert Donald Morton, in *Guillaume Groen van Prinsterer: Selected Studies*, edited by Van Essen and Morton. Ontario: Wedge.

Fernandez, Alfred, and Siegfried Jenkner. 1995. *International Declarations and Conventions on the Right to Education and the Freedom of Education*. Frankfurt am Main: Info3-Verlag.

Fertig, Ludwig. 1984. *Zeitgeist und Erziehungskunst: Eine Einfuehring in die Kulturgeschichte der Erziehung in Deutschland von 1600 bis 1900*. Darmstadt: Wissenschaftliche Buchgesellschaft.

Fichte, Johann Gottlieb. 1978. *Reden an die deutsche Nation*. Hamburg: Felix Meiner Verlag.

Fishman, Sterling. 1976. *The Struggle for German Youth: The Search for Educational Reform in Imperial Germany, 1890–1914*. New York: Revisionist Press.

Fishman, Sterling, and Lothar Martin. 1987. *Estranged Twins: Education and Society in the Two Germanies*. New York: Praeger.

Fontainerie, Guy de la, editor. 1932. *French Liberalism and Education in the Eighteenth Century: The Writings of La Chalotais, Turgot, Diderot, and Condorcet*. New York: McGraw-Hill.

Fraser, Stewart E., and William W. Brickman, editors. 1968. *A History of International and Comparative Education: Nineteenth Century Documents*. Glenview, IL: Scott, Foresman.

Friederich, Gerd. 1987. "Das niedere Schulwesen," in Jeismann and Lundgreen.

Fritz, Stephen G. 1985. "'The center cannot hold.' Educational politics and the collapse of the Democratic middle in Germany: the school bill crisis in Baden, 1927–1928," *History of Education Quarterly* 25, no. 4 (Winter): 413–37.

Fuehr, Christoph, and Carl-Ludwig Furck, editors. 1998. *Handbuch der deutschen Bildungsgeschichte, Band VI, 1945 bis zur Gegenwart, Zweiter Teilband: Deutsche Demokratische Republik und neue Bundeslaender*. Munich: C. H. Beck.

Fuessel, Hans-Peter. 1994. "The Attribution of Powers as to Education within Germany," in *Subsidiarity and Education: Aspects of Comparative Educational Law*, edited by Jan De Groof. Leuven (Belgium): Acco.

—1997. "Developments in educational legislation in Germany: between unification and autonomy," *European Journal for Education Law and Policy* 1: 131–34.

—1998b. "Freedom in the German school system," *European Journal for Education Law and Policy* 2: 139–40.

—1999. "Religious instruction for Islamic pupils: a German discussion," *European Journal for Education Law and Policy* 3: 139–40.

—2000. "Autonomy of the Educational Institutions," in *Autonomy in Education*, edited by W. Berka, J. De Groof, and H. Penneman. Deventer, Kluwer: 357–63.

Fuessl, Karl-Hans, and Christian Kubina. 1985. "Educational reform between politics and pedagogics. The development of education in Berlin after World War II," *History of Education Quarterly* 25, no. 1/2 (Spring–Summer): 133–53.

Furet, François, and Jacques Ozouf. 1977. *Lire et écrire: L'alphabétisation des français de Calvin à Jules Ferry*. Paris: Éditions de Minuit.

Gay, Peter. 1969. *The Enlightenment: The Science of Freedom*. New York: W. W. Norton.

—1977. *The Enlightenment: The Rise of Modern Paganism*. New York: W. W. Norton.

Gebuerek, Konrad , Heike Kaack, and Guenter Lange. 1989. " 'Keine Antwort— M. f. s.': Briefe an den Paedagogischen Kongress '89"; typescript, no date, sent to the author by Lange in May 1991.

Gelderen, J. Van. 1984. " 'Scheuring' en Vereniging—1837–1869," in Bakker.

Gerretson, C. 1978. "Groen van Prinsterer," in Boogman and Tamse.

—1984. "Onbekende factoren van de Afscheiding van 1834," *Rondom het Woord* 26, no. 4 (Winter).

Gilhuis, T. M. 1975. *Memorietafel van het Christelijk Onderwijs: De Geschiedenis van de Schoolstrijd*, 2nd edition. Kampen: Kok.

—1987. *De tien jaren 1879–1889*. Kampen: Kok.

—No date, a. *En tóch is het anders: Over de herkenbaarheid van het christelijk onderwijs*. Kampen: Kok.

—No date, b. *De gezamenlijke school: Vóór of tegen?* Kampen: Kok.

Ginjaar-Maas, N. J. 1976. "Onderwijs in de branding: Een liberale visie op het onderwijs," in Beks.

Giollitto, Pierre. 1991. *Histoire de la Jeunesse sous Vichy*. Paris: Perrin.

Glenn, Charles L. 1988. *The Myth of the Common School*. Amherst, MA: University of Massachusetts Press.

—1989. "Germany," in *Choice of Schools in Six Nations*. Washington, DC: US Department of Education.

—1995. *Educational Freedom in Eastern Europe*. Washington, DC: Cato Institute.

—1999. "The Belgian Model of peace-making in educational policy," in *Het schoolpact van 1958/Le pacte scolaire de 1958*, edited by Els Witte, Jan De Groof and Jeffrey Tyssens. Brussels: VUPress.

Glenn, Charles, and Jan De Groof (2002). *Finding the Right Balance: Freedom, Autonomy and Accountability in Education*, I-II, Utrecht: Lemma.

—2004. *Balancing Freedom, Autonomy, and Accountability in Education, I-III.* Nijmegen (The Netherlands): Wolf Legal Publishing.

Gonon, Philipp. 1997. "Schule im Spannungsfeld zwischen Arbeit, elementarer Bildung und Beruf," in Badertscher and Grunder.

Gontard, Maurice. 1959. *L'enseignement primaire en France de la Révolution à la Loi Guizot.* Paris: Société d'édition Les Belles Lettres.

Gorski, Philip S. 2003. *The Disciplinary Revolution: Calvinism and the Rise of the State in Early Modern Europe.* Chicago: University of Chicago Press.

Graff, Harvey J. 1991. *The Legacies of Literacy.* Bloomington, IN: University of Indiana Press.

Green, J. A. 1914. *The Educational Ideas of Pestalozzi.* London: W. B. Clive.

Grimm, Gerald. 1991. "Expansion, Uniformisierung, Disziplinierung: Zur Sozialgeschichte der Schulerziehung in Oesterreich im Zeitalter des aufgeklaerten Absolutismus," in Schmale and Dodde.

Griscom, John. 1823. *A Year in Europe, Comprising a Journal of Observations . . . in 1818 and 1819*, vols. 1 and 2. New York: Collins.

Groen van Prinsterer, Guillaume. 1837. *De Maatregelen tegen de Afgescheidenen aan het Staatsregt getoetst.* Leiden: Luchtmans.

—1976. *Ongeloof en Revolutie (1847)*, edited by H. Smitskamp. Franeker (The Netherlands): T. Wever.

—No date. *Vrijheid, Gelijkheid Broederschap: Toelichting van de Spreuk der Revolutie (1848)*; reprinted by Groningen: De Vuurbaak.

—1857. *Adviesen in de Tweede Kamer der Staten-Generaal.* Utrecht: Kemink.

—1860. *Le parti Anti-Révolutionnaire et Confessionel dans l'Église Reformée des Pays-Bas.* Amsterdam: Hoeveker.

—1895. *Handboek der Geschiedenis van het Vaderland (1848)*, sixth printing. Amsterdam: Wormser.

Groot, Aart de. 1960. *Leven en Arbeid van J. H. van der Palm.* Wageningen: Veenman.

—1984a. "'God will het Waar Geluk van 't Algemeen,' Nutspublicaties van de eerste vijftig jaar over Godsdienst en Zede," in Mijnhardt and Wichers.

—1984b. "Het vroegnegentiende-eeuwse Nederland," in Bakker and others.

Groot, Aart de, and P. L. Schram, editors. 1984. *Aspecten van de Afscheiding.* Franeker: T. Wever.

Grootaers, Dominique. 1998a. "Cent cinquante ans d'instruction publique, à la poursuite de l'intégration sociale et de la promotion individuelle," in Grootaers.

—1998b. "Tensions et ruptures dans le projet éducatif et culturel des humanités (1830–1950)," in Grootaers.

Grootaers, Dominique, editor. 1998. *Histoire de l'enseignement en Belgique.* Brussels: CRISP.

Grothe, Peter. 1958. *To Win the Minds of Men: The Story of the Communist Propaganda War in East Germany.* Palo Alto: Pacific Books.

Grunder, Hans-Ulrich. 1997b. "Privat oder staatlich? Alternative Schulmodelle in der Schweiz," in Badertscher and Grunder.

Grunz-Stoll, Johannes. 1997. "Pestalozzi und die Pestalozzianer. Schulwirklichkeiten zu Beginn des 19. Jahrhunderts," in Badertscher and Grunder.

Guimps, Roger de. 1890. *Pestalozzi: His Life and Work*. London: Swan Sonnenschein.

Hager, Fritz-Peter. 2000. "Switzerland," in *International Handbook on History of Education*, edited by Kadriya Salimova and Nan L. Dodde. Moscow: Orbita-M.

Hahn, H.-J. 1998. *Education and Society in Germany*. Oxford: Berg.

Hamann, Bruno. 1986. *Geschichte des Schulwesens*. Bad Heilbrunn: Verlag Julius Klinkhardt.

Hammerstein, Notker, and Ulrich Herrmann. 2005. *Handbuch der deutschen Bildungsgeschichte, Band II: 18. Jahrhundert: Vom spaeten 17. Jahrhundert bis zur Neuordnung Deutschlands um 1800*. Munich: C. H. Beck.

Hans, Nicholas. 1965. "Holland in the eighteenth century Verlichting (Enlightenment)," *Paedagogica Historica* 5, no. 1.

Hansen, Erik. 1973. "Marxism, Socialism, and the Dutch Primary Schools," *History of Education Quarterly* 13, no. 4 (Winter): 367–91.

Hansen, Georg. 1986. *Diskriminiert: Uber den Umgang der Schule mit Minderheiten*. Basel: Beltz.

Harp, Stephen L. 1998. *Learning to Be Loyal: Primary Schooling as Nation Building in Alsace and Lorraine, 1850–1940*. DeKalb, IL: Northern Illinois University Press.

Hearndon, Arthur. 1995. "Problems in German secondary education," in *Education in Germany*, edited by David Phillips. London: Routledge.

Heerspink, J. B. F. 1898. *Dr. P. Hofstede de Groot's Leven en Werken*. Groningen: Noordhoff.

Heisler, Martin O. 1977. "Managing Ethnic Conflict in Belgium," *Annals of the American Academy of Political and Social Science* 433: 32–46.

Helsloot, P. N. 1984. "De Nutsbeweging," in Mijnhardt and Wichers.

Helmreich, Ernst Christian. 1959. *Religious Education in German Schools*. Cambridge, MA: Harvard University Press.

—1979. *The German Churches under Hitler: Background, Struggle, and Epilogue*. Detroit: Wayne State University Press.

Herbst, Jurgen. 2006. *School Choice and School Governance: A Historical Study of the United States and Germany*. New York: Palgrave Macmillan.

Herrlitz, H.-G., W. Hopf, and H. Titze. 1986. *Deutsche Schulgeschichte von 1800 bis zur Gegenwart*, 2nd edition. Koenigstein: Athenäum.

Herrmann, U. 1991. "Pädagogisches Denken und Anfänge der Reformpädagogik," in Berg.

—2005. "Paedagogisches Denken," in Hammerstein and Herrmann.

Hickson, W. E. 1840. *An Account of the Present State of Education in Holland, Belgium, and the German States*. London: Taylor.

Hoefnagel, H . J. M. 1994. "Developments in Dutch Education Policy and Responsibility for Education," in *Subsidiarity and Education Aspects of Comparative Educational Law*, edited by Jan De Groof. Leuven (Belgium): Acco.

Hoerner, Wolfgang. 1990. *Bildung und Wissenschaft in der DDR: Ausgangslage und Reform bis Mitte 1990*. Bonn: Bundesministerium für Bildung und Wissenschaft.

Hofer, Walther. 1957. *Der Nationalsozialismus: Dokumente 1933–1945*. Frankfurt am Main: Fischer Buecherei.

Hofman, R. H. 1997a. "Institutionele verankering en legitimatie? Verzuiling op het middenveld," in Dijkstra, Dronkers, and Hofman.

—1997b. "Effectieve besturen? Verzuiling en bestuursvorm," in Dijkstra, Dronkers, and Hofman.

Hofmann, Hans-Georg. 1991. "Von der Spezial- zur Allgemeinbildung—Zukunftsorientierte gesellschaftspolitische Bildungsarbeit in den fuenf neuen Bundeslaendern," in *Unternehmertun—Wirtschaftlicher Aufschwung und sozialer Fortschritt in einem vereinigten Deutschland*, edited by Hermann Linke, Horst-Udo Niedenhoff, and Wilfried Vetter. Cologne: Deutscher Instituts-Verlag.

Hofstede de Groot, Petrus. 1841. "De Denkbeelden van Graser, van Heusde, Cousin, en van Bommel over the Betrekking can de Godsdienst en de Wetenschap tot het Onderwijs medegedeeld en vergeleken," *Waarheid in Liefde* 2.

—1844. *Zijn afzonderlijke scholen voor de verschillende kerkgenootschappen noodig of wenschelijk?* Groningen: Scholtens.

—1845. "Het Belang van Volksopvoeding, door een Voorbeeld uit de Geschiedenis onzer Eeuw opgehelderd," *Waarheid in Liefde* 4.

—1848. *Wat hebben wij van het Ontwerp van gewijzigde Grondwet te verwachten met Betrekking tot Godsdienst en Onderwijs?* Groningen: Van Bolhuis Hoitsema.

—1849. "Over de opvoeding van kinderen in navolging van de opvoeding des menschdoms door God," *Waarheid in Liefde*.

Holtrop, P. N. 1984. "De Afscheiding—breekpunt en kristallisatiepunt," in Bakker, and others.

Horn, Daniel. 1976. "The Hitler Youth and Educational Decline in the Third Reich," *History of Education Quarterly* 16, no. 4 (Winter): 425–47.

Hornstein, Walter, and Werner Schefeld. 1998. "Sozialpaedagogik," in Führ and Furck.

Houston, R. A. 2002. *Literacy in Early Modern Europe: Culture and Education 1500–1800*, 2nd edition. Harlow (England): Pearson Education.

Houston, Susan E., and Alison Prentice. 1988. *Schooling and Scholars in Nineteenth Century Ontario*. Toronto: University of Toronto Press.

Humboldt, Wilhelm von. 1993. *The Limits of State Action*, edited by J. W. Burrow. Indianapolis: Liberty Fund.

Huussen, A. H. 1989. "De Franse Revolutie in het Nederlandse politieke leven tijdens de 19de eeuw—Inleidende opmerkingen," in Koole.

Idenburg, Ph. J. 1957. *Bekostiging der Onderwijsvrijheid*. Amsterdam: De Arbeiderpers.

Jach, Frank-Rüdiger, 1991. *Schulvielfalt als Verfassungsgebot*. Berlin: Duncker and Humblot.

—1999. *Schulverfassung und Buergergesellschaft in Europa*. Berlin: Duncker and Humblot.

Jaeger, Georg, and Heinz-Elmar Tenorth. 1987. "Paedagogisches Denken," in Jeismann and Lundgreen.

Janse, C. S. L. 1985. *Bewaar het pand: De spanning tussen assimilatie en persistentie bij de emancipatie van de bevindelijk gereformeerden*. Houten: Den Hertog.

Jeismann, Karl-Ernst. 1987a. "Zur Bedeutung der 'Bildung' im 19. Jahrhundert," in Jeismann and Lundgreen.

—1987b. "Schulpolitik, Schulverwaltung, Schulgesetzgebung," in Jeismann and Lundgreen.

Jeismann, Karl-Ernst, and Peter Lundgreen, editors. 1987. *Handbuch der deutschen Bildungsgeschichte, Band III, 1800–1870: Von der Neuordnung Deutschlands bis zur Gruendung des Deutschen Reiches*. Munich: C. H. Beck.

Jenkner, Siegfried. 1989. "Schule zwischen Staats- und Selbstverwaltung," *Pädagogik und Schule in Ost und West* 37, no. 1.

—1990a. "Freie Schule und Staat. Erste Internationale Ost-West-Tagung in der Bundesrepublik," *Paedagogik und Schule in Ost und West* 38, no. 1.

—1990b. "Das Recht auf Bildung als Menschenrecht und seine Realisierung in beiden deutschen Staaten," *Paedagogik und Schule in Ost und West* 38, no. 4 ().

—1992. "Deutscher Foederalismus und europaeische Integration unter besonderer Beruecksichtigung des Bildungswesens," in *Politische Bildung im vereinten Deutschland*. Opladen: Leske and Budrich.

Jenkner, Siegfried, editor. 1994. *Das Recht auf Bildung und die Freiheit der Erziehung in Eurpaeischen Verfassungen*. Frankfurt/Main (Germany): Info-3-Verlag.

Jong, Otto de. 1978. *Nederlandse Kerkgeschiedenis*, 2nd edition, Nijkerk: Callenbach.

—1984. "Van de andere kant: Hervormde reacties op de Afscheiding," in Bakker and others.

Jonge, J. de. 1977. "Motivatie voor protestants-christelijk onderwijs," in Box, Dronkers, Molenaar, and Mulder.

Kalsbeek, L. 1976. *Theologische en Wijsgerige Actergronden van de Verhouding van Kerk, Staat, en School in Nederland*. Kampen: Kok.

—No date. *Een school met of zonder Bijbel?* Kampen: Kok.

Kant, Immanuel. 1960. *Education*, translated by Annette Churton. Ann Arbor: University of Michigan Press.

Kaplan, Benjamin J. 2007. *Divided by Faith: Religious Conflict and the Practice of Toleration in Early Modern Europe*. Cambridge, MA: Harvard University Press.

Karsten, S. 1997. "Verzuiling als sociaal en politiek verschijnsel," in Dijkstra, Dronkers, and Hofman.

—2003. "Dutch Social Democrats and the struggle for parental choice in education (1890–1940)," *History of Education* 32, no. 4 (July): 417–31.

Keim, Wolfgang. 1995. *Erziehung unter der Nazi-Diktatur, Band I.* Darmstadt: Wissenschaftliche Buchgesellschaft.

Kelly, Reece C. 1985. "German professoriate under Nazism: a failure of totalitarian aspirations," *History of Education Quarterly* 25, no. 3 (Autumn): 261–80.

Kemenade, J. A. van. 1968. *De Katholieken en hun onderwijs.* Meppel: Boom.

Kemenade, J. A. van, P. L. M. Jungbluth, and J. M. M. Ritzen. 1987. "Onderwijs en samenleving," in Kemenade.

Kemenade, J. A. van, editor. 1987. *Onderwijs: Bestel en Beleid.* Groningen: Walters-Noordhoff.

Kessel, N. T. J. M. van, and A. M. L. van Wieringen. 1997. "Onderwijsvoorzieningen en schoolkeuse," in Dijkstra, Dronkers, and Hofman.

Kesteloot, Chantal. 2004. *Au nom de la Wallonie et de Bruxelles français: Les origines du FDF.* Brussels: Editions Complexe.

Kisjes, A. Joh., and P. A. te Velde, editors. 1983. *Het Gereformeerd Onderwijs: Identiteitsbezinning.* Kampen: Kok.

Kneller, George Frederick. 1941. *The Educational Philosophy of National Socialism.* New Haven, CT: Yale University Press.

Knetsch, F. R. J. 1984. "Het Reveil en de Afscheiding," in Groot and Schram.

Knight, Edgar W., editor. 1930. *Reports on European Education by John Griscom, Victor Cousin, Calvin E. Stowe.* New York: McGraw-Hill.

Knopp, Guido. 2000. *Hitlers Kinder.* Munich: Goldmann.

Koelman, J. B. J. 1987. *Kosten van de verzuiling.* The Hague: Vuga.

Koenig, Hans-Joerg. 1990. "Schulverfassung in der DDR," *Recht der Jugend und des Bildungswesens* 4.

Komlósi, Sándor. 1991. " Schule und Erziehung in Ungarn (1750–1825). Zwischen Systemerhalt und Modernisierung," in Schmale and Dodde.

Koole, R. A., editor. 1989. *Van Bastille tot Binnenhof: De Franse Revolutie en haar invloed op de Nederlandse politieke partijen.* Houten (The Netherlands): Fibula.

Koppejan, J. 1985. "Ontstaan en groei van het reformatorisch onderwijs," in *Belijden en opvoeden: Gedachten over de christelijke school vanuit een reformatorische visie,* edited by M. Golverdingen, and others. Houten (The Netherlands): Den Hertog.

Kossmann, E. H. 2001. *De lage landen 1780–1980: Deel 1 1780–1914.* Olympus.

—2002. *De lage landen 1780–1980: Deel II 1914–1980.* Olympus.

Kraus, Josef, and Günter Lange. 1991. "Schulpolitik im geeinten Deutschland," typescript, no date (received by the author from Lange, May 1991).

Krieger, Leonard. 1970. *Kings and Philosophers 1689–1789.* New York: W. W. Norton and Company.

Kruijt, J. P., and Walter Goddijn. 1962. "Verzuiling en Ontzuiling als sociologisch proces," in *Drift en Koers: Een halve eeuw sociale verandering in Nederland*, edited by A. N. J. Hollander, and others. Assen: Van Gorcum.

Kuhlemann, Frank-Michael. 1991. "Niedere Schulen," in Berg.

Kuiper, J. 1904. *Geschiedenis van het Christelijk Lager Onderwijs in Nederland* (16n. Chr.-1904). Groningen: Wolters.

Kuyper, Abraham. 1869. *De 'Nuts'-beweging*. Amsterdam: Hoeveker.

—1890. *Eenige Kameradviesen uit de jaren 1874 en 1875*. Amsterdam: Wormser.

—1907. *Ons Program*. Hilversum: Hoeveker and Wormser.

—1931. *Lectures on Calvinism (1898)*. Grand Rapids: Eerdmans.

Lamberti, Marjorie. 1989. *State, Society, and the Elementary School in Imperial Germany*. New York: Oxford University Press.

—1992. "Elementary school teachers and the struggle against social democracy in Wilhelmine Germany," *History of Education Quarterly* 32, no. 1 (Spring): 73–97.

—2000. "Radical schoolteachers and the origins of the progressive education movement in Germany, 1900–1914," *History of Education Quarterly* 40, no. 1 (Spring): 22–48.

Lamberts, Emiel. 1972. *Kerk en Liberalisme in het Bisdom Gent (1821–1857)*. Leuven: Universitaire Uitgaven.

Langedijk, D. 1935. *De Schoolstrijd*. The Hague: Van Haeringen.

—1947. *Groen van Prinsterer en de Schoolkwestie*. The Hague: Voorhoeve.

Langewiesehe, Dieter, and Heinz-Elmar Tenorth, editors. 1989. *Handbuch der deutschen Bildungsgeschichte, Band V, 1918–1945: Die Weimarer Republic und die nationalsozialistische Diktatur*. Munich: C. H. Beck

—1989. "Bildung, Formierung, Destruction Grundzüge der Bildungsgeschichte von 1918–1945," in Langewiesehe and Tenorth.

Lannie, Vincent P., editor. 1974. *Henry Barnard: American Educator*. New York: Teachers College Press.

Laveleye, Émile de. 1858. *Débats sur l'enseignement primaire dans les Chambres hollandaises (Session de 1857)*. Ghent: Vanderhaegen.

—1872. *L'instruction du peuple*. Paris: Hachette.

LaVopa, Anthony J. 1980. *Prussian Schoolteachers: Profession and Office, 1763–1848*. Chapel Hill: University of North Carolina Press.

Leeb, I. Leonard. 1973. *The Ideological Origins of the Batavian Revolution*. The Hague: Springer.

Lehman, Albrecht. 1989. "Militaer und Militant zwischen den Weltkriegen," in Langewiesehe and Tenorth.

Leman, Johan. 1985. "The Foyer-Project: How a Confusing Trilingual Situation Can Be Converted into an Advantage for Immigrant Children in Brussels," in *Four Years Bicultural Education in Brussels: An Evaluation*. Brussels: The Foyer Committee of Bicultural Education.

Lijphart, Arend. 1968. *The Politics of Accommodation: Pluralism and Democracy in the Netherlands*. Berkeley: University of California Press.

Lipschits, I. 1977. *De protestants-christelijke stroming tot 1940*. Deventer: Kluwer.

Lorwin, Val R. 1966. "Belgium: Religion, Class, and Language in National Politics," in *Political Oppositions in Western Democracies*, edited by Robert A. Dahl. New Haven, CT: Yale University Press.

Lory, Jacques. 1979. *Libéralisme et instruction primaire 1842–1879: Introduction à l'étude de la lutte scolaire en Belgique*, vols. 1 and 2. Louvain: Éditions Nauwelaerts.

Lost, Christine. 1990. " Bemerkungen zum Umgang mit Reformpaedagogik in der DDR (1945 bis 1989)," *Paedagogische Forschung* 31, nos. 5/6 ().

Lundgreen, Peter. 1980. *Sozialgeschichte der deutschen Schule im Ueberblick, Teil I: 1770–1918*. Göttingen: Vandenhoeck.

—1981. *Sozialgeschichte der deutschen Schule im Ueberblick, Teil II: 1918–1980*. Göttingen: Vandenhoeck.

Luther, Martin. 1962. "To the Councilmen of All Cities in Germany That They Establish and Maintain Christian Schools," translated by Albert Steinhaeuser, in *Luther's Works*, vol. 45. Philadelphia: Fortress Press.

Maizière, Lothar de. 1990. "Aus der Regierungserklaerung von Ministerpraesident Lothar de Maizière vom 19. April 1990," *Bildung und Erziehung* 43, no. 3 (September).

Mallinson, Vernon. 1963. *Power and Politics in Belgian Education, 1815 to 1961*. London: Heinemann.

—1970. *Belgium*. New York: Praeger.

Mallinson, Vernon, and Silvain de Coster. 1960. "Church and state education in Belgium," *Comparative Education Review* 4, no. 1: 43–48.

Mann, Erika. 2001. *Zehn Millionen Kinder: Die Erziehung der Jugend im Dritten Reich (1938)*. Hamburg: Rowohlt.

Mann, Golo. 1958. *Deutsche Geschichte des 19. und 20. Jahrhunderts*. Frankfurt am Main: Fischer.

Mann, Horace. 1844. "A preliminary and critical account of European education," *The Common School Journal*, Boston, VI: 2–12.

Marwijk Kooy-von Baumhauer, Liesbeth. 1984. *Scholen verschillen: een verkennend vergelijkend onderzoek naar het intern functioneren van vijfentwintig school-gemeenschappen vwo-havo-mavo*. Groningen: Wolters Noordhoff.

Max Planck Institute. 1983. *Between Elite and Mass Education: Education in the Federal Republic of Germany*, translated by Raymond Meyer and Adriane Heinrichs-Goodwin. Albany: State University of New York Press.

McKay, Llewelyn R. 1956. "The 'new look' in West German schools," *History of Education Journal* 7, no. 4 (Summer): 144–51.

McLeod, Hugh. 2000. *Secularization in Western Europe, 1848–1914*. New York: St. Martin's Press.

McMahon, Darrin M. 2001. *Enemies of the Enlightenment*. Oxford: Oxford University Press.

Meiden, Anne van der. 1981. *Welzalig is het Volk: De Zwarte-kousen Kerken*. Baarb: Ten Have.

Meinecke, Friedrich. 1977. *The Age of German Liberation, 1795–1815*, edited by Peter Paret. Berkeley: University of California Press.

Melton, James van Horn. 2003. *Absolutism and the Eighteenth-Century Origins of Compulsory Schooling in Prussia and Austria*. Cambridge: Cambridge University Press.

Meulen, S. Boef-Van der, and S. J. Bouhuijs. 1977. "Vrijheid van onderwijs en bevoegd gezag," in Box, Dronkers, Molenaar, and Mulder.

Mijnhardt, W. W. 1984. "Het Nut en de Genootschapsbeweging," in Mijnhardt and Wichers.

Mijnhardt, W. W., and A. J. Wichers, editors. 1984. *Om het Algemeen Volksgeluk: Twee Eeuwen Particulier Initiatief, 1784–1984*. Edam: Maatschappij tot Nut van 't Algemeen.

Mitter, Wolfgang. 1990a. "Allgemeinbildendes Schulwesen: Grundfragen und Ueberblick," in Anweiler and others.

—1990b. "Politische Bildung und Erziehung," in Anweiler and others.

—1998. "Das Deutsche Bildungswesen in Internationale Perspective," in Führ and Furck.

Mueller, Detlef K. 1987. "The Process of Systematisation: The Case of German Secondary Education," in *The Rise of the Modern Educational System: Structural Change and Social Reproduction 1870–1920*, edited by Detlef K. Müller, Fritz Ringer, and Brian Simon. Cambridge: Cambridge University Press.

Mueller-Rolli, Sebastian. 1989. "Lehrer," in Langewiesehe and Tenorth.

Mulder, L. H. 1984a. "Een sociologische visie op de Afscheiding van 1834," *Rondom het Woord* 26, no. 4 (Winter).

—1984b. "De Afscheiding sociaal-wetenschappelijk benaderd," in Groot and Schram.

Navarro Sandalinas, Ramón. 1990. *La enseñanza primaria durante el Franquismo (1936–1975)*. Barcelona: PPU.

Neugebauer, Wolfgang. 2005. "Niedere Schulen und Realschulen," in Hammerstein and Herrmann.

Nipperdey, Thomas. 1983. *Deutsche Geschichte 1800–1866*. Munich: Verlag C. H. Beck.

Oelschlaeger, Guenther. No date. *Weltanschauliche Schulung in der Hitler-Jugend: Inhalte, Schwerpunkte und Methoden*. Selbstverlag G. Oelschläger.

Olson, James M. 1977. "Radical social democracy and school reform in Wilhelmian Germany," *History of Education Quarterly* 17, no. 1 (Spring): 3–16.

Oosterhof, Okko Nanning. 1913. *Isaac da Costa als Polemist*. Kampen: Zalsman.

Osborn, Andrew R. 1934. *Schleiermacher and Religious Education*. London: Oxford University Press.

Osborne, David, and Ted Gaebler. 1992. *Reinventing Government*. Reading, MA: Addison-Wesley.

Osterwalder, Fritz. 1997. "Schule denken: Schule als linear gegliederte, staatliche und öffentliche Institution?" in Badertscher and Grunder.

Otto, Hans-Uwe, and Heinz Suenker, editors. 1991. *Politische Formierung und soziale Erziehung im Nationalsozialismus.* Frankfurt am Main: Suhrkamp.

Passant, E. J. 1962. *A Short History of Germany, 1815–1945.* Cambridge: Cambridge University Press.

Pestalozzi, Johann Heinrich. 1977. *Leonard and Gertrude,* translated by Eva Channing. New York: Gordon Press.

Peukert, Detlev J. K. 1989. "Sozialpaedagogik," in Langewiesehe and Tenorth.

Phillips, David, editor. 1995. *Education in Germany: Tradition and Reform in Historical Context.* London: Routledge.

Ploeg, Tymen J. van der. 1995. "Introduction to the Dutch model of government-non governmental organizations," in *Rethinking the Balance: Government and non-governmental organizations in the Netherlands,* edited by van der Ploeg and John W. Sap. Amsterdam: VU Press.

Poglia, Edo. 1993. "L'Etat et l'éducation: quelques questions actuelles," in *Die Zukunft der öffentlichen Bildung/L'avenir de l'éducation publique,* edited by Philipp Gonon and Jürgen Oelkers. Bern: Peter Lang.

Pommereau, Isabelle de. 2006. "Private schools take off in Germany," *Christian Science Monitor* (January 30): 1–2.

Postma, Andries. 1995. *Handboek van het nederlandse onderwijsrecht.* Zwolle: W. E. J. Tjeenk Willink.

Potz, Richard, and Brigitte Schinkele. 2005. "Religionsunterricht in Oesterreich," in *Religious Education in Public Schools,* edited by José Luis Martínez López-Muñiz, Jan De Groof, and Gracienne Lauwers. Dordrecht: Springer.

Prentice, Alison. 2004 [1977]. *The School Promoters: Education and Social Class in Mid-Nineteenth Century Upper Canada.* University of Toronto Press.

Ramm, Thilo. 1990. "Die Bildungsverfassungen," in Anweiler and others.

Rasker, A. J. 1981. *De Nederlandse Hervormde Kerk vanaf 1795.* Kampen: Kok.

Rawson, W. 1840. "On the decline of popular instruction in Belgium," *Journal of the Statistical Society of London* 2, no. 6: 385–96.

Reble, Albert. 1999. *Geschichte der Paedagogik: Dokumentationsband,* 4th edition. Stuttgart: Klett-Cotta.

—2002. *Geschichte der Paedagogik,* 20th edition. Stuttgart: Klett-Cotta.

Rehm, Stefanie. 1991. "Grusswort sur Eroeffnung des Evangelischen Schulzentrums Leipzig," *Saechsisches Staatsministerium fuer Kultus* (December 6).

Rein, Gerhard, editor. 1989. *Die Opposition in der DDR: Entwuerfe fuer einen anderen Sozialismus.* Berlin: Wichern.

Reisner, Edward H. 1922. *Nationalism and Education since 1789.* New York: Macmillan.

—1930. *The Evolution of the Common School.* New York: Macmillan.

Remak, Joachim, editor. 1960. *The Nazi Years: A Documentary History.* Englewood Cliffs: Prentice-Hall.

Reuter, Lutz R. 1998. "Participation im Schulwesen," in Fuehr and Furck.

Richter, Ingo. 1990. "West Germany, Switzerland and Austria," in Ian K. Birch and Ingo Richter, *Comparative School Law*. Pergamon Press.

—1992. "Privatschulfreiheit fuer die Grundschulen von Sekten?" *Neue Zeitschrift für Verwaltungsrecht* 12: 1162–64.

Riel, Harm van. 1982. *Geschiedenis van het Nederlandse Liberalisme in de 19e Eeuw*. Assen: Van Gorcum.

Rijnsdorp, C. 1979. "'Met vreugd naar school' (Herinnering en tijdbeeld)," in *In het honderdste jaar: Gedenkboek Stichting Unie 'School en Evangelie' 1879-1979*. Kampen: Kok.

Ringer, Fritz. 1979. *Education and Society in Modern Europe*. Bloomington: Indiana University Press.

Robbins, Charles Leonidas. 1912. *Teachers in Germany in the Sixteenth Century: Conditions in Protestant Elementary and Secondary Schools*. New York: Teachers College.

Robinsohn, Saul, and J. Caspar Kuhlmann. 1995. "Two Decades of Non-Reform in West German Education" (1967), in *Education in Germany*, edited by David Phillips. London: Routledge.

Roegiers, J. 1983. "Sociocultureel leven in de Zuidelijke Nederlanden 1794–1814," in *Algemene Geschiedenis der Nederlanden* 11. Weesp: Fibula-Van Dishoeck.

Roeleveld, J. 1997. "Concurrentie tussen scholen? Verzuiling en leerlingenmarkten," in Dijkstra, Dronkers, and Hofman.

Rosanvallon, Pierre. 1985. *Le moment Guizot*. Paris: Gallimard.

Rousseau, Jean-Jacques. 1962 [1773]. "Considerations on the Government of Poland," in *The Minor Educational Writings of Jean Jacques Rousseau*, translated by William Boyd. New York: Teachers College.

—1979 [1762]. *Emile, or On Education*, translated by Allan Bloom. New York: Basic Books.

Rush, Benjamin. 1965. "Plan for the Establishment of Public Schools," in *Essays on Education in the Early Republic*, edited by Frederick Rudolf. Cambridge, MA: Harvard University Press.

Ruether, Beate. 1992. "Vom marxistisch-leninistischen Grundlagenstudium zum Studium generale in der ehemaligen DDR," in Anweiler.

Scandola, Pietro. 1991. "Von der Standesschule zur Staatsschule: Die Entwicklung des Schulwesens in der Schweizerischen Eidgenossenschaft 1750-1830 am Beispiel der Kantone Bern und Zuerich," in Schmale and Dodde.

Schaepman, H. J. A. M. 1895. *Van strijd tot vrede? Nog een woord over Art. 194 der Grondwet*, Utrecht.

Schama, Simon. 1970. "Schools and politics in the Netherlands, 1796–1814," *Historical Journal* 13, no. 4.

—1977. *Patriots and Liberators: Revolution in the Netherlands 1780-1813*. New York: Knopf.

Schelfhout, C. E. 1977. "Sociologie en onderwijs," in Box, Dronkers, Molenaar, and Mulder.

—1979. "Onderwijs en onderwijsvrijheid (het katholiek onderwijs over de protestants christelijke school)," in *In het honderdste jaar: Gedenkboek Stichting Unie 'School en Evangelie' 1879–1979*. Kampen: Kok.

Schiedeck, Jürgen, and Martin Stahlmann. 1991. "Die Inszenierung totalen Erlebens: Lagererziehung im Nationalsozialismus," in Otto and Sünker.

Schleiermacher, Friedrich. 2000. *Texte zur Paedagogik*, vols.1 and 2, edited by Michael Winkler and Jens Brachmann. Frankfurt am Main: Suhrkamp.

Schleunes, Karl A. 1989. *Schooling and Society: The Politics of Education in Prussia and Bavaria 1750–1900*. Oxford, New York, and Munich: Berg.

Schmale, Wolfgang. 1991. "Die Schule in Deutschland im 18. und fruehen 19 Jh. Konjunkturen, Horizonte, Mentalitaeten, Probleme, Ergebnisse," in Schmale and Dodde.

Schmale, Wolfgang, and Nan L. Dodde, editors. 1991. *Revolution des Wissens? Europa und seine Schulen im Zeitalter der Aufklaerung (1750–1825)*. Bochum (Germany): Verlag Dr. Dieter Winkler.

Schmidt, Hanno. 2005. "Die Philanthropine-Musterschulen der Paedagogischen Aufklaerung," in Hammerstein and Herrmann.

Scholtz, Harald. 1985. *Erziehung und Unterricht unterm Hakenkreuz*. Göttingen: Vandenhoeck.

Schoten, Fons van. 1983. "Het publiekrechtelijk karakter van het openbaar onderwijs in gevaar?" in Akkermans and Leune.

Schoten, Fons van, and Hans Wansink. 1984. *De nieuwe schoolstrijd: Knelpunten en conflicten in de hedendaagse onderwijspolitiek*. Utrecht: Bohn, Scheltema and Holkema.

Schram, P. L. 1984. "De Afscheiding van 1834," Rondom het Woord 26, no. 4 (Winter).

Schutte, G. J. 1977. *Mr. G. Groen van Prinsterer*. Goes: Oosterbaan and Le Cointre.

Senden, G. H. Van. 1845. "De dweeperij," *Waarheid in Liefde* 2.

Shirley, Dennis. 1992. *The Politics of Progressive Education: The Odenwaldschule in Nazi Germany*. Cambridge, MA: Harvard University Press.

Siegert, Reinhart. 2005. "Volksbildung im 18. Jahrhundert," in Hammerstein and Herrmann.

Silber, Kate. 1960. *Pestalozzi: The Man and His Work*. London: Routledge and Kegan Paul.

Simons, Ludo. 2002. "Eer Vlanderen vergeet. Over de toekomst van de Vlaamse Beweging," in *Vlaamse Beweging: Welke toekomst?* Leuven: Davidsfonds.

Skillen, James, and Rockne McCarthy. 1991. *Political Order and the Plural Structure of Society*. Atlanta: Scholars Press.

Skopp, Douglas R. 1982. "The elementary school teachers in 'revolt': reform proposals for Germany's Volksschulen in 1848 and 1849," *History of Education Quarterly* (Fall): 341–61.

Sontheimer, Kurt, and Wilhelm Bleek. 1975. *The Government and Politics of East Germany*, translated by Ursula Price. New York: St. Martin's Press.

Spaeni, Martina. 1997. "Umstrittene Faecher in der Paedagogik. Zur Geschichte des Religions- und Turnunterrichts," in Badertscher and Grunder.

Sparn, Walter. 2005. "Religioese und Theologische Aspekte der Bildungsgeschichte im Zeitalter der Aufklaerung," in Hammerstein and Herrmann.

Spiegel, Yorick. 1968. *Theologie der buergerlichen Gesellschaft: Sozialphilosophie und Glaubenslehre bei Friedrich Schleiermacher*. Munich: Chr. Kaiser Verlag.

Spijker, W. van 't. 1984a. "De dogmatische aspecten van de Afscheiding," in Groot and Schram.

—1984b. *De kerk bij Hendrik de Cock*, Apeldoornse studies 21. Kampen: Kok.

Spotts, Frederic. 1973. *The Churches and Politics in Germany*. Middletown, CT: Wesleyan University Press.

Stern, Fritz. 1974. *The Politics of Cultural Despair: A Study in the Rise of the Germanic Ideology*. Berkeley: University of California Press.

Stokvis, P. R. D. 1984. "Afscheiding en emigratie," in Groot and Schram.

Stouten, J. 1984. *Verlichting in de Letteren*. Leiden: Nijhoff.

Stowe, Calvin. 1836. *The Prussian System of Public Instruction and Its Applicability to the United States*. Cincinnati: Truman and Smith.

Strikwerda, Carl. 1997. *A House Divided: Catholics, Socialists, and Flemish Nationalists in Nineteenth-Century Belgium*. London: Rowman and Littlefield.

Stuurman, S. 1983. *Verzuiling, Kapitalisme, en Patriarchaat*. Nijmegen: Socialistiese Uitgeverij.

—1989. "De bezwering van een afwezig spook—Nederlandse opinies over de Franse Revolutie 1848–1900," in Koole.

Swing, Elizabeth Sherman. 1982. "Education for Separatism: The Belgian Experience," in *Issues in International Bilingual Education: The Role of the Vernacular*, edited by Beverly Hartford, Albert Valdman, and Charles R. Foster. New York: Plenum Press.

Tenorth, Heinz-Elmar. 1987. "Lehrerberuf und Lehrerbildung," in Jeismann and Lundgreen.

—1989. "Paedagogisches Denken," in Langewiesehe and Tenorth.

—2000. *Geschichte der Erziehung: Einfuehrung in die Grundzuege ihrer neuzeitlichen Entwicklung*. Weinheim and München: Juventa Verlag.

Tenorth, Heinz-Elmar, and Peter Drewek. 2000. "Germany," in *International Handbook on History of Education*, edited by Kadriya Salimova and Nan L. Dodde. Moscow: Orbita-M.

Tent, James F. 1982. *Mission on the Rhine: Reeducation and Denazification in American-Occupied Germany*. Chicago: University of Chicago Press.

Thiel, Markus. 2000. *Der Erziehungsauftrag des Staates in der Schule: Grundlagen und Grenzen staatlicher Erziehungstaetigkeit im oeffentlichen Schulwese*. Berlin: Duncker and Humblot.

Thielicke, Helmut. 1969. *Theological Ethics, Volume 2: Politics*, edited by William H. Lazareth. Philadelphia: Fortress Press (German 1958, 1959).

Thurlings, J. M. G. 1978. *De wankele Zuil: Nederlandse katholieken tussen assimilatie en pluralisme*, 2nd edition. Deventer: Van Loghum Slaterus.

Tijn, Th. Van. 1977. "Actergronden van de ontwikkeling van het lager onderwijs en van de schoolstrijd in Nederland, 1862–1905," in Box, Dronkers, Molenaar, and Mulder.

Tismaneanu, Vladimir. 1990. "Against Socialist Militarism: The Independent Peace Movement in the German Democratic Republic," in *In Search of Civil Society.* New York: Routledge.

Titze, Hartmut. 1973. *Die Politisierung der Erziehung.* Frankfurt am Main: Fischer Taschenbuch Verlag,

—1991. "Lehrerbildung und Professionalisierung," in Berg.

Tocqueville, Alexis de. 1988. *Democracy in America,* edited by J. P. Mayer, translated by George Lawrence. New York: Harper and Row.

Tveit, Knut. 1991. "Schulische Erziehung in Nordeuropa 1750–1825: Dänemark, Finnland, Island, Norwegen und Schweden," in Schmale and Dodde.

Tyssens, Jeffrey. 1997. *Guerre et paix scolaires, 1950–1958.* Brussels: Be Boeck and Larcier.

—1998. "L'enseignement moyen jusqu'au Pacte scolaire: structuration, expansion, conflits," in Grootaers.

—1999. "Onderwijsconflict en -pacificatie vanuit een comparatief perspectief: België, Nederland, Frankrijk," in *Het schoolpact van 1958/Le pacte scolaire de 1958,* edited by Els Witte, Jan De Groof and Jeffrey Tyssens. Brussels: VUB Press.

Tyssens, Jeffrey, and Els Witte. 1996. *De vrijzinnige traditie in Belgie.* Brussels: VUB Press.

Uhlig, Christa. 1990. "Erziehung zwischen Engagement und Resignation— Gedanken zur Bildungsgeschichte in der DDR," *Paedagogische Forschung* 31, nos. 5/6.

Ulich, Robert. 1935. *A Sequence of Educational Influences.* Cambridge, MA: Harvard University Press.

Urban, Elke. 1991. "Neugruendungen Leipziger Schulen," Schulvielfalt in *Hannover (Theorie und Praxis 37).* Hannover: Fachbereich Erziehungswissenschaften I der Universität Hannover.

Valk, J. 1995. "Religion and the schools: the case of Utrecht," *History of Education Quarterly* 35, no. 2 (Summer): 159–77

Van Dyke, Harry. 1989. *Groen van Prinsterer's Lectures on Unbelief and Revolution.* Jordan Station, ON: Wedge Publishing Foundation.

Venard, Marc. 2003. "L'éducation par l'école (1480–1660)," in François Lebrun, Marc Venard, and Jean Quéniart, *Histoire de l'enseignement et de l'éducation II. De Gutenberg aux Lumières (1480–1789).* Paris: Perrin.

Verhaegen, Pierre. 1905. *La lutte scolaire en Belgique.* Ghent: A. Siffer.

Vogel, Johann Peter. 1972. "Bildungspolitische Perspektiven," in *Freie Schule II. Oeffentliche Verantwortung und freie Initiative.* Stuttgart: Arbeitsgemeinschaft Freier Schulen.

—1991. "Administration statt Konzeption—Bemerkungen zu neuen Schulgesetzen," *Paedagogik und Schulalltag* 46, no. 3.

—2000. "Zahlen freie Schulen 1998," *Recht und Schule* 3/00 (September).

Volkmer, Werner. 1979. "East Germany: Dissenting Views during the Last Decade," in *Opposition in Eastern Europe*, edited by Rudolf L. Tökés. Baltimore: Johns Hopkins University Press.

Voorstel eindtermen. 1993. Ministry of Education, Flemish Community, Brussels.

Vree, J. 1984a. "De Nederlandse Hervormde kerk in de jaren voor de Afscheiding," in Bakker and others.

—1984b. *De Groninger Godgeleerden: De Oorsprongen en de Eerste Periode van hun Optreden (1820–1843).* Kampen: Kok.

Vreeburg, B. 1997. "Religieuze socialisatie en onderwijsverzuiling," in Dijkstra, Dronkers, and Hofman.

Vroede, Maurits (Maurice) de. 1970. *Van schoolmeester tot onderwijzer. De opleiding can de leerkrachten in België en Luxemburg, van het eind van de 18de eeuw tot omstreeks 1842.* Leuven: Universitaire Uitgaven.

—1977. "Onderwijs en opvoeding in de Zuidelijke Nederlanden 1815–circa 1840," in *Algemene Geschiedenis der Nederlanden* 12. Weesp: Fibula-Van Dishoeck.

—1985. "Primary education and the fight against alcoholism in Belgium at the turn of the century," *History of Education Quarterly* 25, no. 4 (Winter): 483–97.

—1991. "Language in Education in Belgium up to 1940," in *Schooling, Educational Policy, and Ethnic Identity*, edited by Janusz Tomiak. New York: New York University Press.

Walz, John A. 1936. *German Influence on American Education and Culture.* Philadelphia: Carl Schurz Memorial Foundation.

Waterkamp, Dietmar. 1986. "Erziehung in der DDR zwischen Optimismus und Resignation," in *Vergleichende Bildungsforschung: DDR, Osteuropa und interkulturelle Perspektiven: Festschrift für Oskar Anweiler zum 60. Geburtstag,* edited by Bernhard Dilger, Friedrich Kuebart and Hans-Peter Schaefer. Berlin: Arno Spitz.

—1990. "Erziehung in der Schule," in Anweiler, and others.

Weber, Hermann, editor. 1986. *DDR: Dokumente zur Geschichte der Deutschen Demokratischen Republik 1945–1985.* Deutscher Taschenbuch Verlag.

Wehler, Hans-Ulrich. 1989a. *Deutsche Gesellschaftsgeschichte, Erster Band: Vom Feudalismus des Alten Reiches bis zur Defensiven Modernisierung der Reformaera, 1700–1815,* 2nd edition. Munich: C. H. Beck.

—1989b. *Deutsche Gesellschaftsgeschichte: Zweiter Band: Von der Reformaera bis zur industriellen und politischen "Deutschen Doppelrevolution," 1815–1845/49.* 2nd edition, Munich: C. H. Beck.

—1995. *Deutsche Gesellschaftsgeschichte, Dritter Band: Von der "Deutschen Doppelrevolution" bis zum Beginn des Ersten Weltkrieges, 1849–1914.* Munich: C. H. Beck.

—2003. *Deutsche Gesellschaftsgeschichte, Vierter Band: Vom Beginn des Ersten Weltkriegs bis zur Gruendung der beiden deutschen Staaten, 1914–1949.* Munich: C. H. Beck.

Weiss, Manfred, and Cornelia Mattern, Manfred. 1991. "The Situation and Development of the Private School System in Germany," in *Social Change and Educational Planning in West Germany*, edited by Hasso von Recum and Manfred Weiss. Frankfurt am Main: Deutsches Institut für internationale Pädagogische Forschung.

Welch, Steven R. 2001. "Revolution and reprisal: Bavarian schoolteachers in the 1848 revolution," *History of Education Quarterly* 41, no. 1 (Spring): 25–57.

Wiedemann, Dieter. 1998. "DDR-Jugend als Gegenstand empirischer Sozialforschung," in Fuehr and Furck.

Wieringa, W. J. 1984. "De Afscheiding en de Nederlandse samenleving," in Bakker and others.

Williamson, Roger. 1981. "East Germany: the federation of Protestant churches," *Religion in Communist Lands* 9, nos. 1–2 (Spring).

Wils, L. 1977. "De politieke ontwikkeling in Belgie 1847–1870," in *Algemene Geschiedenis der Nederlanden* 12. Weesp: Fibula-Van Dishoeck.

Winkler, Michael. 2000. "Einleitung," in Friedrich Schleiermacher, *Texte zur Paedagogik*, vol. 1. Frankfurt am Main: Suhrkam.

Wit, C. H. E. de. 1968. "La République batave, 1795–1803," in *Occupants occupés, 1792–1815*. Brussels: Université Libre.

Witte, Els. 1977. "Het socioculturele leven in Belgie: Vrijdenkersbeweging 1840–1873," in *Algemene Geschiedenis der Nederlanden* 12. Weesp: Fibula-Van Dishoeck.

Witte, Els, and A. Meynen. 1982. "Het maatschappelijk-politieke leven in Belgie 1945–1980," in *Algemene Geschiedenis der Nederlanden* 15. Weesp: Fibula-Van Dishoeck.

Wolfe, Alan. 1989. *Whose Keeper? Social Science and Moral Obligation*. Berkeley: University of California Press.

Wouden, Ries van der, Marieke Ruinaard, Rick Kwekkeboom, Elisabeth ter Borg, Peter Voogt and Wiert Wiertsema. 1994. *Evaluatie sociale vernieuwing: het eindrapport, Rijswijk*. The Netherlands: Sociaal en Cultureel Planbureau.

Wynants, Paul, and Martine Paret. 1998. "École et clivages aux XIXe et XXe siècles," in Grootaers.

Zeps, Michael J. 1987. *Education and the Crisis of the First Republic*. Boulder: East European Monographs.

Zymek, Bernd. 1989. "Schulen," in Langewiesehe and Tenorth.

Index